How to Prepare A Texas Parole Packet

2023

Lawyer X

How to Prepare a Texas Parole Packet
2023
Version 23.1

www.TexasParoleNow.com

Published by Rebellion Books
www.RebellionBooks.com

Developed in the United States

ISBN: 978-0-9840469-3-5
Library of Congress Assignation in progress

Printed in the United States of America

About the Author

Lawyer X is the pen name of a former attorney who now spends all of his time writing and consulting. While in practice, he was involved in both criminal and civil trials across the United States, including picking or helping to pick juries in hundreds of cases.

In addition to his work as a trial lawyer, Lawyer X wrote articles, lectured at continuing legal education seminars, and was active in the legal community for many years.

He maintains anonymity now so that he can provide knowledge from inside and express honest opinions and viewpoints that other members of the legal community would just as soon were not shared.

His goal is to see changes in the legal system that will allow people to represent themselves in cases where lawyers are not needed or cannot be hired for economic reasons yet still have a stranglehold on the system.

Table of Contents

Purpose of this Book

This book is designed to provide a simple, inexpensive, yet informative collection of information and examples to allow an offender or their loved ones to put together a package of information, which will be effective and assist the offender in obtaining parole from the Board of Pardons and Paroles.

It is not intended to, nor does it, offer legal advice, nor is it intended to take the place of a competent attorney well-versed in the procedures and policies of the parole process. If you can afford a parole attorney, then by all means, hire one. If you can't, this package provides a basic format to allow you to present extenuating information to the parole board in an effective manner.

Contained in this book is a general overview of the statutes on parole eligibility. These cover a range of crimes and are for general information only. The statutes are taken directly from the Texas Government Code and/or the Texas Penal Code. Many of the full statutes are attached as appendices at the back of this book. Although they contain legalese and are often hard to understand, the statutes are still a valuable reference point.

The information contained in this book is subject to change at any time, as new laws are enacted, and new policies are adopted by the Texas Department of Criminal Justice and by the Texas Board of Pardons and Paroles.

History of Parole in Texas

The first parole law was enacted by the Texas Legislature in 1905. That law gave power to the Board of Prison Commissioners and the Board of Pardons Advisors, with the approval of the Governor, to make rules and regulations under which certain meritorious prisoners might be paroled. Those who served two years or one-fourth of their terms were eligible for parole, provided they were first-time offenders and had not been sentenced for certain offenses.

In 1911, legislation was passed which empowered the Board of Prison Commissioners alone to make rules and regulations, subject to the Governor's approval, for the parole of prisoners. This law provided that meritorious prisoners were to be eligible for parole after having served the minimum terms fixed by statute for the crime and conviction. It also provided for a parole agent or supervisor to keep the state informed about the conduct of parolees. However, no system of supervision existed. In 1913, the addition of an indeterminate sentence law increased the use of parole and gave the Governor the sole power to grant paroles. The Board of Prison Commissioners still established rules and regulations under which prisoners could be paroled, but such rules and regulations had to be approved by the Governor.

In 1929, the Board of Pardons Advisors was revitalized by the Legislature and a third member was added to create the Board of Pardons and Paroles with power to recommend prisoners for parole to the Governor as well as to advise on clemency matters. Parole applied only to those who had never before been convicted of a crime punishable by sentence to the penitentiary. This restriction was changed in 1930 and only those who had actually been in prison before became ineligible. In 1936, the Constitution was amended to create a constitutional three-member Board of Pardons and Paroles. The amendment gave the Board authority to recommend paroles and all acts of clemency to the Governor (however, the Governor could grant one 30-day capital reprieve without such recommendation), and the Governor was given sole power to revoke paroles and conditional pardons. This act may be said to be the birthplace of parole in Texas.

Parole was to be recommended only if the Board was of the opinion that the prisoner was not incompatible with the welfare of society. The Board was empowered to prescribe conditions of parole and was required to furnish a written copy of such conditions to the parolee. The parolee did not have to have a job to be paroled; but, if offered one, he had to accept. He was not to leave the state without the Board's consent. He was required to support his dependents, make restitution for his crime and abandon evil associates and ways. Upon release from prison, a parolee was given a suit of clothing, two suits of underwear, $5.00, and a railroad ticket to the place of his conviction.

While there were no parole officers, a supervisor of parolees was provided to keep records of parolees; and, if they lapsed into criminal ways or violated any condition of parole, the matter was to be reported to the Governor, who could issue a warrant for the retaking of the prisoner. After his return to prison, the Board was required to hold a hearing to consider the case of the parole violator. A parole violator was required to serve the balance of his maximum sentence calculated from the date of his delinquency. Therefore, the time spent on parole counted as time served on his sentence until parole was revoked. A violator who committed a new offense while on parole was required to serve the balance of his original sentence before beginning to serve the new sentence.

In 1937, the Governor called for the formation of voluntary parole boards. These boards consisted of citizens of the state who performed supervisory services to parolees without compensation. Prior to this time, no actual supervision of parolees was possible since only one supervisor of parolees was provided in the law. Voluntary parole supervisors were appointed in 242 of 254 counties in Texas. They assisted parolees in obtaining jobs and required them to make reports.

The Adult Probation and Parole Law enacted by the 50th Legislature in 1947 established the general framework for how community supervision (probation) and parole operate today. Prior to 1947, parole releases from prison were actually executive clemency and were called conditional pardons or executive paroles. However, since no additional funds for parole operation were appropriated in the 1947 Legislature, supervision of those released on parole or conditional pardon was entirely by the volunteer parole boards.

Many changes continued over the years, leading eventually to the establishment of the current composition of the Board of Pardons and Paroles (7 Board Members and 12 Commissioners). Until September 1, 1989, in addition to parole decisions, the Board was also responsible for the operations of the parole supervision system. When the Legislature merged the Board of Pardons and Paroles, the Texas Adult Probation Commission, and the Texas Department of Corrections into the Texas Department of Criminal Justice (TDCJ), the Board maintained its authority over parole decisions, but the TDCJ Parole Division assumed the other parole-related responsibilities.

The Parole Division Director is appointed by the TDCJ Executive Director and is responsible for the administration and operation of the division.

Overview of Parole

The parole process in Texas is a collaborative effort between the Texas Board of Pardons and Paroles and the Texas Department of Criminal Justice-Parole Division.

The Board of Pardons and Paroles is responsible for the consideration of eligible offenders for Parole or Discretionary Mandatory Supervision; the imposition of appropriate conditions of release; the determination of revocation or other appropriate sanctions for those offenders who have violated the terms of release; and the recommendation of clemency matters to the Governor.

Parole is a type of supervised release from prison. It is offered under the conditional and discretionary powers of the Texas parole panel to grant or deny parole to an offender. Parole is a privilege, not a right.

The Parole Division of the Texas Department of Criminal Justice identifies offenders who are eligible for parole six months prior to their initial parole eligibility date. For subsequent review dates, the offenders are identified four months prior to their review date. At this time their case file is pulled to be worked.

An Institutional Parole Officer conducts a very brief interview with the inmate at the prison, reviews his or her file, and prepares a brief case summary for the people at the Parole Board to review at a later date. Inmates should always be respectful and friendly to the Institutional Parole Officer during this interview.

When parole is an option for an offender, a notice is sent to the victims of the crime, their families, criminal justice professionals and concerned citizens regarding the parole review process. Those registered on the confidential Victim Notification System will receive notice of the parole review process and be given the opportunity to submit protest correspondence for consideration by the Texas Board of Pardons and Parole. Victims defined by Texas Government Code 508.117 may also request an interview to speak to the Texas Board of Pardons and Parole.

There is no right to an interview before the Parole Panel for offenders. The Board has the discretion to grant or deny requests for an interview with the inmate, inmate's family, or other parties supporting or opposing parole.

For most cases, a three-member Parole Panel will vote on the offender's parole release. A majority of two votes is required to determine the outcome. Some cases require a vote of the entire Parole Panel instead of a three-member panel.

Once all votes have been cast, the offender is notified of the Parole Panel's decision.

The review process generally takes approximately four to six months to complete.

Parole Review Process

The parole review process is a comprehensive review and consideration of an offender's case, from conviction offense, to medical and psychological history, to how they have adjusted and behaved in prison. Case files are sent to each Voting Board office (see Appendix 4) or are sent as an electronic file through the Offender Information Management System (OIMS). Each parole panel of the Board reviews files and interviews victims upon request as required by Texas law. Interviews with offenders and other individuals in support or protest of an offender is at the discretion of the parole panel's lead voter.

Parole Panel

A parole panel is composed of one Board Member and two Parole Commissioners who make decisions by majority vote concerning parole and discretionary mandatory release, revocation, and imposing conditions of supervision. For offenders convicted of certain offenses, the law requires a vote of two-thirds of the entire Board Members to be grant parole.

Parole Review

All offenders sentenced to a term of incarceration in the Texas Department of Criminal Justice Correctional Institutions Division (TDCJ CID) are eligible for release on parole, except those sentenced to death or to life imprisonment without parole.

If an offender is denied parole, the Board is required to set a future date for parole reconsideration. If the offender is not convicted of an offense listed in Texas Government Code, Section 508.149(a) (see Appendix 6), this date must be set as soon as practical after the first anniversary of the denial date. If the offender is serving a sentence for an offense listed in Section 508.149(a), Government Code, or an offense punishable as a felony of the second or third degree under Section 22.04, Penal Code, the date may be set up to five years from the denial date. If the offender is serving a sentence under Section 22.021, Penal Code, or a life sentence for a capital felony, the date may be set up to ten years from the denial date.

Parole Review Process Overview

1. The Parole Division of the Texas Department of Criminal Justice identifies offenders six months prior to their initial parole eligibility, and

four months prior to subsequent review dates, and directs the case file to be pulled for review.

2. Notice is sent to trial officials, victims, and victim family members.

3. An Institutional Parole Officer (IPO) of the Texas Board of Pardons and Paroles interviews the offender and prepares a parole case summary for the Board.
4. An interview with the offender is at the discretion of the Parole Panel member, as are interviews with individuals in support or protest of an offender's release to parole.

5. Parole Panel members must grant an interview to victims, as defined by statute, upon request.

6. The offender's file is sent to the designated board office for review and vote by a Parole Panel.

   A panel consists of three voting members and a majority of two votes is needed for a final decision. Voting is sequential, with one panel member recording their vote and passing it to the next panel member. If the first two votes are the same, the vote is final. If the first two votes differ, the third panel member reviews the case and breaks the tie.

7. The offender is notified of the Parole Panel's decision via correspondence.

   A denial will include the next review date. An approval may include special conditions.

Types of Release

Parole

The release of an offender by the decision of a parole panel, to serve the remainder of his or her sentence under the supervision of a parole officer. Offenders may only be paroled if they receive approval from a parole panel and if they have served enough of their sentence to be eligible by law for parole. Parole is a privilege, not a right. Parolees include offenders released on "MRIS" (Medically Recommended Intensive Supervision previously known as "Special Needs Parole") which is an early release program for non-violent offenders who are terminally ill, physically handicapped, mentally ill, or have an intellectual developmental disorder and pose no threat to public safety.

Mandatory Supervision Release

Mandatory supervision (MS) is a type of release from prison that was first implemented for offenses occurring on or after August 31, 1977. At that time MS was just that, mandatory with no requirement for the approval from the Parole Board. (There is no MS date for life sentences.) For offenders whose offenses occurred between August 31, 1977, and August 31, 1996, the Parole Board was required to order the release of an inmate to MS when the actual calendar time the inmate had served plus any accrued good conduct time equaled the term to which the inmate was sentenced. For eligible offenses committed on or after September 1, 1996, MS became discretionary.

It is important to know that not all offenders are eligible for Mandatory Supervision. Offenders convicted of offenses listed under r §508.149(a) Government Code, are not eligible. (See Parole Review Periods section for the list of offenses not eligible for Mandatory Supervision).

Discretionary Mandatory Supervision

For offenses committed on or after September 1, 1996, the Parole Board is required to vote on Discretionary Mandatory Supervision for inmates whose accrued good conduct time plus their actual calendar time equals the term of which they were sentenced for possible release. The Board must review eligible offenders for possible release to discretionary mandatory supervision on or before their eligibility date. The Board has the discretion to grant or deny release is they believe the offender's release would endanger the public or the accrued good conduct time is not an accurate reflection of rehabilitative potential.

Direct Discharge

Offenders who are not granted parole and who are not eligible for mandatory supervision release must remain in the prison system until they have served their entire court-ordered sentence and are discharged from state custody. No post-release supervision requirements can be imposed on such discharged offenders.

Difference Between Parole and Mandatory Release

Parole is discretionary and always involves a decision on the part of a Parole Panel. Although an initial parole eligibility date may be reached months or even years before an offender's mandatory supervision date, a Parole Panel is in no way required to approve parole at the time of initial or subsequent parole reviews.

Under the law in effect until August 31, 1996, release to mandatory supervision was automatic, with no Parole Panel decision involved. All offenders serving time for offenses committed prior to August 31, 1996, and classified as eligible for mandatory supervision, based on the nature of their offenses, must be released on their "minimum expiration date" when calendar time served and accrued "good time" add up to equal their entire sentence.

In 1995, the 74th Legislature gave the Board authority to review scheduled mandatory supervision releases for offenders with offenses committed on or after September 1, 1996. Specifically, a Parole Panel may deny mandatory supervision releases on a case-by-case basis when the panel determines that an offender's good conduct time does not accurately reflect the potential for rehabilitation and that the offender's release would endanger the public.

Parole and mandatory supervision are similar in that the Parole Division supervises both categories of offenders. They must report to Parole Officers, must abide by the same rules in the community, and are subject to arrest and re-incarceration if they violate the conditions of release.

Medically Recommended Intensive Supervision (MRIS)

In 1991, the Texas Legislature authorized the early parole review and release of certain categories of offenders who are elderly, intellectually disabled, terminally ill, physically handicapped, require long-term care, or have a mental illness are eligible for MRIS parole regardless of whether they have reached their initial parole eligibility date. With approval from the Parole Panel, such offenders may be released to the MRIS program.

All MRIS applicants are carefully screened by the Texas Correctional Office for Offenders with Medical or Mental Impairments (TCOOMMI) and Correctional Managed Health Care and, prior to MRIS approval, the Parole Panel must determine that the offender is no longer a threat to public safety and poses no risk of committing future offenses due to his or her medical and/or psychiatric condition. An offender, other than an offender who is serving a sentence of death, may be released on MRIS on a date designated by a Parole Panel, with the following exceptions:

- An offender with a 3g offense, as described in Article 42.12, Code of Criminal Procedure (see Appendix 6), may only be considered if a medical condition of terminal illness or long-term care has been diagnosed.

- An offender with a reportable conviction or adjudication under Chapter 62, Code of Criminal Procedure may only be considered if in a persistent vegetative state or being with an organic brain syndrome with significant to total mobility impairment.

- An offender who is not a citizen of the United States may be released to immigration authorities pending deportation if the Parole Panel determines that upon release the offender would be deported to another country and that the offender does not constitute a threat to public safety in the other country or this country and is unlikely to reenter this country illegally.

Once a determination is made that an individual meets the medical requirements for MRIS, there is a specially designated parole panel that votes whether to approve MRIS. The panel may only grant MRIS if they make a determination that the offender "does not constitute a threat to the public safety." TCOOMMI must then approve the supervision plan.

Good Conduct Time

Good Conduct Time Credit or "Good Time Credit" is time credited to an offender for good behavior or for participating in work or self-improvement programs while incarcerated. For most offender the good conduct time credits are added to the actual calendar time served to calculate the offender's eligibility for parole or mandatory supervision.

Every offender who enters the Texas Department of Criminal Justice (TDCJ) system is assigned a Line Class. The Line Class is a designation used within the TDCJ which determines the amount of Good Conduct Time Credit an inmate can earn for their behavior and their diligent participation in certain programs. The amount of Good Time Credit an offender can earn is set by law in the Texas Government Code Section 498.003.

The Line Class and Good Conduct Time accrued is only used for parole and mandatory supervision eligibility, otherwise the classification does not affect the offender's term.

The majority of the offenders are assigned a Line Class of 1 upon entering the TDCJ system. The classification is subjective and is based on the offender's conduct during the intake process.

Although you do not need to know every nuance in the law concerning the granting of good conduct time credit you do need to understand what good time can be earned and how to use it.

It is important to know that good conduct timo, parolo, and mandatory supervision do not apply to offenders convicted of what are what known as "State Jail Felonies". State Jail offenders can receive Diligent Participation Credit which is calculated and awarded differently than Good Conduct Time Credit.

Time Earning Status and Good Conduct Time Credit

When offenders enter the TDCJ facilities, during the intake process the offender is evaluated and assigned a time-earning status of Line Class I to Line Class III. Most new inmates are assigned Line Class I. Line Class 1 earns the most credits and Line Class 3 earns the least amount of credits. Each time-earning status is linked to a set number of days good conduct time that can be earned each month. The earned amount is fixed by the Legislature.

Inmates can work their way into a higher time-earning status or be placed into a lower time-earning status, dependent upon their behavior. New inmates that are processed into TDCJ with a Line Class of 2 or 3 must wait six months before they are eligible for promotion in time-earning status.

There are two types of time-earning statuses: Line Class status ranging from Line Class I to Line Class III and State-Approved Trusty (SAT) status ranging from SAT II to SAT IV.

The amount of good conduct time credits awarded to an inmate is based on the laws in effect ***when the crime was committed.***

Good Time Credit For Offenses Committed Before 09/01/1987

Offenders who committed their crimes before September 1, 1987 are known as Pre-70th Legislature Offenders or 65th Legislature Offenders. They are awarded good conduct time credits each month based on their time-earning status.

Classification	Flat Time	Good Conduct Time Credit for completion of academic or vocation programs or on-the-job training
Line Class 1 - Initial classification of new inmates.	30 Days	Up to 15 Days for "A", "B", or "C" credits.
Line Class 2 - Inmates with disciplinary status	30 Days	Up to 15 Days for "A", "B", or "C" credits.
Line Class 3- Inmates with security custody. No good time credit earned.	30 Days	No Good Time Credit earned
Inmate on Parole or Mandatory Supervision - No good time credit can be earned.	30 Days	No Good Time Credit earned
While **confined in a county jail**	30 Days	Up to 20 Days

Good Time Credit For Offenses Committed On or After 09/01/1987

Offenders who committed their crimes on or after September 1, 1987 are known as 70th Legislature Offenders. They are awarded good conduct time credits for their behavior and Diligent Participation Credits for their participation in work, industrial, educational, or vocational programs.

Classification	Flat Time	Good Conduct Time Credits	Diligent Participation Good Conduct Time Credits for participation in Work, Industrial, Educational or Vocational Program
Trusty Status (any classification)	30 Days	Up to 20 Days (May not award more than 10 extra days for each 30 days actually served)	Up to 15 Days
Line Class 1 - Initial classification of new inmates.	30 Days	Up to 20 Days	Up to 15 Days
Line Class 2 - Inmates with disciplinary status	30 Days	Up to 10 Days	Up to 15 Days
Line Class 3- Inmates with security custody. No good time credit earned.	30 Days	0 Days - Not Eligible for this credit.	0 Days - Not Eligible for this credit.
Inmates assigned to **Administrative Segregation**	30 Days	Can receive Good Conduct Time Credits based on their Time-Earning Status of Line Class 1, 2 or 3.	0 Days - Not Eligible for this credit.
Inmate while **on Parole or Mandatory Supervision -** No	30 Days	0 Days - Not Eligible for this credit.	0 Days - Not Eligible for this credit.

good time credit can be earned.			
While confined in a county jail	30 Days	Up to 20 Days	Up to 15 Days for voluntary work program operated by the Sheriff

Good Time Credit While Confined to County Jail

If an offender is confined in a county jail after being sentenced, TDCJ will award good conduct time to the offender up to an amount earned by an inmate in the entry level time earning class of Line Class I. The offender can also earn Diligent Participation credits by participating in a voluntary work program operated by a sheriff under Article 43.101, Code of Criminal Procedure. To receive credit, the sheriff of must attach a certification of the number of days the inmate diligently participated in the volunteer work program when the inmate is transferred to a TDCJ facility.

Reduction of Good Time Credit

If an inmate commits an offense or violates a rule, TDCJ may remove or reduce all or any part of the inmate's accrued good conduct time or place any or all of the inmate's good conduct time in suspension. Good conduct time forfeited cannot be restored. However, good conduct time placed in suspension can be reinstated. TDCJ can also restore good conduct time forfeited on a revocation that does not involve a new criminal conviction after the inmate has served at least three months of good behavior in TDCJ.

Any or all good conduct time can also be forfeited by the offender if the offender attempts to contact the victim or victim's family by letter, telephone, or any other means directly or indirectly.

Good conduct time can be forfeited by the filing of frivolous lawsuits from the offender. The judge must make a finding in the "final order" that the lawsuit was dismissed as frivolous or malicious.

Other Factors in Determining Parole Eligibility

There are many other factors which are used to determine if and when an offender is eligible for parole or mandatory supervision. These factors include:

- The date the crime was committed.

- The type of crime committed.
- Was the conviction a 3g offense?
- Was the conviction an aggravated crime?
- Did the conviction have an enhancement?
- Did the conviction occur in a drug free zone?
- The length of the sentence.
- The amount of actual time served.
- Is the offender serving consecutive sentences?

In essence, the line class assigned to an offender determines how much good conduct time credit and diligent participation good conduct time credit an inmate receives thus affecting when the prisoner will be eligible for parole or mandatory supervision.

Parole Eligibility

The rules regarding parole eligibility are complicated as you will see in this section. Parole eligibility is governed by the laws in effect when the crime was committed.

To find the information on parole eligibility, locate the section in which the offense date is within the appropriate Legislative date range.

55th Legislature	Prior to 01/01/1966	
Offense	**Parole Eligibility**	**Comments**
All Offenses	Calendar Time= 1/3, including any bonus & blood donations. Maximum of 15 yrs.	Code of Criminal Procedure (CCP), Article 42.12 was amended 01/01/1966 to allow good time and ¼ time for all persons confined in TDO.

59th Legislature	01/01/1966 - 08/31/1967	
Offense	**Parole Eligibility**	**Comments**
All Offenses	Calendar Time+ Good Time =*1/4, including any bonus & blood donations. Maximum of 15 yrs.	* Effective 01/01/1966

60th Legislature	09/01/1967 - 08/31/1977	
Offense	**Parole Eligibility**	**Comments**
All Offenses	Calendar Time+ Good Time =*1/3, including any bonus & blood donations. Maximum of *20 yrs.	No Mandatory Supervision: offender discharges sentence when calendar time + good time = total sentence.
	*Due to court rulings during that time period, ma calculates eligibility dates on all offenses prior to 08/28/1977 utilizing calendar time + good time= 1/3, regardless of the law in effect when the offense was committed.	Sentence is effectively reduced by the amount of good time earned. * Effective 01/01/1967

65th Legislature	09/01/1977 - 08/31/1989	
Offense	**Parole Eligibility**	**Comments**
*3g Offenses: - Aggravated Kidnapping-20.04 - Aggravated Robbery-29.03 -Aggravated Sexual Assault-22.021 - Any offense with Affirmative finding of Deadly Weapon - Capital Murder--19.03	Calendar Time = ¼ Minimum of 2 yrs. Maximum of 15 yrs.	CCP, Art. 42.12 CCP, Art. 42.18 *Effective 09/01/1987
All other offenses	Calendar Time + Good Time = 1/4, including work credits and bonus time. Maximum of 15 yrs.	CCP, Art. 42.18
*The offenses listed below are NOT eligible for Mandatory Supervision: - Aggravated Assault, 2nd or 3rd	Ineligible for Mandatory Supervision.	CCP, Art. 42.18 * Effective 09/01/1987

Degree--22.02 -Aggravated Kidnapping, 1st or 2nd Degree -20.04 - Aggravated Robbery, 1st Degree-29.03 - Aggravated Sexual Assault, 1st Degree--22.021 - Any offense with Affirmative finding of Deadly Weapon -Arson, 1st Degree-28.02 - Burglary of a Habitation, 1st Degree-30.02{ d2)(d3) (armed with explosives or deadly weapon or causes injury while in commission of offense) - Capital Murder--19.03 - Deadly Assault on Law or Corrections Officer; Court Participant; Probation Personnel; Member or Employees of the BPP; Employees of TYC, 1st Degree--22.03 - Injury to a Child or Elderly, 1st Degree--22.04 - Murder, 1st Degree--19.02 - Robbery, 2nd Degree--29.02 - Sexual Assault, 2nd Degree-22.011		
*CU offenses	Time credit on all sentences, one after another, until eligibility is reached on last sentence.	CCP, Art. 42.08{a) CCP, Art. 42.18 * Effective 09/01/1987

69th Legislature	09/01/1983-08/31/1987	
Offense	Parole Eligibility	Comments
- Aggravated Kidnapping-20.04 - Aggravated Robbery--29.03 - *Aggravated Sexual Assault--22.021 - Any offense with affirmative finding of Deadly Weapon - Capital Murder-19.03	Calendar Time= 1/3 Minimum of 2 yrs. Maximum of 20 yrs.	CCP, Art. 42.12 Sec. 3f * Effective 08/31/1983.
All other offenses	Calendar Time+ Good Time= 1/3, including any credits and bonus. Maximum of 20 yrs.	CCP, Art. 42.12 Sec. 15b (Parole calculations) - CCP, Art. 42.12 Sec. 15c (Mandatory Supervision calculations) - 09/01/1985 Parole laws effectively moved from CCP, 42.12 to CCP, 42.18 -All offenses eligible for Mandatory Supervision.

70th Legislature	09/01/198-08/31/198	
Offense	Parole Eligibility	Comments
- Aggravated Kidnapping-20.04 - Aggravated Robbery--29.03 - *Aggravated Sexual Assault--22.021 - Any offense with affirmative finding of Deadly Weapon - Capital Murder-19.03	Calendar Time= 1/3 Minimum of 2 yrs. Maximum of 20 yrs.	CCP, Art. 42.12 Sec. 3f * Effective 08/31/1983.
All other offenses	Calendar Time+ Good Time= 1/3, including any credits and bonus. Maximum of 20 yrs.	CCP, Art. 42.12 Sec. 15b (Parole calculations) - CCP, Art. 42.12 Sec. 15c (Mandatory Supervision calculations) - 09/01/1985 Parole laws effectively moved from CCP, 42.12 to CCP, 42.18 -All offenses eligible for Mandatory Supervision.

71st & 72nd Legislature	09/01/1989 - 08/31/1993	
Offense	**Parole Eligibility**	**Comments**
Capital Murder (Capital Felony)- *Life Sentence-19.03 1) Murder of a peace officer or fireman on official duty, 2) Intentionally murders a person in the course of committing or attempting to commit a kidnapping, burglary, robbery, aggravated sexual assault, arson 3) Murders for remuneration, or promise of remuneration or employs another to commit the murder for remuneration or the promise of remuneration, 4) Murders while escaping or attempting to escape from a penal institution, 5) Murders an employee of a penal institution while incarcerated, 6) Murders more than one person during the same criminal transaction or during different criminal transactions but the murders are committed pursuant to the same scheme, or course of conduct.	Calendar Time= ¼ Minimum of 2 yrs. Maximum of 15 yrs. ** Calendar Time = 35 yrs.	CCP42.18 * Effective 09/01/1989 ** Effective 09/01/1991
3g Offenses: -Aggravated Kidnapping-20.04 -Aggravated Robbery--29.03 -Aggravated Sexual Assault-22.021 - Any offense with Affirmative finding of Deadly Weapon - Capital Murder-19.03	Calendar Time= ¼ Minimum of 2 yrs. Maximum of 15 yrs.	CCP, Art. 42.12 CCP, Art. 42.18
All other offenses	Calendar Time+ Good Time = 1/4, including work credits and bonus time. Maximum of 15 yrs. Supervision.	CCP, Art. 42.18(8)(b)(4)
CU offenses	Time credit on all sentences, one after another, until eligibility is reached on last sentence.	CCP, Art. 42.08{a) CCP, Art. 42.18
The offenses listed below are NOT eligible for Mandatory Supervision: - Aggravated Assault, 2nd or 3rd Degree - 22.02 - Aggravated Kidnapping, 1st or 2nd Degree - 20.04 - Aggravated Robbery, 1st Degree - 29.03 - Aggravated Sexual Assault, 1st Degree - 22.021 - Any offense with Affirmative finding of Deadly Weapon - Arson, 1st Degree - 28.02 - Burglary of a Habitation, 1st Degree - 30.02 (d2) {d3){armed with explosives or deadly weapon or causes injury while in commission of offense) - Capital Murder -19.03 - Deadly Assault on Law or Corrections Officer; Court Participant; Probation Personnel; Member or Employees of the BPP; Employees of TYC, 1st	Ineligible for Mandatory Supervision.	CCP, Art. 42.18

Degree -22.03 - Injury to a Child or Elderly, 1st Degree -22.04 - Murder, 1st Degree -19.02 - Robbery, 2nd Degree - 29.02 - Sexual Assault, 2nd Degree - 22.011		

73rd Legislature	09/01/1993 - 08/31/1995	
Offense	**Parole Eligibility**	**Comments**
Capital Murder (Capital Felony)- Life Sentence -19.03 1) Murder of a peace officer or fireman on official duty, 2) Intentionally murders a person in the course of committing or attempting to commit a kidnapping, burglary, robbery, aggravated sexual assault, arson, *obstruction or retaliation, 3) Murders for remuneration, or promise of remuneration or employs another to commit the murder for remuneration or the promise of remuneration, 4) Murders while escaping or attempting to escape from a penal institution, 5) Murders an employee of a penal institution while incarcerated, *6) Murders with intent to establish, maintain, or participate in an alliance, or in the profits of an alliance, of individuals, while incarcerated, *7) A person convicted of and serving a sentence for Murder (19.02) who murders while incarcerated, *8) Murders while serving a sentence of Life or 99 years for Aggravated Kidnapping, Aggravated Sexual Assault, or Aggravated Robbery, 9) Murders more than one person during the same criminal transaction, or during different criminal transactions but the murders are committed pursuant to the same scheme, or course of conduct, *10) Murders an individual under six years of age.	* Calendar Time= 40 yrs.	CCP, Art. 42.18 * Effective 09/01/1993
3g Offenses: - Aggravated Kidnapping - 20.04 - Aggravated Robbery- 29.03 - Aggravated Sexual Assault - 22.021 - Any offense with Affirmative finding of Deadly Weapon - Capital Murder--19.03 - *Indecency w/Child (Sexual Contact) 2nd Degree - 21.ll(a)(l) - *Murder, 19.02 -**A Felony Increased Under Health & Safety Code 481.134 (c), (d), (e), or (f) (Drug-Free Zones), if it is shown that there is a previous conviction for an offense which punishment was	*Calendar Time=½ Minimum of 2 yrs. *Maximum of 30 yrs.	CCP, Art. 42.12 * Effective 09/01/1993 **Effective 05/30/1995

increased under any of those subsections.		
All other 1st, 2nd, and 3rd degree felony offenses (****a court may reduce the punishment of a 3rd degree felony by imposing the confinement of a Class A Misdemeanor category offense (may or may not have been prosecuted under the lesser category offense title)).	Calendar Time+ Good Time = 1/4, including work credits and bonus time. Maximum of 15 yrs.	CCP, Art. 42.18 (8)(b)(5) ****Effective thru 08/31/1995
*Drug-Free Zones-481.134	*Calendar Time = 5 yrs. or maximum term, whichever is less.	CCP, Art. 42.18 (8)(b)(4) * Effective 09/01/1993
CU offenses	Time credit on all sentences, one after another, until eligibility is reached on last sentence.	CCP, Art. 42.08(a) CCP, Art. 42.18
**State Jail Felonies - a court may enhance the punishment by imposing the confinement of a 2nd or 3rd degree felony. - a court may reduce the punishment by imposing the confinement of a Class B Misdemeanor category offense (may or may not have been prosecuted under the lesser category offense title).	Parole Eligibility is NOT applicable.	PC 12.35 * *Confinement is to a state jail for any term of not more than two years or less than 180 days. ** Effective 09/01/1994
The offenses listed below are NOT eligible for Mandatory Supervision: -Aggravated Assault, *1st or 2nd Degree - 22.02 -Aggravated Kidnapping, 1st or 2nd Degree - 20.04 - Aggravated Robbery, 1st Degree - 29.03 - Aggravated Sexual Assault, 1st Degree - 22.021 - Any offense with Affirmative finding of Deadly Weapon - Arson, 1st Degree - 28.02 - Burglary of a Habitation, 1st Degree - 30.02 - **(d2)(d3) (armed with explosives or deadly weapon or causes injury while in commission of offense) - ***with intent to commit FELONY other than felony Theft - (d2) and (d3) are no longer applicable -Capital Murder-19.03 - Injury to a Child or Elderly, *or Disabled Individual, 1st Degree - 22.04 - Murder, 1st Degree-19.02 - Robbery, 2nd Degree - 29.02 - Sexual Assault, 2nd Degree - 22.011 * A Felony Increased Under Health & Safety Code 481.134 (Drug-Free Zones).	Ineligible for Mandatory Supervision.	CCP, Art. 42.18 *Effective 09/01/1993 ** Effective until 08/31/1994 ***Effective 09/01/1994

74th Legislature	09/01/1995 - 08/31/1997	
Offense	**Parole Eligibility**	**Comments**
Capital Murder (Capital Felony)- Life Calendar TI me= 40 yrs. Sentence -19.03 1) Murder of a peace officer or fireman on official duty, 2) Intentionally murders a person in the course of committing or attempting to commit a kidnapping, burglary, robbery, aggravated sexual assault, arson, obstruction or retaliation, 3) Murders for remuneration, or promise of remuneration or employs another to commit the murder for remuneration or the promise of remuneration, 4) Murders while escaping or attempting to escape from a penal institution, 5) Murders an employee of a penal institution while incarcerated, 6) Murders with intent to establish, maintain, or participate in an alliance, or in the profits of an alliance, of individuals, while incarcerated, 7) A person convicted of and serving a sentence for Murder (19.02) who murders while incarcerated, 8) Murders while serving a sentence of Life or 99 years for Aggravated Kidnapping, Aggravated Sexual Assault, or Aggravated Robbery, 9) Murders more than one person during the same criminal transaction, or during different criminal transactions but the murders are committed pursuant to the same scheme, or course of conduct, 10) Murders an individual undor six years of age.	Calendar Time= 40 yrs.	CCP, Art. 42.18
* Offender is serving a Life Sentence for one of the following listed offenses: - Aggravated Kidnapping (with intent to violate or abuse the victim sexually)--20.04(a)(4) - Aggravated Sexual Assault-22.021 - Burglary of Habitation with Intent to Commit any of the following listed sexual offenses:--30.02 -Aggravated Sexual Assault-22.021 - Indecency w/Child-21.11 - Sexual Assault--22.011 - Aggravated Kidnapping (with intent to violate or abuse the victim sexually)--20.04(a)(4) **AND** has a previous conviction for: *TWO felony offenses, at least one of which is of the following offenses: - Burglary of Habitation with Intent to Commit any of the following listed sexual offenses:--30.02 -Aggravated Kidnapping (with intent to violate or abuse the victim	Calendar Time = 35 yrs.	CCP, Art. 42.18 PC 12.42 (d)(2) *Effective 09/01/1995

sexually)--20.04(a)(4) -Indecency w/Child-21.11 - Sexual Assault--22.011 - Prohibited Sexual Conduct-25.02 -Aggravated Sexual Assault--22.021 - Possession or Promotion of Child Pornography--43.26 - Sexual Performance by a Child--43.25		
3g Offenses: -Aggravated Kidnapping- 20.04 - Aggravated Robbery- 29.03 - Aggravated Sexual Assault- 22.021 - Any offense with Affirmative finding of Deadly Weapon - Capital Murder-19.03 - Indecency w/Child (Sexual Contact) 2nd Degree- 21.ll(a) (1) - Murder-19.02 - *Sexual Assault (of a Child)- 22.0ll(a) (2) A Felony Increased Under Health & Safety Code 481.134 (c), (d), (e), or (f) (Drug-Free Zones), if it is shown that there is a previous conviction for an offense which punishment was increased under any of those subsections.	Calendar Time= ½ Minimum of 2 yrs. Maximum of 30 yrs.	CCP, Art. 42.12 CCP, Art. 42.18 * Effective 09/01/1995
All other 1st, 2nd, and 3rd degree felony offenses	Calendar Time+ Good Time = 1/4, including work credits and bonus time. Maximum of 15 yrs.	CCP, Art. 42.18 (8)(b)(5)
Drug-Free Zones 481.134	calendar Time= 5 yrs. or maximum term, whichever is less.	CCP, Art. 42.18 (8)(b)(4)
CU offenses	Time credit on all sentences, one after another, until eligibility is reached on last sentence.	CCP, Art. 42.08 (a) CCP, Art. 42.18
State Jail Felonies - a court may enhance the punishment by imposing the confinement of a 2nd or 3rd degree felony - a court may reduce the punishment by imposing the confinement of a *Class A Misdemeanor category offense (may or may not have been prosecuted under the lesser category offense title.)	Parole Eligibility is NOT applicable.	PC 12.35 Confinement is to a state jail for any term of not more than two years or less than 180 days. * Effective 09/01/1995 60
The offenses listed below are NOT eligible for Mandatory Supervision: - Aggravated Assault, 1st or 2nd Degree - 22.02 - Aggravated Kidnapping, 1st or 2nd Degree - 20.04 - Aggravated Robbery, 1st Degree - 29.03 - Aggravated Sexual Assault, 1st Degree - 22.021 - Any offense with Affirmative finding of Deadly Weapon - Arson, 1st Degree - 28.02 - Burglary of a Habitation, 1st Degree - 30.02 with intent to commit felony other than Theft - Capital Murder -19.03 - *** Indecency w/Child 2nd or 3rd Degree-21.11 - Injury to a Child or Elderly or Disabled	Ineligible for Mandatory Supervision.	CCP, Art. 42.18 ** Effective 09/01/1996 *** Effective 05/23/1997

Individual, 1st Degree - 22.04 - Murder, 1st or ***2nd Degree- 19.02 - Robbery, 2nd Degree - 29.02 - Sexual Assault, 2nd Degree - 22.011 A Felony Increased Under Health & Safety Code 481.134 (Drug-Free Zones). **Any offense committed on or after 09/01/1996 with a prior conviction to include any above listed offenses.		
** Discretionary Mandatory Supervision		CCP, Art. 42.18 (8)(c-1) ** An offender may be denied mandatory supervision by a parole panel for the following reasons: - ** Offender will endanger the public AND - ** Offender's accrued good conduct time is not an accurate reflection of the offender's potential for rehabilitation. ** Effective 09/01/1996

75th Legislature	09/01/1997 - 08/31/1999	
Offense	**Parole Eligibility**	**Comments**
Capital Murder (Capital Felony)- Life Calendar TI me= 40 yrs. Sentence--19.03 1) Murder of a peace officer or fireman on official duty, 2) Intentionally murders a person in the course of committing or attempting to commit a kidnapping, burglary, robbery, aggravated sexual assault, arson, obstruction or retaliation, 3) Murders for remuneration, or promise of remuneration or employs another to commit the murder for remuneration or the promise of remuneration, 4) Murders while escaping or attempting to escape from a penal institution, 5) Murders an employee of a penal institution while incarcerated, 6) Murders with intent to establish, maintain, or participate in an alliance, or in the profits of an alliance, of individuals, while incarcerated, 7) A person convicted of and serving a sentence for Murder (19.02) who murders while incarcerated, 8) Murders while serving a sentence of Life or 99 years for Aggravated Kidnapping, Aggravated Sexual Assault, or Aggravated Robbery, 9) Murders more than one person during the same criminal transaction, or during different criminal transactions but the murders are committed pursuant to the same scheme, or course of conduct, 10) Murders an individual under six	Calendar Time= 40 yrs.	*Gov't Code 508.046 *CCP, Art. 42.18 repealed effective 9-1-1997. Parole and Mandatory Supervision law now codified in Govt. Code 508.

years of age.		
Offender is serving a Life Sentence for one of the following listed offenses: -Aggravated Kidnapping (with intent to violate or abuse the victim sexually)--20.04(a)(4) -Aggravated Sexual Assault-22.021 - *Sexual Assault-22.011 - Burglary of Habitation with Intent to Commit any of the following listed sexual offenses:--30.02 - Aggravated Kidnapping (with intent to violate or abuse the victim sexually)--20.04(a)(4) -Aggravated Sexual Assault--22.021 - Indecency w/Child-21.11 - Sexual Assault-22.011	Calendar Time= 35 yrs.	*Gov't Code 508.145(c) PC 12.42(c)(2) *CCP, Art. 42.18 repealed effective 9-1-1997. Parole and Mandatory Supervision law now codified in Govt. Code 508.
AND has a previous conviction for *one of the following offenses: -Aggravated Kidnapping (with intent to violate or abuse the victim sexually)--20.04(a)(4) -Aggravated Sexual Assault-22.021 -Indecency w/Child--21.11 - Possession or Promotion of Child Pornography-43.26 - Prohibited Sexual Conduct--25.02 - Sexual Assault-22.011 - Sexual Performance by a Child-43.25 - Burglary of Habitation with Intent to Commit any of the following listed sexual offenses:--30.02 -Aggravated Kidnapping (with intent to violate or abuse the victim sexually)--20.04(a)(4) -Aggravated Sexual Assault--22.021 - Indecency w/Child-21.11 - Prohibited Sexual Conduct-25.02 - Sexual Assault-22.011 *Offense in another state substantially similar to any of above offenses.		*Effective 09/01/1997
3g Offenses: - Aggravated Kidnapping-20.04 -Aggravated Robbery--29.03 -Aggravated Sexual Assault-22.021 - Any offense with Affirmative finding of Deadly Weapon - Capital Murder-19.03 - Indecency w/Child (Sexual Contact) 2nd Degree-21.ll(a) (1) - Murder--19.02 - Sexual Assault (of a Child), 22.0ll(a)(2) A Felony Increased Under Health & Safety Code 481.134 (c), (d), (e), or (f) (Drug-Free Zones), if it is shown that there is a previous conviction for an offense which punishment was increased under any of those subsections.	Calendar Time = ½ Minimum of 2 yrs. Maximum of 30 yrs.	CCP, Art. 42.12 *Gov't Code 508.046 *CCP, Art. 42.18 repealed effective 9-1-1997. Parole and Mandatory Supervision law now codified in Govt. Code 508.
All other 1st, 2nd, and 3rd degree felony offenses	Calendar Time+ Good TI me= 1/4, including work credits and bonus time. Maximum of 15 yrs	*Gov't code 508.145(f)
Drug-Free Zones 481.134	Calendar Time = 5 yrs. or maximum term, whichever is less.	*Gov't code 508.145(e)
CU Offenses	Time credit on all sentences, one after	CCP, Art. 42.08(a)

	another, until eligibility is reached on last sentence.	*Gov't Code 508.150
State Jail Felonies - a court may enhance the punishment by imposing the confinement of a 2nd or 3rd degree felony. - a court may reduce the punishment by imposing the confinement of a Class A Misdemeanor category offense (may or may not have been prosecuted under the lesser category offense title.)	Parole Eligibility is NOT applicable.	PC 12.35 Confinement is to a state jail for any term of not more than two years or less than 180 days.
The offenses listed below are NOT eligible for Mandatory Supervision: - Aggravated Assault, 1st or 2nd Degree--22.02 - Aggravated Kidnapping, 1st or 2nd Degree--20.04 - Aggravated Robbery, 1st Degree-29.03 - Aggravated Sexual Assault, 1st Degree--22.021 - Any offense with Affirmative finding of Deadly Weapon - Arson, 1st Degree-28.02 - Burglary of a Habitation, 1st Degree--30.02 with intent to commit felony other than Theft - Capital Murder--19.03 - Indecency w/Child 2nd or 3rd Degree-21.11 - Injury to a Child or Elderly or Disabled Individual, 1st Degree--22.04 - Murder, 1st or 2nd Degree--19.02 - Robbery, 2nd Degree--29.02 - Sexual Assault, 2nd Degree-22.011 A Felony Increased Under Health & Safety Code 481.134 (Drug-Free Zones). Any offense committed on or after 09/01/1996 with a prior conviction to include any above listed offenses.	Ineligible for Mandatory Supervision.	*Gov't Code 508.149 *CCP, Art. 42.18 repealed effective 09/01/97. Parole and mandatory supervision law now codified in Gov't Code 508.
Discretionary Mandatory Supervision		Gov't Code 508.149(b) An offender may be denied mandatory supervision by a parole panel for the following reasons: - Offender will endanger the public AND - Offender's accrued good conduct time is not an accurate reflection of the offender's potential for rehabilitation.

76th Legislature	09/01/1999 - 08/31/2001	
Offense	**Parole Eligibility**	**Comments**
Capital Murder (Capital Felony)- Life Sentence-19.03 1) Murder of a peace officer or fireman on official duty, 2) Intentionally murders a person in the course of committing or attempting to commit a kidnapping, burglary, robbery, aggravated sexual assault, arson, obstruction or retaliation,	Calendar Time= 40 yrs. Sentence-19.03	Gov't Code 508.046

3) Murders for remuneration, or promise of remuneration or employs another to commit the murder for remuneration or the promise of remuneration, 4) Murders while escaping or attempting to escape from a penal institution, 5) Murders an employee of a penal institution while incarcerated, 6) Murders with intent to establish, maintain, or participate in an alliance, or in the profits of an alliance, of individuals, while incarcerated, 7) A person convicted of and serving a sentence for Murder (19.02) who murders while incarcerated, 8) Murders while serving a sentence of Life or 99 years for Aggravated Kidnapping, Aggravated Sexual Assault, or Aggravated Robbery, 9) Murders more than one person during the same criminal transaction, or during different criminal transactions but the murders are committed pursuant to the same scheme, or course of conduct, 10) Murders an individual under six years of age.		
Offender is serving a Life Sentence for one of the following listed offenses: - Aggravated Kidnapping (with intent to violate or abuse the victim sexually)--20.04{a){4) - Aggravated Sexual Assault-22.021 - Sexual Assault-22.011 - Burglary of Habitation with Intent to Commit any of the following listed sexual offenses:--30.02 - Aggravated Kidnapping (with intent to violate or abuse the victim sexually)--20.04{a)(4) -Aggravated Sexual Assault--22.021 - Indecency w/Child-21.11 - Sexual Assault--22.011	Calendar Time = 35 yrs.	Gov't Code 508.145(c) PC 12.42 (c)(2)
AND has a previous conviction for one of the following offenses: -Aggravated Kidnapping (with intent to violate or abuse the victim sexually)--20.04{a)(4) -Aggravated Sexual Assault-22.021 -Indecency w/Child-21.11 - Possession or Promotion of Child Pornography--43.26 - Prohibited Sexual Conduct--25.02 - Sexual Assault-22.011 - Sexual Performance by a Child--43.25 - Burglary of Habitation with Intent to Commit any of the following listed sexual offenses:--30.02 -Aggravated Kidnapping (with intent to violate or abuse the victim sexually)--20.04{a)(4) -Aggravated Sexual Assault--22.021 -Indecency w/Child-21.11 - Prohibited Sexual Conduct-25.02		

- Sexual Assault-22.011 Offense in another state substantially similar to any of the above offenses.		
3g Offenses: - Aggravated Kidnapping-20.04 - Aggravated Robbery-29.03 -Aggravated Sexual Assault-22.021 - Any offense with Affirmative finding of Deadly Weapon - Capital Murder--19.03 - Indecency w/Child (Sexual Contact) 2nd Degree-21.ll(a) (1) - Murder-19.02 - Sexual Assault, *all subsections--22.011 A Felony Increased Under Health & Safety Code 481.134 (c), (d), (e), or (f) (Drug-Free Zones), if it is shown that there is a previous conviction for an offense which punishment was increased under any of those subsections. **A Felony Increased Under Health & Safety Code 481.140 (Use of Child in Commission of Offense).	Calendar Time = ½ Minimum of 2 yrs. Maximum of 30 yrs.	CCP, Art. 42.12 Gov't Code 508.046 * Effective 09/01/1999 ** Effective 06/14/2001
All other 1st, 2nd, and 3rd degree felony offenses	Calendar Time+ Good Time= 1/4, including work credits and bonus time. Maximum of 15 yrs.	Gov't code 508.145(f)
Drug-Free Zones 481.134	Calendar Time = 5 yrs. or maximum term, whichever is less.	Gov't code 508.145(e)
CU offenses	Time credit on all sentences, one after another, until eligibility is reached on last sentence.	CCP, Art. 42.08 (a) Gov't Code 508.150
State Jail Felonies - a court may enhance the punishment by imposing the confinement of a 2nd or 3rd degree felony. - a court may reduce the punishment by imposing the confinement of a Class A Misdemeanor category offense (may or may not have been prosecuted under the lesser category offense title.)	Parole Eligibility is NOT applicable.	PC12.35 Confinement is to a state jail for any term of not more than two years or less than 180 days.
The offenses listed below are NOT eligible for Mandatory Supervision: - Aggravated Assault, 1st or 2nd Degree--22.02 -Aggravated Kidnapping, 1st or 2nd Degree--20.04 - Aggravated Robbery, 1st Degree-29.03 - Aggravated Sexual Assault, 1st Degree--22.021 - Any offense with Affirmative finding of Deadly Weapon - Arson, 1st Degree-28.02 - Burglary of a Habitation, 1st Degree-30.02 with intent to commit felony other than Theft - Capital Murder-19.03 - Indecency w/Child 2nd *or* 3rd Degree-21.11 - Injury to a Child or Elderly or Disabled Individual, 1st Degree--22.04 Murder, 1st or 2nd Degree--19.02 - Robbery, 2nd Degree--29.02 - Sexual Assault, 2nd Degree-22.011	Ineligible for Mandatory Supervision.	Gov't Code 508.149 ** Effective 06/14/2001

A Felony Increased Under Health & Safety Code 481.134 (Drug-Free Zones). **A Felony Increased Under Health & Safety Code 481.140 (Use of Child in Commission of Offense). Any offense committed on or after 09/01/1996 with a prior conviction to include any above listed offenses.		
Discretionary Mandatory Supervision		Gov't Code 508.149(b) An offender may be denied mandatory supervision by a parole panel for the following reasons: - Offender will endanger the public **AND** - Offender's accrued good conduct time is not an accurate reflection of the offender's potential for rehabilitation

77th Legislature	09/01/2001 - 08/31/2003	
Offense	**Parole Eligibility**	**Comments**
Capital Murder (Capital Felony)- Life Sentence-19.03 1) Murder of a peace officer or fireman on official duty, 2) Intentionally murders a person in the course of committing or attempting to commit a kidnapping, burglary, robbery, aggravated sexual assault, arson, obstruction or retaliation, 3) Murders for remuneration, or promise of remuneration or employs another to commit the murder for remuneration or the promise of remuneration, 4) Murders while escaping or attempting to escape from a penal institution, 5) Murders an employee of a penal institution while incarcerated, 6) Murders with intent to establish, maintain, or participate in an alliance, or in the profits of an alliance, of individuals, while incarcerated, 7) A person convicted of and serving a sentence for Murder (19.02) who murders while incarcerated, 8) Murders while serving a sentence of Life or 99 years for Aggravated Kidnapping, Aggravated Sexual Assault, or Aggravated Robbery, 9) Murders more than one person during the same criminal transaction, or during different criminal transactions but the murders are committed pursuant to the same scheme, or course of conduct, 10) Murders an individual under six years of age.	Calendar Time= 40 yrs.	Gov't Code 508.046
Offender is serving a Life Sentence for one of the following listed offenses: - Aggravated Kidnapping (with intent	Calendar Time = 35 yrs.	Gov't Code 508.145(c) PC 12.42 (c)(2)

to violate or abuse the victim sexually)--20.04(a)(4) - Aggravated Sexual Assault-22.021 - Sexual Assault-22.011 - Burglary of Habitation with Intent to Commit any of the following listed sexual offenses:--30.02 - Aggravated Kidnapping (with intent to violate or abuse the victim sexually)--20.04(a)(4) -Aggravated Sexual Assault--22.021 - Indecency w/Child-21.11 - Sexual Assault--22.011		
AND has a previous conviction for one of the following offenses: -Aggravated Kidnapping (with intent to violate or abuse the victim sexually)--20.04(a)(4) -Aggravated Sexual Assault-22.021 -Indecency w/Child-21.11 - Possession or Promotion of Child Pornography--43.26 - Prohibited Sexual Conduct--25.02 - Sexual Assault-22.011 - Sexual Performance by a Child--43.25 - Burglary of Habitation with Intent to Commit any of the following listed sexual offenses:--30.02 -Aggravated Kidnapping (with intent to violate or abuse the victim sexually)--20.04(a)(4) -Aggravated Sexual Assault--22.021 -Indecency w/Child-21.11 - Prohibited Sexual Conduct-25.02 - Sexual Assault-22.011 Offense in another state substantially similar to any of the above offenses.		
3g Offenses: -Aggravated Kidnapping-20.04 -Aggravated Robbery--29.03 -Aggravated Sexual Assault-22.021 - Any offense with Affirmative finding of Deadly Weapon - Capital Murder-19.03 - Indecency w/Child (Sexual Contact) 2nd Degree-21.ll(a) (1) - Murder--19.02 - Sexual Assault, all subsections-22.011 A Felony Increased Under Health & Safety Code 481.134 (c), (d), (e), or (f) (Drug-Free Zones), if it is shown that there is a previous conviction for an offense which punishment was increased under any of those subsections. A Felony Increased Under Health & Safety Code 481.140 (Use of Child in Commission of Offense).	Calendar Time= ½ Minimum of 2 yrs. Maximum of 30 yrs.	CCP, Art. 42.12 Gov't Code 508.046
All other 1st, 2nd, and 3rd degree felony offenses	Calendar Time+ Good Time= 1/4, including work credits and bonus time. Maximum of 15 yrs.	Gov't code 508.145(f)
Drug-Free Zones 481.134	Calendar Time = 5 yrs. or maximum term, whichever is less.	Gov't code 508.145(e)
CU offenses	Time credit on all sentences, one after another, until eligibility is reached on	CCP, Art. 42.08 (a) Gov't Code 508.150

	last sentence.	
State Jail Felonies - a court may enhance the punishment by imposing the confinement of a 2nd or 3rd degree felony. - a court may reduce the punishment by imposing the confinement of a Class A Misdemeanor category offense (may or may not have been prosecuted under the lesser category offense title.)	Parole Eligibility is NOT applicable.	PC12.35 Confinement is to a state jail for any term of not more than two years or less than 180 days.
The offenses listed below are NOT eligible for Mandatory Supervision: - Aggravated Assault, 1st or 2nd Degree--22.02 - Aggravated Kidnapping, 1st or 2nd Degree--20.04 - Aggravated Robbery, 1st Degree-29.03 - Aggravated Sexual Assault, 1st Degree--22.021 - Any offense with Affirmative finding of Deadly Weapon - Arson, 1st Degree-28.02 - Burglary of a Habitation, 1st Degree-30.02 with intent to commit felony other than theft - Capital Murder-19.03 - Indecency w/Child 2nd or 3rd Degree-21.11 - Injury to a Child or Elderly or Disabled Individual, 1st Degree--22.04 - Murder, 1st or 2nd Degree--19.02 - Robbery, 2nd Degree--29.02 - Sexual Assault, 2nd Degree-22.011 A Felony Increased Under Health & Safety Code 481.134 (Drug-Free Zones). A Felony Increased Under Health & Safety Code 481.140 (Use of Child in Commission of Offense). Any offense committed on or after 09/01/1996 with a prior conviction to include any above listed offenses.	Ineligible for Mandatory Supervision.	Gov't Code 508.149
Discretionary Mandatory Supervision		Gov't Code 508.149(b) An offender may be denied mandatory supervision by a parole panel for the following reasons: - Offender will endanger the public **AND** - Offender's accrued good conduct time is not an accurate reflection of the offender's potential for rehabilitation

78th Legislature	09/01/2003 - 08/31/2005	
Offense	**Parole Eligibility**	**Comments**
Capital Murder (Capital Felony)- Life Calendar TI me= 40 yrs. Sentence--19.03 1) Murder of a peace officer or fireman on official duty, 2) Intentionally murders a person in the course of committing or attempting to commit a kidnapping, burglary, robbery, aggravated sexual	Calendar Time= 40 yrs.	Gov't Code 508.046 *Effective 09/01/2003

assault, arson, obstruction or retaliation, or *terroristic threat-22.07(a)(l,3,4,5, or 6), 3) Murders for remuneration, or promise of remuneration or employs another to commit the murder for remuneration or the promise of remuneration, 4) Murders while escaping or attempting to escape from a penal institution, S) Murders an employee of a penal institution while incarcerated, 6) Murders with intent to establish, maintain, or participate in an alliance, or in the profits of an alliance, of individuals, while incarcerated, 7) A person convicted of and serving a sentence for Murder (19.02) who murders while incarcerated, 8) Murders while serving a sentence of Life or 99 years for Aggravated Kidnapping, Aggravated Sexual Assault, or Aggravated Robbery, 9) Murders more than one person during the same criminal transaction, or during different criminal transactions but the murders are committed pursuant to the same scheme, or course of conduct, 10) Murders an individual under six years of age.		
Offender is serving a Life Sentence for one of the following listed offenses: -Aggravated Kidnapping (with intent to violate or abuse the victim sexually)--20.04{a}{4) - Aggravated Sexual Assault-22.021 - Sexual Assault-22.011 - Burglary of Habitation with Intent to Commit any of the following listed sexual offenses:--30.02 - Aggravated Kidnapping (with intent to violate or abuse the victim sexually)--20.04{a)(4) -Aggravated Sexual Assault--22.021 - Indecency w/Child-21.11 - Sexual Assault-22.011	Calendar Time= 35 yrs.	Gov't Code 508.145(c) PC 12.42{c)(2)
AND has a previous conviction for one of the following offenses: -Aggravated Kidnapping (with intent to violate or abuse the victim sexually)--20.04{a)(4) -Aggravated Sexual Assault-22.021 -Indecency w/Child-21.11 - *Obscenity (images of child under the age of 18)--43.23{h) - Possession or Promotion of Child Pornography-43.26 - Prohibited Sexual Conduct--25.02 - Sexual Assault-22.011 - Sexual Performance by a Child-43.25 - Burglary of Habitation with Intent to Commit any of the following listed sexual offenses:--30.02 -Aggravated Kidnapping (with intent		* Effective 09/01/2003

to violate or abuse the victim sexually)--20.04{a){4) -Aggravated Sexual Assault--22.021 -Indecency w/Child-21.11 - Prohibited Sexual Conduct-25.02 - Sexual Assault-22.011 Offense in another state substantially similar to any of the above offenses.		
3g Offenses: - Aggravated Kidnapping-20.04 -Aggravated Robbery--29.03 -Aggravated Sexual Assault-22.021 - Any offense with Affirmative finding of Deadly Weapon - Capital Murder-19.03 - Indecency w/Child (Sexual Contact) 2nd Degree-21.ll(a) (1) - Murder--19.02 - Sexual Assault, all subsections-22.011 A Felony Increased Under Health & Safety Code 481.134 (c), (d), (e), or (f) (Drug-Free Zones), if it is shown that there is a previous conviction for an offense which punishment was increased under any of those subsections. A Felony Increased Under Health & Safety Code 481.140 (Use of Child in Commission of Offense).	Calendar Time= ½ Minimum of 2 yrs. Maximum of 30 yrs.	CCP, Art. 42.12 Gov't Code 508.046
All other 1st, 2nd, and 3rd degree felony offenses	Calendar Time+ Good Time= 1/4, including work credits and bonus time. Maximum of 15 yrs.	Gov't code 508.145(f)
Drug-Free Zones 481.134	Calendar Time= 5 yrs. or maximum term, whichever is less.	Gov't code 508.145(e)
CU offenses	Time credit on all sentences, one after another, until eligibility is reached on last sentence.	CCP, Art. 42.08 (a) Gov't Code 508.150
State Jail Felonies - a court may enhance the punishment by imposing the confinement of a 2nd or 3rd degree felony. - a court may reduce the punishment by imposing the confinement of a Class A Misdemeanor category offense (may or may not have been prosecuted under the lesser category offense title.)	Parole Eligibility is NOT applicable.	PC 12.35 Confinement is to a state jail for any term of not more than two years or less than 180 days.
The offenses listed below are NOT eligible for Mandatory Supervision: - Aggravated Assault, 1st or 2nd Degree--22.02 - Aggravated Kidnapping, 1st or 2nd Degree--20.04 - Aggravated Robbery, 1st Degree-29.03 - Aggravated Sexual Assault, 1st Degree--22.021 - Any offense with Affirmative finding of Deadly Weapon - Arson, 1st Degree-28.02 - Burglary of a Habitation, 1st Degree-30.02 with intent to commit felony other than theft - Capital Murder--19.03 - Indecency w/Child 2nd or 3rd Degree-21.11	Ineligible for Mandatory Supervision	Gov't Code 508.149

- Injury to a Child or Elderly or Disabled Individual, 1st Degree--22.04 - Murder, 1st or 2nd Degree--19.02 - Robbery, 2nd Degree--29.02 - Sexual Assault, 2nd Degree-22.011 A Felony Increased Under Health & Safety Code 481.134 (Drug-Free Zones). A Felony Increased Under Health & Safety Code 481.140 (Use of Child in Commission of Offense). Any offense committed on or after 09/01/1996 with a prior conviction to include any above listed offenses.		
Discretionary Mandatory Supervision		Gov't Code 508.149(b) An offender may be denied mandatory supervision by a parole panel for the following reasons: - Offender will endanger the public **AND** - Offender's accrued good conduct time is not an accurate reflection of the offender's potential for rehabilitation

79th Legislature	09/01/2005 - 08/31/2007	
Offense	**Parole Eligibility**	**Comments**
Capital Murder (Capital Felony)* Death or Life without Parole--19.03 1) Murder of a peace officer or fireman on official duty, 2) Intentionally murders a person in the course of committing or attempting to commit a kidnapping, burglary, robbery, aggravated sexual assault, arson, obstruction or retaliation, or terroristic threat--22.07(a)(l,3,4,5, or 6), 3) Murders for remuneration, or promise of remuneration or employs another to commit the murder for remuneration or the promise of remuneration, 4) Murders while escaping or attempting to escape from a penal institution, 5) Murders an employee of a penal institution while incarcerated, 6) Murders with intent to establish, maintain, or participate in an alliance, or in the profits of an alliance, of individuals, while incarcerated, 7) A person convicted of and serving a sentence for Murder (19.02) who murders while incarcerated, 8) Murders while serving a sentence of Life or 99 years for Aggravated Kidnapping, Aggravated Sexual Assault, or Aggravated Robbery, 9) Murders more than one person during the same criminal transaction, or during different criminal transactions but the murders are committed pursuant to the same scheme, or course of conduct,	*Not eligible for Parole or MS release (40 yrs. flat repealed effective 09/01/2005) *Punishable by Death or Life without Parole only. * Prohibits anyone younger than 18yrs. of age to be punished by Death.	Govt. Code 508.145 * Effective 09/01/2005

10) Murders an individual under six years of age, 11) *Murders in retaliation for/on account of service/status as a judge or justice of courts.		
Offender is serving a Life Sentence for. one of the following listed offenses: - Aggravated Kidnapping (with intent to violate or abuse the victim sexually)--20.04{a){4) - Aggravated Sexual Assault-22.021 - Sexual Assault-22.011 - Burglary of Habitation with Intent to Commit any of the following listed sexual offenses:--30.02 - Aggravated Kidnapping (with intent to violate or abuse the victim sexually)--20.04{a)(4) -Aggravated Sexual Assault--22.021 - Indecency w/Child-21.11 - Sexual Assault--22.011	Calendar Time = 35 yrs.	Gov't Code 508.145(c) PC 12.42{c}{2J
AND has a previous conviction for one of the following offenses: -Aggravated Kidnapping (with intent to violate or abuse the victim sexually)--20.04{a)(4) -Aggravated Sexual Assault-22.021 -Indecency w/Child-21.11 - Obscenity (images of child under the age of 18)--43.23{h) - Possession or Promotion of Child Pornography--43.26 - Prohibited Sexual Conduct--25.02 - Sexual Assault-22.011 - Sexual Performance by a Child--43.25 - Burglary of Habitation with Intent to Commit any of the following listed sexual offenses:--30.02 -Aggravated Kidnapping (with intent to violate or abuse the victim sexually)--20.04{a){4) -Aggravated Sexual Assault--22.021 -Indecency w/Child-21.11 - Prohibited Sexual Conduct-25.02 - Sexual Assault-22.011 Offense in another state substantially similar to any of the above offenses.		
3g Offenses: - Aggravated Kidnapping-20.04 - Aggravated Robbery-29.03 -Aggravated Sexual Assault-22.021 - Any offense with Affirmative finding of Deadly Weapon - Capital Murder--19.03 - Indecency w/Child (Sexual Contact) 2nd Degree-21.ll(a) (1) - Murder--19.02 - Sexual Assault, all subsections-22.011 A Felony Increased Under Health & Safety Code 481.134 (c), (d), (e), or (f) (Drug-Free Zones), if it is shown that there is a previous conviction for an offense which punishment was increased under any of those subsections.	Calendar Time = ½ Minimum of 2 yrs. Maximum of 30 yrs.	CCP, Art. 42.12 Gov't Code 508.046

A Felony Increased Under Health & Safety Code 481.140 (Use of Child in Commission of Offense).		
All other 1st, 2nd, and 3rd degree felony offenses	Calendar Time+ Good Time= 1/4, including work credits and bonus time. Maximum of 15 yrs.	Gov't code 508.145(f)
Drug-Free Zones 481.134	Calendar Time = 5 yrs. or maximum term, whichever is less.	Gov't code 508.145(e)
CU offenses	Time credit on all sentences, one after another, until eligibility is reached on last sentence.	CCP, Art. 42.08 (a) Gov't Code 508.150
State Jail Felonies - a court may enhance the punishment by imposing the confinement of a 2nd or 3rd degree felony. - a court may reduce the punishment by imposing the confinement of a Class A Misdemeanor category offense (may or may not have been prosecuted under the lesser category offense title.)	Parole Eligibility is NOT applicable.	PC12.35 Confinement is to a state jail for any term of not more than two years or less than 180 days.
The offenses listed below are NOT eligible for Mandatory Supervision: - Aggravated Assault, 1st or 2nd Degree--22.02 -Aggravated Kidnapping, 1st or 2nd Degree--20.04 - Aggravated Robbery, 1st Degree-29.03 - Aggravated Sexual Assault, 1st Degree--22.021 - Any offense with Affirmative finding of Deadly Weapon - Arson, 1st Degree-28.02 - Burglary of a Habitation, 1st Degree-30.02 with intent to commit felony other than theft - Capital Murder-19.03 - Indecency w/Child 2nd or 3rd Degree-21.11 - Injury to a Child or Elderly or Disabled Individual, 1st Degree--22.04 - Murder, 1st or 2nd Degree--19.02 - Robbery, 2nd Degree--29.02 - Sexual Assault, 2nd Degree-22.011 A Felony Increased Under Health & Safety Code 481.134 (Drug-Free Zones). A Felony Increased Under Health & Safety Code 481.140 (Use of Child in Commission of Offense). Any offense committed on or after 09/01/1996 with a prior conviction to include any above listed offenses.	Ineligible for Mandatory Supervision	Gov't Code 508.149
Discretionary Mandatory Supervision		Gov't Code 508.149(b) An offender may be denied mandatory supervision by a parole panel for the following reasons: - Offender will endanger the public **AND** - Offender's accrued good conduct time is not an accurate reflection of the offender's potential for rehabilitation.

80th Legislature	09/01/2007 - 08/31/2009	
Offense	**Parole Eligibility**	**Comments**
Capital Murder (Capital Felony)-Death or Life without Parole-19.03 1) Murder of a peace officer or fireman on official duty, 2) Intentionally murders a person in the course of committing or attempting to commit a kidnapping, burglary, robbery, aggravated sexual assault, arson, obstruction or retaliation, or terroristic threat--22.07(a)(l,3,4,5, or 6), 3) Murders for remuneration, or promise of remuneration or employs another to commit the murder for remuneration or the promise of remuneration, 4) Murders while escaping or attempting to escape from a penal institution, 5) Murders an employee of a penal institution while incarcerated, 6) Murders with intent to establish, maintain, or participate in an alliance, or in the profits of an alliance, of individuals, while incarcerated, 7) A person convicted of and serving a sentence for Murder (19.02) who murders while incarcerated, 8) Murders while serving a sentence of Life or 99 years for Aggravated Kidnapping, Aggravated Sexual Assault, or Aggravated Robbery, 9) Murders more than one person during the same criminal transaction, or during different criminal transactions but the murders are committed pursuant to the same scheme, or course of conduct, 10) Murders an individual under six years of age, 11) Murders in retaliation for/on account of service/status as a judge or justice of courts.	Not eligible for Parole or MS release Punishable by Death or Life without Parole only. Prohibits anyone younger than 18yrs. of age to be punished by Death.	Gov't Code 508.145
Offender is serving a Life Sentence for Calendar TI me = 35 yrs. one of the following listed offenses: -Aggravated Kidnapping (with intent to violate or abuse the victim sexually) - 20.04(a)(4) *22.021(f) does not apply -* Aggravated Sexual Assault- 22.021 - Indecency w/Child - 21.ll(a)(l) - Sexual Assault- 22.011 - Burglary of Habitation with Intent to Commit any of the following listed sexual offenses: - 30.02 -Aggravated Kidnapping (with intent to violate or abuse the victim sexually) - 20.04(a)(4) - Aggravated Sexual Assault- 22.021 - Indecency w/Child - 21.11 - Sexual Assault- 22.011	Calendar Time = 35 yrs. *22.021(f) does not apply	Gov't Code 508.145(c) PC 12.42(c)(2) *Effective 9-1-2007
AND has a previous conviction one of the following offenses:		

-Aggravated Kidnapping (with intent to violate or abuse the victim sexually)--20.04(a)(4) -Aggravated Sexual Assault-22.021 - Indecency w/Child--21.11 - Obscenity (images of child under the age of 18)--43.23(h) - Possession or Promotion of Child Pornography--43.26 - Prohibited Sexual Conduct--25.02 - Sexual Assault-22.011 - Sexual Performance by a Child--43.25 - Burglary of Habitation with Intent to Commit any of the following listed sexual offenses:--30.02 -Aggravated Kidnapping (with intent to violate or abuse the victim sexually)--20.04(a)(4) -Aggravated Sexual Assault-22.021 - Indecency w/Child-21.11 - Sexual Assault-22.011 - Prohibited Sexual Conduct-25.02 Offense in another state similar to any above offenses.		
3g Offenses: -Aggravated Kidnapping-20.04 -Aggravated Robbery--29.03 -*Aggravated Sexual Assault-22.021 - Any offense with Affirmative finding of Deadly Weapon - Capital Murder-19.03 - Indecency w/Child (Sexual Contact) 2nd Degree-21.ll(a) (1) - *Injury to a Child, Elderly, or Disabled Individual, 1st Degree--22.04 (a)(l) (applies only to Child victim 14 or younger) - Murder--19.02 - Sexual Assault-22.011 - *Sexual Performance by a Child--43.25, all subsections A Felony Increased Under Health & Safety Code 481.134 (c), (d), (e), or (f) (Drug-Free Zones), if it is shown that there is a previous conviction for an offense which punishment was increased under any of those subsections. A Felony Increased Under Health & Safety Code 481.140 (Use of Child in Commission of Offense).	Calendar Time= ½ Minimum of 2 yrs. Maximum of 30 yrs. *22.021(f) does not apply	CCP, Art. 42.12 Gov't Code 508.046 *Effective 09/01/2007
All other 1st, 2nd, and 3rd degree felony offenses	Calendar Time+ Good Time= 1/4, including work credits and bonus time. Maximum of 15 yrs.	Gov't code 508.145(f)
Drug-Free Zones 481.134	Calendar Time= 5 yrs. or maximum term, whichever is less.	Gov't code 508.145(e)
CU offenses	Time credit on all sentences, one after another, until eligibility is reached on last sentence.	CCP, Art. 42.08 (a) Gov't Code 508.150
State Jail Felonies - a court may enhance the punishment by imposing the confinement of a 2nd or 3rd degree felony. - a court may reduce the punishment by imposing the confinement of a Class A Misdemeanor category offense (may	Parole Eligibility is NOT applicable.	PC 12.35 Confinement is to a state jail for any term of not more than two years or less than 180 days.

or may not have been prosecuted under the lesser category offense title.)		
The offenses listed below are NOT eligible for Mandatory Supervision: - Aggravated Assault, 1st or 2nd Degree--22.02 - Aggravated Kidnapping, 1st or 2nd Degree--20.04 - Aggravated Robbery, 1st Degree-29.03 - Aggravated Sexual Assault, 1st Degree--22.021 - Any offense with Affirmative finding of Deadly Weapon - Arson, 1st Degree-28.02 - Burglary of a Habitation, 1st Degree-30.02 with intent to commit felony other than theft - Capital Murder-19.03 - Indecency w/Child--21.11 - Injury to a Child or Elderly or Disabled Individual, 1st Degree--22.04 - Murder, 1st or 2nd Degree--19.02 - Robbery, 2nd Degree--29.02 - Sexual Assault, --22.011 - *Sexual Performance by a Child-43.25 A Felony Increased Under Health & Safety Code 481.134 (Drug-Free Zones). A Felony Increased Under Health & Safety Code 481.140 (Use of Child in Commission of Offense). Any offense committed on or after 09/01/1996 with a prior conviction to include any above listed offenses.	Ineligible for Mandatory Supervision.	Gov't Code 508.149 *Effective 09/01/2007
Discretionary Mandatory Supervision.		Gov't Code 508.149(b) An offender may be denied mand supervision by a parole panel for t following reasons: - Offender will endanger the public AND - Offender's accrued good conduct time is not an accurate reflection of the offender's potential for rehabilitation.
* The offenses listed below are NOT eligible for Parole or Mandatory Supervision: - Aggravated Sexual Assault - 22.021(f) * Effective 09/01/2007 - Continuous Sexual Abuse of a Young Child or Children - 21.02	Ineligible for Parole. Ineligible for Mandatory Supervision.	Gov't Code 508.145(a) Gov't Code 508.149 * Effective 09/01/2007

81st Legislature	09/01/2009 - 08/31/2011	
Offense	**Parole Eligibility**	**Comments**
Capital Murder {Capital Felony)-Death or Life without Parole-19.03 1) Murder of a peace officer or fireman on official duty, 2) Intentionally murders a person in the course of committing or attempting to commit a kidnapping, burglary, robbery, aggravated sexual	**Not eligible for Parole or Mandatory Supervision release. **Punishable by Death or Life without Parole only. *Calendar Time= 40 years served without consideration of good time. (Life sentence). Prohibits anyone younger than 18yrs.	Gov't Code 508.145 * Effective 09/01/2009 ****unless** transferred to the court under Section 54.02, Family Code. (Life sentence)

assault, arson, obstruction or retaliation, or terroristic threat--22.07(a)(l,3,4,5, or 6), 3) Murders for remuneration, or promise of remuneration or employs another to commit the murder for remuneration or the promise of remuneration, 4) Murders while escaping or attempting to escape from a penal institution, 5) Murders an employee of a penal institution while incarcerated, 6) Murders with intent to establish, maintain, or participate in an alliance, or in the profits of an alliance, of individuals, while incarcerated, 7) A person convicted of and serving a sentence for Murder {19.02) who murders while incarcerated, 8) Murders while serving a sentence of Life or 99 years for Aggravated Kidnapping, Aggravated Sexual Assault, or Aggravated Robbery, 9) Murders more than one person during the same criminal transaction, or during different criminal transactions but the murders are committed pursuant to the same scheme, or course of conduct, 10) Murders an individual under six years of age, 11) Murders in retaliation for/on account of service/status as a judge or justice of courts.	of age to be punished by Death.	
Offender is serving a Life Sentence for one of the following listed offenses: -Aggravated Kidnapping (with intent to violate or abuse the victim sexually) - 20.04(a)(4) *22.021(f) does not apply -* Aggravated Sexual Assault- 22.021 - Indecency w/Child - 21.ll(a)(l) - Sexual Assault - 22.011 - Burglary of Habitation with Intent to Commit any of the following listed sexual offenses: - 30.02 -Aggravated Kidnapping (with intent to violate or abuse the victim sexually) - 20.04(a)(4) - Aggravated Sexual Assault- 22.021 - Indecency w/Child - 21.11 - Sexual Assault- 22.011	Calendar Time= 35 yrs. *22.021(f) does not apply	Gov't Code 508.145(c) PC 12.42(c)(2)
AND has a previous conviction for one of the following offenses: -Aggravated Kidnapping (with intent to violate or abuse the victim sexually)--20.04(a)(4) -Aggravated Sexual Assault-22.021 - Indecency w/Child--21.11 - Obscenity (images of child under the age of 18)--43.23(h) - Possession or Promotion of Child Pornography-43.26 - Prohibited Sexual Conduct--25.02 - Sexual Assault-22.011 - Sexual Performance by a Child-43.25		

- Burglary of Habitation with Intent to Commit any of the following listed sexual offenses:--30.02 -Aggravated Kidnapping (with intent to violate or abuse the victim sexually)--20.04(a)(4) -Aggravated Sexual Assault-22.021 - Indecency w/Child-21.11 - Sexual Assault-22.011 - Prohibited Sexual Conduct-25.02 Offense in another state substantially similar to any of the above offenses.		
3g Offenses: - Aggravated Kidnapping-20.04 - Aggravated Robbery- 29.03 -* Aggravated Sexual Assault- 22.021 - Any offense with Affirmative finding of Deadly Weapon - **Criminal Solicitation, 1st Degree-15.03 - Capital Murder-19.03 - Indecency w/Child (Sexual Contact)2nd Degree- 21.ll(a)(l) - Injury to a Child or Elderly or Disabled Individual, 1st Degree -22.04 (a)(l) (applies only to Child victim 14 or younger) - Murder, -19.02 - Sexual Assault--22.011 - Sexual Performance by a Child -43.25, all subsections A Felony Increased Under Health & Safety Code 481.134 (c), (d), (e), or (f) (Drug-Free Zones), if it is shown that there is a previous conviction for an offense which punishment was increased under any of those subsections. A Felony Increased Under Health & Safety Code 481.140 (Use of Child in Commission of Offense).	Calendar Time = ½ Minimum of 2 yrs. Maximum of 30 years. *22.021(f) does not apply **For every 12 months that elapse between date of arrest warrant and actual arrest date, initial Parole eligibility date is delayed by 3 years for the offenses of: - Murder-19.02 - Sexual Assault--22.011 -Aggravated Sexual Assault--22.021	CCP, Art. 42.12 Gov't Code 508.046 **Effective 09/01/2009
All other 1st, 2nd, and 3rd degree felony offenses	Calendar Time+ Good Time= 1/4, including work credits and bonus time. Maximum of 15 yrs.	Gov't code 508.145(f)
Drug-Free Zones 486.184	Calendar Time = 5 yrs. or maximum term, whichever is less.	Gov't code 508.145(e)
CU offenses	Time credit on all sentences, one after another, until eligibility is reached on last sentence.	CCP, Art. 42.08 (a) Gov't Code 508.150
State Jail Felonies - a court may enhance the punishment by imposing the confinement of a 2nd or 3rd degree felony. - a court may reduce the punishment by imposing the confinement of a Class A Misdemeanor category offense (may or may not have been prosecuted under the lesser category offense title.)	Parole Eligibility is NOT applicable.	PC 12.35 Confinement is to a state jail for any term of not more than two years or less than 180 days.
The offenses listed below are NOT eligible for Mandatory Supervision: - Aggravated Assault, 1st or 2nd Degree - 22.02 - Aggravated Kidnapping, 1st or 2nd Degree - 20.04 - Aggravated Robbery, 1st Degree-29.03	Ineligible for Mandatory Supervision.	Gov't Code 508.149 *Effective 09/01/2009

- Aggravated Sexual Assault, 1st Degree--22.021 - Any offense with Affirmative finding of Deadly Weapon - Arson, 1st Degree-28.02 - Burglary of a Habitation, 1st Degree-30.02 with intent to commit felony other than theft - Capital Murder--19.03 -*Criminal Solicitation, 1st Degree-15.03 - Indecency w/Child--21.11 - Injury to a Child or Elderly or Disabled Individual, 1st Degree--22.04 - Murder, 1st or 2nd Degree--19.02 - Robbery, 2nd Degree--29.02 - Sexual Assault-22.011 - Sexual Performance by a Child--43.25 A Felony Increased Under Health & Safety Code 481.134 (Drug-Free Zones). A Felony Increased Under Health & Safety Code 481.140 (Use of Child in Commission of Offense). Any offense committed on or after 09/01/1996 with a prior conviction to include any above listed offenses.		
Discretionary Mandatory Supervision		Gov't Code 508.149(b) An offender may be denied mandatory supervision by a parole panel for the following reasons: - Offender will endanger the public **AND** - Offender's accrued good conduct time is not an accurate reflection of the offender's potential for rehabilitation.
The offenses listed below are NOT eligible for Parole or Mandatory Supervision: - Aggravated Sexual Assault - 22.021(f) - Continuous Sexual Abuse of a Young Child or Children - 21.02	Ineligible for Parole. Ineligible for Mandatory Supervision.	Gov't Code 508.145(a) Gov't Code 508.149

82nd Legislature	09/01/2011 - 08/31/2013	
Offense	**Parole Eligibility**	**Comments**
Capital Murder {Capital Felony)-Death or Life without Parole-19.03 1) Murder of a peace officer or fireman on official duty, 2) Intentionally murders a person in the course of committing or attempting to commit a kidnapping, burglary, robbery, aggravated sexual assault, arson, obstruction or retaliation, or terroristic threat--22.07{a)(l,3,4,5, or 6), 3) Murders for remuneration, or promise of remuneration or employs another to commit the murder for remuneration or the promise of remuneration, 4) Murders while escaping or attempting to escape from a penal institution,	**Not eligible for Parole or Mandatory Supervision release. **Punishable by Death or Life without Parole only. Calendar TI me= 40 years served without consideration of good time (Life sentence) Prohibits anyone younger than 18yrs. of age to be punished by Death.	Gov't Code 508.145 *Effective 09/01/2011 ****unless** transferred to the court under Section 54.02, Family Code. (Life sentence)

5) Murders an employee of a penal institution while incarcerated, 6) Murders with intent to establish, maintain, or participate in an alliance, or in the profits of an alliance, of individuals, while incarcerated, 7) A person convicted of and serving a sentence for Murder {19.02) who murders while incarcerated, 8) Murders while serving a sentence of Life or 99 years for Aggravated Kidnapping, Aggravated Sexual Assault, or Aggravated Robbery, 9) Murders more than one person during the same criminal transaction or during different criminal transactions but the murders are committed pursuant to the same scheme, or course of conduct, 10) Murders an individual under *ten years of age, 11) Murders in retaliation for/on account of service/status as a judge or justice of courts.		
Offender is serving a Life Sentence for. one of the following listed offenses: -Aggravated Kidnapping (with intent to violate or abuse the victim sexually) - 20.04(a)(4) -**Aggravated Sexual Assault-22.021 - Indecency w/Child - 21.ll(a)(l) - Sexual Assault- 22.011 -*Trafficking of Persons-20A.02(a)(7) or (a)(8), (involves a child) - Burglary of Habitation with Intent to Commit any of the following : - 30.02 -Aggravated Kidnapping (with intent to violate or abuse the victim sexually) - 20.04(a)(4) - Aggravated Sexual Assault- 22.021 - Indecency w/Child - 21.11 - Sexual Assault- 22.011 -*Trafficking of Persons-20A.02 (a)(7) or (a)(8), (involves a child)	Calendar Time = 35 yrs **22.021(f) does not apply	Gov't Code 508.145(c) PC 12.42(c)(2) *Effective 09/01/2011
AND has a previous conviction for one of the following offenses: -Aggravated Kidnapping (with intent to violate or abuse the victim sexually)--20.04(a)(4) -Aggravated Sexual Assault-22.021 - Indecency w/Child--21.11 - Obscenity (images of child under the age of 18)--43.23(h) - Possession or Promotion of Child Pornography--43.26 - Prohibited Sexual Conduct--25.02 - Sexual Assault-22.011 -*Trafficking of Persons--20A.02 (a)(7) or (a)(8), (involves a child) - Sexual Performance by a Child-43.25 - Burglary of Habitation with Intent to Commit any of the following: -Aggravated Kidnapping (with intent to violate or abuse the victim sexually)--20.04(a)(4) -Aggravated Sexual Assault-22.021		*Effective 09/01/2011

- Indecency w/Child-21.11 - Sexual Assault--22.011 - Prohibited Sexual Conduct-25.02 -*Trafficking of Persons-20A.02 (a) (7) or **(a)(8),** (involves a child) Offense in another state substantially similar to any of the above offenses.		
3g Offenses: - Aggravated Kidnapping-20.04 - Aggravated Robbery- 29.03 -** Aggravated Sexual Assault- 22.021 - Any offense with Affirmative finding of Deadly Weapon - Criminal Solicitation, 1st Degree-15.03 - Capital Murder--19.03 - Indecency w/Child (Sexual Contact)2nd Degree- 21.II(a)(I) - Injury to a Child or Elderly or Disabled Individual, 1st Degree -22.04(a)(I) (applies only to Child victim 14 or younger) - Murder-19.02 - Sexual Assault--22.011 - Sexual Performance by a Child -43.25, all subsections A Felony Increased Under Health & Safety Code 481.134 (c), (d), (e), or (f) (Drug-Free Zones), if it is shown that there is a previous conviction for an offense which punishment was increased under any of those subsections. A Felony Increased Under Health & Safety Code 481.140 (Use of Child in Commission of Offense).	Calendar Time = ½ Minimum of 2 yrs. Maximum of 30 years. **22.021(f) does not apply For every 12 months that elapse between date of arrest warrant and actual arrest date, initial Parole eligibility date is delayed by 3 years for the offenses of: - Murder-19.02 - Sexual Assault--22.011 -Aggravated Sexual Assault--22.021 * Continuous Trafficking of Persons--20A.03 **-NOT3g** - Calendar Time = 1/2 - Minimum 2 years - Maximum 30 years * Compelling Prostitution--43.05 and Trafficking of Persons--20A.02 are listed as "3g" offenses in CCP 42.12, but were omitted from 3g parole eligibility flat time requirements under Gov't Code 508.145.	CCP, Art. 42.12 Gov't Code 508.046 *Effective 09/01/2011
All other 1st, 2nd, and 3rd degree felony offenses	Calendar TI me+ Good TI me= 1/4, including work credits and bonus time. Maximum of 15 yrs.	Gov't Code 508.145(f)
Drug-Free Zones 481.134	Calendar Time = 5 yrs. or maximum term, whichever is less.	Gov't Code 508.145(e)
CU offenses	Time credit on all sentences, one after another, until eligibility is reached on last sentence.	CCP, Art. 42.08(a) Gov't Code 508.150
State Jail Felonies - a court may enhance the punishment by imposing the confinement of a 2nd or 3rd degree felony. a court may reduce the punishment by imposing the confinement of a Class A Misdemeanor category offense (may or may not have been prosecuted under the lesser category offense title.)	Parole Eligibility is NOT applicable.	PC 12.35 Confinement is to a state jail for any term of not more than two years or less than 180 days.
The offenses listed below are NOT eligible for Mandatory Supervision: - Aggravated Assault, 1st or 2nd Degree - 22.02 -Aggravated Kidnapping, 1st or 2nd Degree - 20.04 - Aggravated Robbery, 1st Degree - 29.03 Aggravated Sexual Assault, 1st Degree- 22.021	Ineligible for Mandatory Supervision.	Gov't Code 508.149 #Effective 09/01/2011

- Any offense with Affirmative finding of Deadly Weapon - Arson, 1st Degree - 28.02 - Burglary of a Habitation, 1st Degree - 30.02 with intent to commit felony other than theft - Capital Murder-19.03 - Indecency w/Child - 21.11 - Injury to a Child or Elderly or Disabled Individual, 1st Degree- 22.04 - Criminal Solicitation, 1st Degree- 15.03 - *Compelling Prostitution-43.05 - *Trafficking of Persons-20A.02 - *Continuous Trafficking of Persons- 20A.03 - Murder, 1st or 2nd Degree -19.02 - Robbery, 2nd Degree - 29.02 - Sexual Assault, 2nd Degree - 22.011 - Sexual Performance by a Child -43.25 A Felony Increased Under Health & Safety Code 481.134 (Drug-Free Zones). A Felony Increased Under Health & Safety Code 481.140 (Use of Child in Commission of Offense). Any offense committed on or after 09/01/1996 with a prior conviction to include any above listed offenses.		
Discretionary Mandatory Supervision		
The offenses listed below are NOT eligible for Parole or Mandatory Supervision: - Aggravated Sexual Assault - 22.021(f) - Continuous Sexual Abuse of a Young Child or Children - 21.02	Ineligible for Parole. Ineligible for Mandatory Supervision.	Gov't Code 508.149(b) An offender may be denied mandatory supervision by a parole panel for the following reasons: -Offender will endanger the public AND -Offender's accrued good conduct time i not an accurate reflection of the offender's potential for rehabilitation.
-**Injury to a Child, Elderly or Disabled Individual, 2nd or 3rd Degree - 22.04	**Eligible for up to a five year set-off following a decision of parole denial by the BPP voting panel per HB 431	**Effective 06/14/2013

83rd Legislature	09/01/2013 - 08/31/2015	
Offense	**Parole Eligibility**	**Comments**
Capital Murder (Capital Felony)-Death or Life without Parole-19.03 1) Murder of a peace officer or fireman on official duty, 2) Intentionally murders a person in the course of committing or attempting to commit a kidnapping, burglary, robbery, aggravated sexual assault, arson, obstruction or retaliation, or terroristic threat-- 22.07(a)(I,3,4,5, or 6), 3) Murders for remuneration, or promise of remuneration or employs another to commit the murder for remuneration or the promise of remuneration, 4) Murders while escaping or attempting to escape from a penal institution,	**Not eligible for Parole or Mandatory Supervision release. **Punishable by Death or Life without Parole only. Calendar TI me= 40 years served without consideration of good time (Life sentence). Prohibits anyone younger than 18yrs. of age to be punished by Death.	Gov't Code 508.145 **Unless transferred to the court under Section 54.02, Family Code (Life sentence).

5) Murders an employee of a penal institution while incarcerated, 6) Murders with intent to establish, maintain, or participate in an alliance, or in the profits of an alliance, of individuals, while incarcerated, 7) A person convicted of and serving a sentence for Murder (19.02) who murders while incarcerated, 8) Murders while serving a sentence of Life or 99 years for Aggravated Kidnapping, Aggravated Sexual Assault, or Aggravated Robbery, 9) Murders more than one person during the same criminal transaction, or during different criminal transactions but the murders are committed pursuant to the same scheme, or course of conduct, 10) Murders an individual under ten years of age, 11) Murders in retaliation for/on account of service/status as a judge or justice of courts.		
Offender is serving a Life Sentence for one of the following listed offenses: -Aggravated Kidnapping (with intent to violate or abuse the victim sexually)--20.04(a)(4) -* Aggravated Sexual Assault--22.021 *22.021(f) does not apply - Indecency w/Child--21.II(a)(I) - Sexual Assault-22.011 -Trafficking of Persons-20A.02 (a)(7) or (a)(8), (involves a child) - Burglary of Habitation with Intent to Commit any of the following: -30.02 -Aggravated Kidnapping (with intent to violate or abuse the victim sexually) - 20.04(a)(4) -Aggravated Sexual Assault--22.021 - Indecency w/Child-21.11 - Sexual Assault--22.011 -Trafficking of Persons-20A.02 (a)(7) or (a)(8), (involves a child)	Calendar Time = 35 yrs. **22.021(f) does not apply.	Gov't Code 508.145(c) PC 12.42(c)(2)
AND has a previous conviction for one of the following offenses: -Aggravated Kidnapping (with intent to violate or abuse the victim sexually)--20.04(a)(4) -Aggravated Sexual Assault-22.021 - Indecency w/Child--21.11 - Obscenity (images of child under the age of 18)--43.23(h) - Possession or Promotion of Child Pornography--43.26 - Prohibited Sexual Conduct--25.02 - Sexual Assault-22.011 - Sexual Performance by a Child--43.25 -Trafficking of Persons-20A.02 (a)(7) or (a)(8), (involves a child) - Burglary of Habitation with Intent to Commit any of the following:--30.02 -Aggravated Kidnapping (with intent to violate or abuse the victim sexually)--20.04(a)(4)		

-Aggravated Sexual Assault--22.021 - Indecency w/Child-21.11 - Prohibited Sexual Conduct-25.02 - Sexual Assault--22.011 -Trafficking of Persons-20A.02 (a)(7) or (a)(8), (involves a child) Offense in another state substantially similar to any of the above offenses.		
3g Offenses: -Aggravated Kidnapping-20.04 -Aggravated Robbery--29.03 -**Aggravated Sexual Assault--22.021 - Any offense with Affirmative finding of Deadly Weapon Criminal Solicitation, 1st Degree--15.03 Capital Murder--19.03 - Indecency w/Child (Sexual Contact) 2nd Degree-21.ll(a)(l) - Injury to a Child or Elderly or Disabled Individual, 1st Degree--22.04(a)(1) (applies only to Child victim 14 or younger) - Murder--19.02 - Sexual Assault-22.011 - Sexual Performance by a Child-43.25 -*Compelling Prostitution-43.05 -*Trafficking of Persons-20A.02 -* Burglary of Habitation with Intent to Commit any of the following:-30.02 -Continuous Sexual Abuse of a Young Child or Children-21.02 - Indecency w/Child-21.11 - Sexual Assault-22.011 -Aggravated Sexual Assault--22.021 - Prohibited Sexual Conduct-25.02 A Felony Increased Under Health & Safety Code 481.134 (c), (d), (e), or (f) (Drug-Free Zones), if it is shown that there is a previous conviction for an offense which punishment was increased under any of those subsections. A Felony Increased Under Health & Safety Code 481.140 (Use of Child in Commission of Offense).	Calendar Time = ½ Minimum of 2 yrs. Maximum of 30 years. **22.021(f) does not apply For every 12 months that elapse between date of arrest warrant and actual arrest date, initial Parole eligibility date is delayed by 3 years for the offenses of: - Murder--19.02 - Sexual Assault-22.011 -Aggravated Sexual Assault-22.021; -Continuous Trafficking of Persons--20A.03 -*Engaging in Organized Criminal Activity-- 71.02 -*Directing Activities of Criminal Street Gangs-71.023 **-NOT 3g** - Calendar Time = 1/2 - Minimum 2 years - Maximum 30 years	CCP, Art. 42.12 Gov't Code 508.046 *Effective 09/01/2013
All other 1st, 2nd, and 3rd degree felony offenses	Calendar Time + Good Time = 1/4, including work credits and bonus time. Maximum of 15 yrs.	Gov't code 508.145(f)
Drug-Free Zones 481.134	Calendar Time = 5 yrs. or maximum term, whichever is less.	Gov't code 508.145(e)
CU offenses	Time credit on all sentences, one after another, until eligibility is reached on last sentence.	CCP, Art. 42.08 (a) Gov't Code 508.150
State Jail Felonies - a court may enhance the punishment by imposing the confinement of a 2nd or 3rd degree felony. - a court may reduce the punishment by imposing the confinement of a Class A Misdemeanor category offense (may or may not have been prosecuted under the lesser category offense title.)	Parole Eligibility is NOT applicable.	PC 12.35 Confinement is to a state jail for term of not more than two years less than 180 days.
The offenses listed below are NOT eligible for Mandatory Supervision: - Aggravated Assault, 1st or 2nd	Ineligible for Mandatory Supervision	Gov't Code 508.149 *Effective 09/01/2013

Degree- 22.02 - Aggravated Kidnapping, 1st or 2nd Degree-20.04 -Aggravated Robbery, 1st Degree-29.03 - Aggravated Sexual Assault, 1st Degree- 22.021 - Any offense with Affirmative finding of Deadly Weapon - Arson, 1st Degree-28.02 - Burglary of Habitation, 1st Degree-30.02 with intent to commit felony other than Theft -Capital Murder-19.03 - Compelling Prostitution--43.05 - Continuous Traffi::king of Persons-20A.03 - Criminal Solicitation, 1st Degree-15.03 - Indecencyw/Child-21.11 - Injury to a Child or Elderly or Disabled Individual, 1st Degree-22.04 - Murder, 1st or 2nd Degree-19.02 - Robbery, 2nd Degree-29.02 - Sexual Assault, 2nd Degree-22.011 - Sexual Performance by a Child--43.25 - Traffi::king of Persons-20A.02 -*Engaging in Organized Criminal Activity, 1st Degree- 71.02 -*Directing Activities of Criminal Street Gangs, 1st Degree-71.023 A Felony Increased Under Health & Safety Code 481.134 (Drug-Free Zones). A Felony Increased Under Health & Safety Code 481.140 (Use of Child in Commission of Offense). Any offense committed on or after 09/01/1996 with a prior conviction to include any above listed offenses.		
Discretionary Mandatory Supervision		Gov't Code 508.149(b) An offender may be denied mandatory supervision by a parole panel for the following reasons: - Offender will endanger the public AND - Offender's accrued good conduct time is not an accurate reflection of the offender's potential for rehabilitation.
The offenses listed below are NOT eligible for Parole or Mandatory Supervision: -Aggravated Sexual Assault-22.021(f) - Continuous Sexual Abuse of a Young Child or Children-21.02	Ineligible for Parole. Ineligible for Mandatory Supervision.	Gov't Code 508.145(a) Gov't Code 508.149
- Injury to a Child, Elderly or Disabled Individual, 2nd or 3rd Degree-22.04	Eligible for up to a five year set-off following a decision of parole denial by the BPP voting panel per HB 431.	Effective 06/14/2013

84th Legislature	09/01/2015 - 08/31/2017	
Offense	**Parole Eligibility**	**Comments**
Capital Murder (Capital Felony)-Death or Life without Parole-19.03 1) Murder of a peace officer or fireman on official duty,	**Not eligible for Parole or Mandatory Supervision release. **Punishable by Death or Life without Parole only.	Gov't Code 508.145 **Unless transferred to the court under Section 54.02, Family Code (Life

2) Intentionally murders a person in the course of committing or attempting to commit a kidnapping, burglary, robbery, aggravated sexual assault, arson, obstruction or retaliation, or terroristic threat--22.07(a)(l,3,4,5, or 6), 3) Murders for remuneration, or promise of remuneration or employs another to commit the murder for remuneration or the promise of remuneration, 4) Murders while escaping or attempting to escape from a penal institution, 5) Murders an employee of a penal institution while incarcerated, 6) Murders with intent to establish, maintain, or participate in an alliance, or in the profits of an alliance, of individuals, while incarcerated, 7) A person convicted of and serving a sentence for Murder (19.02) who murders while incarcerated, 8) Murders while serving a sentence of Life or 99 years for Aggravated Kidnapping, Aggravated Sexual Assault, or Aggravated Robbery, 9) Murders more than one person during the same criminal transaction, or during different criminal transactions but the murders are committed pursuant to the same scheme, or course of conduct, 10) Murders an individual under ten years of age, 11) Murders in retaliation for/on account of service/status as a judge or justice of courts.	Calendar Time= 40 years served without consideration of good time (Life sentence). Prohibits anyone younger than 18yrs. of age to be punished by Death.	sentence).
Offender is serving a Life Sentence for one of the following listed offenses: -Aggravated Kidnapping (with intent to violate or abuse the victim sexually)--20.04(a)(4) -* Aggravated Sexual Assault--22.021 *22.021(f) does not apply - Indecency w/Child--21.ll(a)(l) - Sexual Assault-22.011 -Trafficking of Persons-20A.02 (a)(7) or (a)(8), (involves a child) - Burglary of Habitation with Intent to Commit any of the following: -30.02 -Aggravated Kidnapping (with intent to violate or abuse the victim sexually) - 20.04(a)(4) -Aggravated Sexual Assault--22.021 - Indecency w/Child-21.11 - Sexual Assault--22.011 -Trafficking of Persons-20A.02 (a)(7) or (a)(8), (involves a child)	Calendar Time = 35 yrs. **22.021(f) does not apply.	Gov't Code 508.145(c) PC 12.42(c)(2)
AND has a previous conviction for one of the following offenses: -Aggravated Kidnapping (with intent to violate or abuse the victim sexually)--20.04(a)(4) -Aggravated Sexual Assault-22.021		

- Indecency w/Child--21.11 - Obscenity (images of child under the age of 18)--43.23(h) - Possession or Promotion of Child Pornography--43.26 - Prohibited Sexual Conduct--25.02 - Sexual Assault-22.011 - Sexual Performance by a Child--43.25 -Trafficking of Persons-20A.02 (a)(7) or (a)(8), (involves a child) - Burglary of Habitation with Intent to Commit any of the following:--30.02 -Aggravated Kidnapping (with intent to violate or abuse the victim sexually)--20.04(a)(4) -Aggravated Sexual Assault--22.021 - Indecency w/Child-21.11 - Prohibited Sexual Conduct-25.02 - Sexual Assault--22.011 -Trafficking of Persons-20A.02 (a)(7) or (a)(8), (involves a child) Offense in another state substantially similar to any of the above offenses.		
3g Offenses: -Aggravated Kidnapping-20.04 -Aggravated Robbery--29.03 -**Aggravated Sexual Assault--22.021 - Any offense with Affirmative finding of Deadly Weapon Criminal Solicitation, 1st Degree--15.03 Capital Murder--19.03 - Indecency w/Child (Sexual Contact) 2nd Degree-21.ll(a)(l) - Injury to a Child or Elderly or Disabled Individual, 1st Degree--22.04(a)(1) (applies only to Child victim 14 or younger) - Murder--19.02 - Sexual Assault-22.011 - Sexual Performance by a Child-43.25 -*Compelling Prostitution-43.05 -*Trafficking of Persons-20A.02 -* Burglary of Habitation with Intent to Commit any of the following:-30.02 -Continuous Sexual Abuse of a Young Child or Children-21.02 - Indecency w/Child-21.11 - Sexual Assault-22.011 -Aggravated Sexual Assault--22.021 - Prohibited Sexual Conduct-25.02 A Felony Increased Under Health & Safety Code 481.134 (c), (d), (e), or (f) (Drug-Free Zones), if it is shown that there is a previous conviction for an offense which punishment was increased under any of those subsections. A Felony Increased Under Health & Safety Code 481.140 (Use of Child in Commission of Offense).	Calendar Time = ½ Minimum of 2 yrs. Maximum of 30 years. **22.021(f) does not apply For every 12 months that elapse between date of arrest warrant and actual arrest date, initial Parole eligibility date is delayed by 3 years for the offenses of: - Murder--19.02 - Sexual Assault-22.011 -Aggravated Sexual Assault-22.021; -Continuous Trafficking of Persons--20A.03 -*Engaging in Organized Criminal Activity-- 71.02 -*Directing Activities of Criminal Street Gangs-71.023 **-<u>NOT</u> 3g** - Calendar Time = 1/2 - Minimum 2 years - Maximum 30 years	CCP, Art. 42.12 Gov't Code 508.046
All other 1st, 2nd, and 3rd degree felony offenses	Calendar Time + Good Time = 1/4, including work credits and bonus time. Maximum of 15 yrs.	Gov't code 508.145(f)

Drug-Free Zones 481.134	Calendar Time = 5 yrs. or maximum term, whichever is less.	Gov't code 508.145(e)
CU offenses	Time credit on all sentences, one after another, until eligibility is reached on last sentence.	CCP, Art. 42.08 (a) Gov't Code 508.150
State Jail Felonies - a court may enhance the punishment by imposing the confinement of a 2nd or 3rd degree felony. - a court may reduce the punishment by imposing the confinement of a Class A Misdemeanor category offense (may or may not have been prosecuted under the lesser category offense title.)	Parole Eligibility is NOT applicable.	PC 12.35 Confinement is to a state jail for term of not more than two years less than 180 days.
The offenses listed below are NOT eligible for Mandatory Supervision: - Aggravated Assault, 1st or 2nd Degree- 22.02 - Aggravated Kidnapping, 1st or 2nd Degree-20.04 -Aggravated Robbery, 1st Degree-29.03 - Aggravated Sexual Assault, 1st Degree- 22.021 - Any offense with Affirmative finding of Deadly Weapon - Arson, 1st Degree-28.02 - Burglary of Habitation, 1st Degree-30.02 with intent to commit felony other than Theft -Capital Murder-19.03 - Compelling Prostitution--43.05 - Continuous Traffi::king of Persons-20A.03 - Criminal Solicitation, 1st Degree-15.03 - indecency w/Child-21.11 - Injury to a Child or Elderly or Disabled Individual, 1st Degree-22.04 - Murder, 1st or 2nd Degree-19.02 - Robbery, 2nd Degree-29.02 - Sexual Assault, 2nd Degree-22.011 - Sexual Performance by a Child--43.25 - Traffi::king of Persons-20A.02 -*Engaging in Organized Criminal Activity, 1st Degree- 71.02 -*Directing Activities of Criminal Street Gangs, 1st Degree-71.023 A Felony Increased Under Health & Safety Code 481.134 (Drug-Free Zones). A Felony Increased Under Health & Safety Code 481.140 (Use of Child in Commission of Offense). Any offense committed on or after 09/01/1996 with a prior conviction to include any above listed offenses.	Ineligible for Mandatory Supervision	Gov't Code 508.149
Discretionary Mandatory Supervision		Gov't Code 508.149(b) An offender may be denied mandatory supervision by a parole panel for the following reasons: - Offender will endanger the public AND - Offender's accrued good conduct time is not an accurate reflection of the offender's potential for rehabilitation.
The offenses listed below are NOT	Ineligible for Parole. Ineligible for	Gov't Code 508.145(a)

eligible for Parole or Mandatory Supervision: -Aggravated Sexual Assault-22.021(f) - Continuous Sexual Abuse of a Young Child or Children-21.02	Mandatory Supervision.	Gov't Code 508.149
- Injury to a Child, Elderly or Disabled Individual, 2nd or 3rd Degree-22.04	Eligible for up to a five year set-off following a decision of parole denial by the BPP voting panel per HB 431.	Effective 06/14/2013
- *Aggravated Sexual Assault-22.021 - *Capital Murder-19.03 (LIFE) - includes all statutory precursor offenses to both	*Eligible for up to a ten year set -off following a decision of parole denial by the BPP voting panel per HB 1914.	*Effective 09/01/2015
		Effective 1/1/2017 offenses in CCP 42 section 3G are moving to CCP 42A.054

85th Legislature	09/01/2017 - 08/31/2019	
Offense	Parole Eligibility	Comments
Capital Murder (Capital Felony) Death or Life without Parole—19.03 1) Murder of a peace officer or fireman on official duty; 2) Intentionally murders a person in the course of committing or a mp ng to commit a kidnapping, burglary, robbery, aggravated sexual assault, arson, obstruction or retaliation, or terrorist threat—22.07(a)(1), (3), (4), (5), or (6); 3) Murders for remuneration or promise of remuneration or employs another to commit the murder for remuneration or the promise of remuneration; 4) Murders while escaping or attempting to escape from a penal Institution; 5) While incarcerated, murders an employee of a penal ins tu on or murders with intent to establish, maintain, or par cipate in an alliance, or in the profits of an alliance, of individuals; 6) A person convicted of and serving a sentence for Murder (19.02) who murders while incarcerated or murders while serving a sentence of Life or 99 years for Aggravated Kidnapping (20.04), Aggravated Sexual Assault (22.021), or Aggravated Robbery (29.03); 7) Murders more than one person during the same criminal transaction, or during different criminal transactions but the murders are committed pursuant to the same scheme, or course of conduct; 8) Murders an individual under ten years of age; or 9) Murders in retaliation for/on account of service/status as a judge or justice of courts.	**Not eligible for Parole or Mandatory Supervision release. **Punishable by Death or Life without Parole only. Calendar Time = 40 years served without consideration of good e (Life sentence) if under 18 years of age when serving a life sentence for a capital felony. PC 12.31(a)(1), Gov't Code 508.145(b). Offenses of continuous sexual abuse of young child or children (21.02) and super aggravated sexual assault of a child (22.021(f)) also are not eligible for Parole or Mandatory Supervision release. Gov't Code 508.145(a)	Gov't Code 508.145, Gov't Code 508.149 PC 12.31 **Unless transferred to the court under Section 54.02, Family Code (Life sentence).
Offender is serving a Life Sentence for	Calendar Time = 35 yrs.	Gov't Code 508.145(c)

one of the following listed offenses: - Aggravated Kidnapping (with intent to violate or abuse the victim sexually)—20.04(a)(4) - *Aggravated Sexual Assault—22.021 - Indecency w/Child—21.11(a)(1) - Sexual Assault—22.011 - Trafficking of Persons—20A.02 (a)(7) - or (a)(8) (involves a child) - Burglary of Habitation with Intent to Commit any of the following: — 30.02 - Aggravated Kidnapping (with intent to violate or abuse the victim sexually)—20.04(a)(4) - Aggravated Sexual Assault— 22.021 - Indecency w/Child—21.11 - Sexual Assault—22.011 - Trafficking of Persons—20A.02 (a)(7) or (a)(8), (involves a child)	*22.021(f) is not eligible for parole	PC 12.42(c)(2)
AND has a previous conviction for one of the following offenses: - Aggravated Kidnapping (with intent to violate or abuse the victim sexually)—20.04(a)(4) - Aggravated Sexual Assault—22.021 - Indecency w/Child—21.11 - Obscenity (images of child under the age of 18)—43.23(h) - Possession or Promotion of Child Pornography—43.26 - Prohibited Sexual Conduct—25.02 - Sexual Assault—22.011 - Sexual Performance by a Child— 43.25 – Trafficking of Persons— 20A.02 (a)(7) or (a)(8), (involves a child) - Burglary of Habitation with Intent to Commit any of the following--30.02: - Aggravated Kidnapping (with intent to violate or abuse the victim sexually)—20.04(a)(4) - Aggravated Sexual Assault— 22.021 - Indecency w/Child—21.11 - Sexual Assault—22.011 - Prohibited Sexual Conduct—25.02 - Trafficking of Persons—20A.02 (a)(7) or (a)(8) (involves a child) -Offense in another state substantially similar to any of the above offenses.		
CCP 42A.054(a)* Offenses: -Aggravated Kidnapping-20.04 -Aggravated Robbery--29.03 -**Aggravated Sexual Assault--22.021 - Any offense with Affirmative finding of Deadly Weapon Criminal Solicitation, 1st Degree--15.03 Capital Murder--19.03 - Indecency w/Child (Sexual Contact) 2nd Degree-21.ll(a)(l) - Injury to a Child or Elderly or Disabled Individual, 1st Degree--22.04(a)(1)	Calendar Time = ½ Minimum of 2 yrs. Maximum of 30 years. **22.021(f) does not apply For every 12 months that elapse between date of arrest warrant and actual arrest date, initial Parole eligibility date is delayed by 3 years for the offenses of: - Murder--19.02 - Sexual Assault-22.011 -Aggravated Sexual Assault-22.021;	**Effective 01/01/2017 offenses in CCP art. 42.12 Section 3g(a) were re-codified at CCP 42A.054(a).** Gov't Code 508.046 (extraordinary vote required for certain offenses)

(applies only to Child victim 14 or younger) - Murder--19.02 - Sexual Assault-22.011 - Sexual Performance by a Child-43.25 -*Compelling Prostitution-43.05 -*Trafficking of Persons-20A.02 -* Burglary of Habitation with Intent to Commit any of the following:-30.02 -Continuous Sexual Abuse of a Young Child or Children-21.02 - Indecency w/Child-21.11 - Sexual Assault-22.011 -Aggravated Sexual Assault--22.021 - Prohibited Sexual Conduct-25.02 A Felony Increased Under Health & Safety Code 481.134 (c), (d), (e), or (f) (Drug-Free Zones), if it is shown that there is a previous conviction for an offense which punishment was increased under any of those subsections. A Felony Increased Under Health & Safety Code 481.140 (Use of Child in Commission of Offense).	Not on list in 42A.054(a): Engaging in Organized Criminal Activity-- 71.02 -*Directing Activities of Criminal Street Gangs-71.023	
All other 1st, 2nd, and 3rd degree felony offenses	Calendar Time + Good Time = 1/4, including work credits and bonus time. Maximum of 15 yrs.	Gov't code 508.145(f)
Drug-Free Zones 481.134	Calendar Time = 5 yrs. or maximum term, whichever is less.	Gov't code 508.145(e)
CU offenses	Time credit on all sentences, one after another, until eligibility is reached on last sentence.	CCP, Art. 42.08 (a) Gov't Code 508.150
State Jail Felonies - a court may enhance the punishment by imposing the confinement of a 2nd or 3rd degree felony. - a court may reduce the punishment by imposing the confinement of a Class A Misdemeanor category offense (may or may not have been prosecuted under the lesser category offense title.)	Parole Eligibility is NOT applicable.	PC 12.35 Confinement is to a state jail for term of not more than two years less than 180 days.
The offenses listed below are **NOT** eligible for Mandatory Supervision: - Any offense with Affirmative finding of Deadly Weapon - Murder, 1st or 2nd Degree—19.02 - Capital Murder—19.03 - Aggravated Kidnapping, 1st or 2nd Degree—20.04 - Aggravated Assault, 1st or 2nd Degree— 22.02 - Robbery, 2nd Degree—29.02 - Aggravated Robbery, 1st Degree—29.03 - Arson, 1st Degree—28.02 - Burglary of Habitation, 1st Degree 30.02 with intent to commit felony other than Theft - Aggravated Sexual Assault, 1st Degree 22.021 - Compelling Prostitution —43.05 - Trafficking of Persons—20A.02	Ineligible for Mandatory Supervision Also, any offense committed on or after 09/01/1996 with a prior conviction of any of the listed offenses, including predecessor offenses, are ineligible for Mandatory Supervision	Gov't Code 508.149

- Continuous Trafficking of Persons —20A.03 - Criminal Solicitation, 1st Degree—15.03 - Continuous sexual abuse of a child—21.02 - Indecency w/Child—21.11 - Sexual Assault, 2nd Degree—22.011 - Sexual Performance by a Child—43.25 - Injury to a Child or Elderly or Disabled Individual, 1st Degree—22.04 - Engaging in Organized Criminal Activity, 1st Degree—71.02 - Directing Activities of Criminal Street Gangs, 1st Degree—71.023 - A Felony Increased Under Health & Safety Code 481.134 (Drug–Free Zones). - A Felony Increased Under Health & Safety Code 481.140(Use of Child in Commission of Offense).		
Discretionary Mandatory Supervision for offense dates on or after 09/01/1996		Gov't Code 508.149(b) An offender may be denied mandatory supervision by a parole panel for the following reasons: - Offender will endanger the public AND - Offender's accrued good conduct time is not an accurate reflection of the offender's potential for rehabilitation.
The offenses listed below are **NOT** eligible for Parole or Mandatory Supervision: - Super Aggravated Sexual Assault of a child—22.021(f) - Continuous Sexual Abuse of a Young Child or Children—21.02	Ineligible for Parole. Ineligible for Mandatory Supervision.	Gov't Code 508.145(a) Gov't Code 508.149 Also see, PC 12.42(c)(4)(repeat offender)
- Injury to a Child, Elderly or Disabled Individual, 2nd or 3rd Degree-22.04	Eligible for up to a five year set-off following a decision of parole denial by the BPP voting panel per HB 431.	Effective 06/14/2013 Gov't Code 508.141
- *Aggravated Sexual Assault-22.021 - *Capital Murder-19.03 (LIFE) - includes all statutory precursor offenses to both	*Eligible for up to a ten year set -off following a decision of parole denial by the BPP voting panel per HB 1914.	*Effective 09/01/2015 Gov't Code 508.141

86th Legislature	09/01/2019 - 08/31/2021	
Offense	**Parole Eligibility**	**Comments**
Offender is serving a Life Sentence for one of the following listed offenses: - Aggravated Kidnapping (with intent to violate or abuse the vic m sexually)—20.04(a)(4) - *Aggravated Sexual Assault—22.021 - Indecency w/Child—21.11(a)(1) - Sexual Assault—22.011 - Trafficking of Persons—20A.02 (a)(7) or (a)(8) (involves a child) - Burglary of Habitation with Intent to Commit any of the following--30.02: - Aggravated Kidnapping (with intent to violate or abuse the vic m sexually)—20.04(a)(4) - Aggravated Sexual Assault—	Calendar Time = 35 yrs. *22.021(f) is not eligible for parole	Gov't Code 508.145(c) PC 12.42(c)(2)

22.021 - Indecency w/Child—21.11 - Sexual Assault—22.011 - Trafficking of Persons—20A.02 (a)(7) or (a)(8) (involves a child)		
AND has a previous conviction for one of the following offenses: - Aggravated Kidnapping (with intent to violate or abuse the victim sexually)—20.04(a)(4) - Aggravated Sexual Assault—22.021 - Indecency w/Child—21.11 - Obscenity (images of child under the age of 18)—43.23(h) - Possession or Promotion of Child Pornography—43.26 - Prohibited Sexual Conduct—25.02 - Sexual Assault—22.011 - Sexual Performance by a Child—43.25 – Trafficking of Persons—20A.02 (a)(7) or (a)(8) (involves a child) - Burglary of Habitation with Intent to Commit any of the following:—30.02 - Aggravated Kidnapping (with intent to violate or abuse the vic m sexually)—20.04(a)(4) - Aggravated Sexual Assault—22.021 - Indecency w/Child—21.11 - Prohibited Sexual Conduct—25.02 - Sexual Assault—22.011 - Trafficking of Persons—20A.02 (a)(7) or (a)(8) (involves a child) - Offense in another state substantially similar to any of the above offenses.		
CCP 42A.054(a)* Offenses: - Aggravated Kidnapping—20.04 - Aggravated Robbery—29.03 - * *Aggravated Sexual Assault—22.021 - Any offense with affirmative finding of Deadly Weapon - Criminal Solicitation, 1st Degree—15.03 - **Indecency w/Child 2nd & 3rd Degree—21.11** - Injury to a Child or Elderly or Disabled Individual, 1st Degree—22.04(a)(1) (applies only to child victim 14 or younger) - Murder—19.02 - Sexual Assault—22.011 - Sexual Performance by a Child—43.25 – Compelling Prostitution—43.05 - Trafficking of Persons—20A.02 - **Continuous Trafficking of Persons—20A.03** - **Aggravated Promotion of Prostitution—43.04** - 1st Degree Burglary of Habitation (30.02) with Intent to Commit any of the following: - Continuous Sexual Abuse of a	Calendar Time = ½ Minimum of 2 yrs. Maximum of 30 years. **22.021(f) is not eligible for Parole For every 12 months that elapse between date of arrest warrant and actual arrest date, initial Parole eligibility date is delayed by 3 years for the offenses of: - Murder--19.02 - Sexual Assault-22.011 -Aggravated Sexual Assault-22.021; Not on list in 42A.054(a): Engaging in Organized Criminal Activity-- 71.02 Directing Activities of Criminal Street Gangs-71.023	**Effective 01/01/2017 offenses in CCP art.42.12 Section 3g(a) were re-codified at CCP 42A.054(a).** Gov't Code 508.046 (extraordinary vote required for certain offenses) ***New offenses added to list in 42A.054(a) effec ve 09/01/2019:** **- Indecency w/Child 3rd Degree—21.11(a)(2)** **- Con nuous Trafficking of Persons—20A.03** **- Aggravated Promo on of Prostitution—43.04**

Young Child or Children—21.02 - Indecency w/Child—21.11 - Sexual Assault—22.011 - Aggravated Sexual Assault—22.021 - Prohibited Sexual Conduct—25.02 - A Felony Increased under Health & Safety Code 481.134 (c), (d), (e), or (f) (Drug–Free Zones), if it is shown that there is a previous conviction for an offense which punishment was increased under any of those subsections. - A Felony Increased Under Health & Safety Code 481.140 (Use of Child in Commission of Offense).		
All other 1st, 2nd, and 3rd degree felony offenses	Calendar Time + Good Time = 1/4, including work credits and bonus time. Maximum of 15 yrs.	Gov't code 508.145(f)
Drug-Free Zones 481.134	Calendar Time = 5 yrs. or maximum term, whichever is less.	Gov't code 508.145(e)
CU offenses	Time credit on all sentences, one after another, until eligibility is reached on last sentence.	CCP, Art. 42.08 (a) Gov't Code 508.150
State Jail Felonies - a court may enhance the punishment by imposing the confinement of a 2nd or 3rd degree felony. - a court may reduce the punishment by imposing the confinement of a Class A Misdemeanor category offense (may or may not have been prosecuted under the lesser category offense title.)	Parole Eligibility is NOT applicable.	PC 12.35 Confinement is to a state jail for term of not more than two years less than 180 days.
The offenses listed below are **NOT** eligible for Mandatory Supervision: - Any offense with Affirmative finding of Deadly Weapon - Murder, 1st or 2nd Degree—19.02 - Capital Murder—19.03 - Aggravated Kidnapping, 1st or 2nd Degree—20.04 - Aggravated Assault, 1st or 2nd Degree— 22.02 - Robbery, 2nd Degree—29.02 - Aggravated Robbery, 1st Degree—29.03 - Arson, 1st Degree—28.02 - Burglary of Habitation, 1st Degree—30.02 with intent to commit felony other than Theft - Aggravated Sexual Assault, 1st Degree— 22.021 - Compelling Prostitution —43.05 - Trafficking of Persons—20A.02 - Continuous Trafficking of Persons —20A.03 - Criminal Solicitation, 1st Degree—15.03 - Continuous sexual abuse of a child—21.02 - Indecency w/Child—21.11 - Sexual Assault, 2nd Degree—22.011 - Sexual Performance by a Child—43.25	Ineligible for Mandatory Supervision Also, any offense committed on or after 09/01/1996 with a prior conviction of any of the listed offenses, including predecessor offenses, are ineligible for Mandatory Supervision	Gov't Code 508.149

- Injury to a Child or Elderly or Disabled Individual, 1st Degree—22.04 - Engaging in Organized Criminal Activity, 1st Degree—71.02 - Directing Activities of Criminal Street Gangs, 1st Degree—71.023 - A Felony Increased Under Health & Safety Code 481.134 (Drug–Free Zones). - A Felony Increased Under Health & Safety Code 481.140(Use of Child in Commission of Offense).		
Discretionary Mandatory Supervision for offense dates on or after 09/01/1996		Gov't Code 508.149(b) An offender may be denied mandatory supervision by a parole panel for the following reasons: - Offender will endanger the public AND - Offender's accrued good conduct time is not an accurate reflection of the offender's potential for rehabilitation.
The offenses listed below are **NOT** eligible for Parole or Mandatory Supervision: - Super Aggravated Sexual Assault of a child—22.021(f) - Continuous Sexual Abuse of a Young Child or Children—21.02	Ineligible for Parole. Ineligible for Mandatory Supervision.	Gov't Code 508.145(a) Gov't Code 508.149 Also see, PC 12.42(c)(4)(repeat offender)
- Injury to a Child, Elderly or Disabled Individual, 2nd or 3rd Degree-22.04	Eligible for up to a five year set-off following a decision of parole denial by the BPP voting panel per HB 431.	Effective 06/14/2013 Gov't Code 508.141
- *Aggravated Sexual Assault-22.021 - *Capital Murder-19.03 (LIFE) - includes all statutory precursor offenses to both	*Eligible for up to a ten year set -off following a decision of parole denial by the BPP voting panel per HB 1914.	*Effective 09/01/2015 Gov't Code 508.141

Parole Review Periods

Offenders receive an annual review, except those convicted of an offense under Government Code Section 508.149(a). Those offenders with 2nd and 3rd degree Injury to a Child may have their reviews set off for up to five years (up to ten years where indicated below) by vote of a parole panel of the Board. If a parole panel designates an offender as Serve All (SA), the offender will not be reviewed again prior to discharging the sentence.

Offenders not eligible for mandatory supervision (those serving a sentence for a violent offense as listed in Section 508.149(a) of the Texas Government Code):

- Aggravated Assault, 1st or 2nd Degree
- Aggravated Kidnapping, 1st or 2nd Degree
- Aggravated Robbery, 1st Degree
- Aggravated Sexual Assault, 1st Degree (up to ten year set-off)
- Any Offense with an Affirmative Finding of a Deadly Weapon
- Arson, 1st Degree
- Burglary, 1st Degree
- Capital Murder (up to ten year set-off)
- Compelling Prostitution
- Continuous Sex Abuse of a Young Child or Children
- Indecency with a Child
- Injury to a Child, Elderly, or Disabled Individual, 1st Degree
- Murder, 1st or 2nd Degree
- Robbery, 2nd Degree
- Sexual Assault
- Sexual Performance by a Child
- Trafficking of Persons
- A Felony Increased Under Health and Safety Code (Drug-Free Zones or Use of Child in Commission of Offense)

Special Review

The Board may receive and consider information not previously available to a parole panel when an offender has been denied parole or mandatory supervision release. If the panel based their decision upon erroneous information or an administrative file processing error, the case file may be returned to the original panel to reconsider their vote. This is referred as a "Special Review." All requests for Special Review shall be in writing and signed by the offender, his or her attorney, or in cases where the offender is unable to sign due to a mental or physical impairment, by a person acting on his or her behalf.

Requests for a Special Review should be filed with:

Texas Board of Pardons and Paroles
Board Administrator
8610 Shoal Creek Blvd.
Austin, Texas 78757.

Parole Guidelines

For more than a decade, the Parole Board has been using a two prong Guideline to determine an offender's likelihood of parole. In appearance, the Guidelines are objective but the actual application appears to be completely subjective, with parole being granted and/or denied to different offenders with apparently the same scores.

Composition of Guidelines

The guidelines to parole contain two major components which combine to provide a single score. The first is the Risk Assessment Instrument which has both static and dynamic factors and the second is the Offense Severity Class. These work together to, theoretically, provide an offender's likelihood of parole in a single score.

Risk Assessment

The Risk Assessment Instrument contains two sections: Static Risk Factors and Dynamic Risk Factors.

An offender can be assigned 0 to 10 points on the Static Factors and 0 to 9 points on the Dynamic Factors (see the Risk Assessment Worksheet on the next page). A low score is associated with a low risk of recidivism. The higher the score, the greater the risk of parole failure.

Risk Assessment Worksheet

Static Factors

Question	Select One	Your Score
The Commitment Offense: Does the commitment offense include an UUMV, Burglary Of A Habitation, Burglary of a Motor Vehicle, or Forgery charge?	No = 0 Points Yes = 1 Point	
History of Supervisory release Revocations for felony offenses: Is there a history of supervisory release revocations for felony offenses?	No probation, parole or mandatory supervision revocations = 0 Points One Revocation = 1 Point More than one revocation = 3 Points	
Prior Incarcerations: Does the offender have prior incarcerations?	None = 0 Points One or two prior incarcerations = 1 Point Three or more prior incarcerations = 3 Points	
Employment History: Does the offender's employment history include six months of continuous full-time employment or school attendance in the two years before incarceration?	Yes = 0 Points No = 1 Point	
Age at first admission: What was the offender's age at first admission to a juvenile or adult correctional facility?	26 or older = 0 Points 18 to 25 = 1 Point 17 or Under = 2 Points	
Total Static Points		

To complete the Risk Assessment Static Factors, read the question in column one, look at the number next to the answer in column two, and write that number down in column three.

Once all five questions have been answered, add the numbers in column three and write the total down at the bottom. This number is the Total Static Points.

Dynamic Factors

Question	Select One	Your Score
What is the Offender's Current Age?	Under 25 years old = 3 Points 25-34 years old = 2 Points 35-44 years old = 1 Point Over 45 = 0 Points	
Is the offender a confirmed member of a security threat group (Gang)?	Active STG (Gang) Member = 1 Point No Gang "Tag" = 0 Points	
Were there any educational, vocational, or certified on-the-job training programs completed during the present incarceration?	Yes = 0 Points No = 1 Point	
Is there any prison disciplinary conduct in the last eighteen months?	None = 0 Points Demoted below entry level OR good time lost = 1 Point Zero balance of good time = 2 Points	
What is the offender's current prison custody level?	Minimum Out (outside trusty S-2) = 0 Point Minimum In (inside trusty S-3) = 1 Point Medium, close custody or Ad. Seg. = 2 Points	
Total Dynamic Points		

To complete the Risk Assessment Dynamic Factors, read the question in column one, look at the number next to the answer in column two, and write that number down in column three.

Once all five questions have been answered, add the numbers in column three and write the total down at the bottom. This number is the Total Dynamic Points.

Total Risk Assessment Points

Total Static Points	
Total Dynamic Points	
Your Total Points	

Enter the Total Static and Dynamic points on the Total Risk Assessment Points worksheet. Add the numbers together to get "Your Total Points" or the Total Risk Assessment Factor Points.

Next, Look at the chart below. Locate the block that contains the number range of Total Risk Assessment Factor Points in the column with the correct gender. Once that is found, looked in the first column and find the Assigned Risk Level on the row with the correct number of points.

For example, if the Total Risk Assessment Factor Points was 11 for a male, then the Assigned Risk Level is "High Risk"

Score Assigned Risk Level 2022

Assigned Risk Level	Male (Total Points)	Female (Total Points)
Low Risk	3 or less	5 or less
Moderate Risk	4-6	6-9
High Risk	7-9	10+
Highest Risk	10+	N/A

* Please note the new points beginning 01/01/2021. The Supplemental DWI Risk Assessment Factors and Scales were discontinued.

Offense Severity Class

Every felony offense in the Texas Penal Code has been assigned an Offense Severity Rating, which the Board is required to periodically review. The Offense Severity Classes range from Low (for non-violent crimes) to Highest (for capital murder), with the most serious active offense providing the rating in the event there are multiple concurrent offenses.

Look at the chart in Appendix 2 to determine your Offense Severity Level and enter it below.

Offense Severity Level	

Parole Guideline Score

The two components of the guidelines, Risk Assessment and Offense Severity, are merged into a matrix that creates the offender's Parole Guideline Score. There are separate risk scales for male and female offenders.

Parole Guidelines Scores range from one, for an individual with the poorest probability for success, to seven, for an offender with the greatest probability of success while on parole.

The guidelines are neither automatic nor presumptive of whether an offender will receive parole. Parole panel members retain the discretion to vote outside the guidelines when circumstances of an individual case merit doing so.

After determining both the Offense Severity Level and the Total Risk Assessment Factor Points, these two components are then merged to determine the Parole Guideline Score (PGS)..

The PGS is determined by locating the intersection of the total number of Risk Assessment Factor Points from the Risk Assessment worksheet and the Offense Severity Level ranking.

Look at the charts below. Locate on the chart that corresponds to the inmates gender. Look at the top row of the chart and locate the column that contains the number of the Total Risk Assessment Factor points calculated earlier. Now follow that column down until you reach the row that contains the Offense Severity Ranking Level found in the column on the left. The number where the Total Risk Assessment Factor Points and the Offense Severity Ranking Level intersect is the Parole Guideline Score.

As an example, a Risk Assessment Factor Point of 2 with a Moderate Offense Severity Level for a male would result in a Parole Guideline Level of 6, as indicated in the 4th box down in the far right column of the chart below.

Risk Levels for Males

Offense Severity Class	16 Risk Factor Points Highest **H+**	9-15 Risk Factor Points High **H**	4-8 Risk Factor Points Moderate **M**	0-3 Risk Factor Points Low **L**
Highest **H+**	Parole Guideline Score: **1**	Parole Guideline Score: **2**	Parole Guideline Score: **2**	Parole Guideline Score: **3**
High **H**	Parole Guideline Score: **2**	Parole Guideline Score: **3**	Parole Guideline Score: **4**	Parole Guideline Score: **4**
Moderate **M**	Parole Guideline Score: **2**	Parole Guideline Score: 3	Parole Guideline Score: **5**	Parole Guideline Score: **6**
Low **L**	Parole Guideline Score: **3**	Parole Guideline Score: **4**	Parole Guideline Score: **6**	Parole Guideline Score: **7**

Risk Levels for Females

Offense Severity Class	Risk Level: Highest (10+)	Risk Level: Moderate (4-9)	Risk Level: Low (3 or less)
Highest H+	Parole Guideline Score: 2	Parole Guideline Score: 2	Parole Guideline Score: 3
High H	Parole Guideline Score: 3	Parole Guideline Score: 4	Parole Guideline Score: 4
Moderate M	Parole Guideline Score: 3	Parole Guideline Score: 5	Parole Guideline Score: 6
Low L	Parole Guideline Score: 4	Parole Guideline Score: 6	Parole Guideline Score: 7

The Parole Approval Rates by Guideline Level chart in the Parole Analysis section provides the most recent statistics for the parole approval rates for each Guideline Score.

Other Factors That Influence the Parole Board

Not every aspect of an offender's case is measured by the parole guidelines. Board members and parole commissioners also consider other factors, such as 1) the original offense, 2) sentence length, 3) behavior since incarceration, 4) programs completed, and 5) support systems strength and parole plans.

During a parole review, voters consider:

Seriousness of the original crime or crimes an individual committed.;
Sentence length/amount of time served;
Offender's age;
Offender's criminal history;
Other arrests;
Juvenile history;
Drug and alcohol involvement;
Conduct in prison;
Life before prison;

Victim statements;
Protests from trial officials;
Completion of prison programs;
Number of prison incarcerations;

Institutional adjustment (participation in proposed or specialized prison programs)
The post-prison parole plan;
Parole support letters;
Parole package.

Parole Voting Options

Now that the voting members have calculate the offender's Parole Guideline Score, they have several options on voting. Other than a **Serve-All** (offender serves all remaining time) or a **Set Off** (parole not granted - offender is reviewed in 6 months to 10 years), the members of the Board have several options.

A parole panel consists of three parole panel members. The members for each area are listed in Appendix 3. The first voting member will review the file and cast a vote. The file will move to the second voting member to cast a vote. If both votes are the same the parole file is completed. If the first two votes are different then the parole file will move to the third panel member for a vote to break the tie. There must be a majority of two votes to become final.

Approval Votes

FI-1 Release offender on parole supervision when eligible.

FI-2 Release on parole on a specified future date.

FI-3R Transfer to a TDCJ rehabilitation program, such as Changes/Life skills, Voyager, or Segovia Pre-Release Center no earlier than a specified date at least three months with release on parole after completion. Release to parole only after completion of the program.

F1-4R Transfer to a Sex Offender Education Program (SOEP) no earlier than a specified date for at least four months from specified date.

FI-5 Transfer to an In-Prison Therapeutic Community Program (IPTC), with release to an aftercare component after completion of the program.

FI-6 Transfer to DWI rehabilitation program with release to continuum of care program.

FI-6R Transfer to a rehabilitation program, such as the Pre-Release Therapeutic Community (PRTC) or Pre-Release Substance Abuse Program (PRSAP), no earlier than specified date for at least six months with release on parole after completion.

FI-7R Transfer to Serious and Violent Offender Reentry Initiative (SVORI), then released to parole only after program completion and no earlier than specified date for at least seven months.

FI-9R Transfer to the Sex Offender Treatment Program (SOTP-9) no earlier than specified date for at least nine months, with release on parole after completion but not earlier than nine months from specified date.

FI-18R Transfer to the Sex Offender Treatment Program (SOTP-18) or the InnerChange Freedom Initiative (IFI) no earlier than specified date for at least 18 months, with release on parole after completion.

CU-FI Designates the date an offender serving consecutive sentences would have been eligible for parole if single sentence.

RMS Release to mandatory supervision

Denial Votes

NR (Next Review): Deny parole and set time for next parole consideration. State law requires annual reviews except for certain violent or sexual cases.

SA (Serve All): Deny parole with no regular subsequent review, requiring offender to serve the balance of their sentence if the discharge date occurs in less than three years.

CU-NR Deny favorable action and set next review in consecutive sentence case.

CU-SA Require offender to serve all of current sentence in consecutive sentence case.

DMS Denies Mandatory Supervision (and sets next review date) because offender's accrued good conduct time does not accurately reflect potential for rehabilitation and offender's release would endanger the public.

SB 45 Cases Which Requires A Full Board Vote

SB 45 cases involve capital felons who are eligible for parole, persons convicted of an offense under Section 20A.03 [Continuous Trafficking of

Persons], Section 21.02 [Continuous Sexual Abuse of Young Child or Children], Section 21.11(a)(1) [Indecency with a Child], or Section 22.021 [Aggravated Sexual Assault] of the Penal Code or offenders that are required to serve at least 35 calendar years before becoming eligible for parole have more limited set of voting options as stated in Senate Bill 45 of the 74th Legislature. These cases require two-thirds majority vote of the full Board for parole approval.

SB 45 cases are eligible for up to a five year set-off. This means the offender's next parole eligibility date could be up to five years in the future.

SB 45 Voting Options

FI-1 Release when eligible with conditions (if any).

F1-4R Transfer to a TDCJ Sex Offender Education Program (SOEP). Release to parole only after program completion and not earlier than four months from a specified date.

FI-9R Transfer to an TDCJ Sex Offender Treatment Program (SOTP-9) then released to parole only after program completion and not earlier than nine months from specified date.

FI-18R Transfer to an TDCJ rehabilitation treatment program. Release to parole only after program competition and no earlier than eighteen months from the specified date. TDCJ programs may include Sex Offender Treatment Program (SOTP-18), or the InnerChange Freedom Initiative (IFI). The specified date cannot be more than three years from the current panel decision date.

CU-FI Designates the date an offender serving consecutive sentences would have been eligible for parole if single sentence.

RMS Release to mandatory supervision.

Denial Votes:

NR (Next Review): Deny release and set the next review date for 36 or 60 months following the panel decision date.

SA (Serve All): Deny parole with no regular subsequent review, in the event the offender's minimum or maximum expiration date is less than 60 months away.

CU-NR Deny favorable action and set next review in consecutive sentence case.

CU-SA Require offender to serve all of current sentence in consecutive sentence case.

DMS Deny release to mandatory supervision and set the next mandatory supervision review date one year from the panel decision date.

HB 1914 Cases Which Requires A Full Board Vote

HB 1914 cases involve capital felons who are eligible for parole, persons convicted of an offense under Section 20A.03 [Continuous Trafficking of Persons], Section 21.02 [Continuous Sexual Abuse of Young Child or Children], Section 21.11(a)(1) [Indecency with a Child], or Section 22.021 [Aggravated Sexual Assault] of the Penal Code, or persons required under Texas Government Code Section 508.145(c) to serve 35 calendar years before becoming eligible for release on parole. These cases have a limited set of voting options require two-thirds majority vote of the full Board for parole approval.

HB 1914 cases are eligible for up to a ten year set-off. This means the offender's next parole eligibility date could be up to ten years in the future.

HB 1914 Voting Options

FI-1 Release when eligible with conditions (if any).

F1-4R Transfer to a TDCJ Sex Offender Education Program (SOEP). Release to parole only after program completion and not earlier than four months from a specified date.

FI-9R Transfer to an TDCJ Sex Offender Treatment Program (SOTP-9) then released to parole only after program completion and not earlier than nine months from specified date.

FI-18R Transfer to an TDCJ rehabilitation treatment program. Release to parole only after program competition and no earlier than eighteen months from the specified date. TDCJ programs may include Sex Offender Treatment Program (SOTP-18), or the InnerChange Freedom Initiative (IFI). The specified date cannot be more than three years from the current panel decision date.

CU-FI Designates the date an offender serving consecutive sentences would have been eligible for parole if single sentence.

RMS Release to mandatory supervision.

Denial Votes:

NR (Next Review): Deny release and set the next review date for 36 or 60 months following the panel decision date.

SA (Serve All): Deny parole with no regular subsequent review, in the event the offender's minimum or maximum expiration date is less than 60 months away.

CU-NR Deny favorable action and set next review in consecutive sentence case.

CU-SA Require offender to serve all of current sentence in consecutive sentence case.

DMS Deny release to mandatory supervision and set the next mandatory supervision review date one year from the panel decision date.

* **NOTE** * The main difference between SB 45 and HB 1914 is SB 45 convicted offenders can get a set-off of up to 5 years and HB 1914 convicted offenders can get a set-off of up to 10 years.

HB 1433 Cases - Discretionary Mandatory Supervision Voting Options

This legislation requires the Board to review some offenders prior to release to mandatory supervision. To deny mandatory supervision, a parole panel must determine that accrued good conduct time is not an accurate reflection of the offender's potential for rehabilitation AND that the offender's release would endanger the public.

HB 1433 only applies to an offender eligible for release to mandatory supervision if the sentence is for an offense committed on or after September 1, 1996.

The two voting options are:

DMS Deny release to mandatory supervision and set the next mandatory supervision review date one year from the panel decision date. The vote is either D-1 or D-2 to deny DMS.

- D-1 - The record indicates the inmate accrued good conduct time is not an accurate reflection of the inmates potential for rehabilitation
- D-2 The record indicates that the inmate's release would endanger the public.

RMS Release to mandatory supervision.

Rule 145.13 Cases - Voting Options

This voting option is designed for offenders with consecutive sentences if each of the offenses committed were on or after September 1, 1987.

CU/FI Designate the date on which the offender would have been eligible for release on parole if the offender had been sentenced to serve a single sentence. This date shall be within a three-year incarceration period following the panel decision

CU/NU Deny favorable parole action and set the next review date at one year from the panel decision date. If the offender is serving an offense under Section 508.149(a), Government Code, or second or third degree under Section 22.04, Penal Code; the next review date (month/year) may be set at any date in the five-year incarceration period following the panel decision date, but in no event shall it be less than one calendar year from the panel decision date.

CU/SA- If the offender is serving an offense under Section 508.149(a), Government Code, or second or third degree under Section 22.04, Penal Code; deny release and order serve-all, but in no event shall this be utilized if the offender's maximum expiration date is over five years from the date of the panel decision. If the offender is not serving an offense under Section 508.149(a),
Government Code, deny release and order serve-all, but in no event shall this be utilized if the offender's maximum expiration date is over one year from the date of the panel decision.

MRIS Voting Options

Medically Recommended Intensive Supervision (MRIS) Program is for offenders who are mentally ill, mentally retarded, elderly, terminally ill, physically handicapped, or require long-term care are considered for release by a parole panel. The panel, based on the offender's condition and medical evaluation, may release an offender who does not constitute a threat to public safety or a threat to commit an offense.

A special MRIS panel determines the discretionary release of MRIS identified offenders. The two voting options are:

FI-1 Approve MRIS and impose Special Condition "0" which specifies the offender shall comply with the terms and conditions of MRIS Program and abide by the approved release plan. The offender will remain under the care of a physician and in a medically suitable place while under Special Condition "0".

Deny Deny MRIS release.

Special Conditions Attached to Parole

Texas Board of Pardons and Paroles (Board) determine conditions of parole and mandatory supervision. Special conditions are conditions imposed in addition to the standard conditions of parole or mandatory supervision. Unless otherwise provided, any condition may be imposed before or after release and shall remain in effect until specifically removed by a parole panel.

Condition	Name	Description
O.01	Residence During Release	Unless otherwise provided, the offender shall reside in the county where he resided at the time he committed the offense for which he was sentenced to the Correction Institutions Division (CID), or the county of the offense for which the offender was sentenced to the CID, if the offender was not a resident of the State of Texas. This condition appears on almost all parolees.
O.03	Controlled Substance Testing	This condition appears for the release of all offenders. It is the random drug testing while under supervision.
O.04	Post Secondary Education Reimbursement (PSER)	This condition appears for the release of all offenders who enroll in such courses at a TDCJ facility on or after 09/01/1995. It is the reimbursement for post-secondary education programs.
O.05	Substance Abuse Treatment	This condition shall be imposed immediately before release after completion of the In-Prison Therapeutic Community (IPTC) program, established under Section 501.0931 of the Texas Government Code, to ensure participation in a drug and alcohol continuum of care treatment program, post release.
O.06	Child Safety Zone	This condition shall be imposed for offenders whose victim was a child younger than seventeen (17) years of age and are serving a

		sentence for any of the following listed offenses and/or Texas Penal Codes: □ 20.04(a)(4) Aggravated Kidnapping with intent to inflict bodily injury or violate or abuse sexually •21.02 Continuous Sexual Abuse of Young Child or Children • 21.11 Indecency with a Child • 22.011 Sexual Assault (formerly Rape) • 22.021 Aggravated Sexual Assault • 25.02 Prohibited Sexual Conduct (formerly Incest) 08/15/17 PD/POP-2.2.25 Page 4 of 11 • 43.25 Sexual Performance by a Child • 43.26 Possession or Promotion of Child Pornography • 30.02(d) Burglary of a Habitation with intent to commit a violation of an offense listed above
O.07	Community Service for Certain Releasees	This condition shall be imposed for offenders serving a sentence for certain crimes committed because of bias or prejudice. With this condition, offenders are required to perform not less than 300 hours of community service at projects that serve the persons or groups who were the targets of the offender. This condition requires an affirmative finding by the sentencing court under Article 42.014 of the Texas Code of Criminal Procedure. The affirmative finding must be noted on the Judgment and Sentence. Those offenses are listed under the following Texas Penal Code: • 28.02 Arson • 28.03 Criminal Mischief • 28.08 Graffiti
C	Prohibited Financial Activities	This condition prohibits certain financial activities by offenders who have been convicted of theft or fraud or who have an established propensity for engaging in theft or fraudulent criminal behavior. At any time Special Condition "C" is in effect the offender shall:

		- Not open or maintain more than one checking account; - Not open or maintain more than one savings account; - Not obtain or maintain more than one credit or debit card; and - Not participate in electronic financial transmissions without prior written approval of the offender's supervising parole officer
D	Release to Detainer	Release the offender to a detainer for deportation or transfer to Immigration and Customs Enforcement (ICE) or another law enforcement or correctional agency.
E	Educational Skill Level	This condition shall be imposed for mentally competent offenders who have not attained a 6th grade education level prior to release. The parolee must participate in education or vocational programs. This can include ESL, literacy classes, adult basic education classes, vocational training, or other appropriate training as instructed by the supervising parole officer.
I	Employer Notification	Special Condition "I" is intended to inform any prospective employer of an offender's criminal history if the offender will be employed in a position of financial responsibility.
ISF	Intermediate Sanction Facility	A special condition imposed by a parole panel that will serve to punish, rehabilitate, or reform an offender in response to a violation of a condition of release to parole or mandatory supervision following a hearing or proceeding concerning alleged violations under Chapter 146 of the Board Rules.
L	Maximum Level of Supervision	A higher level of supervision is needed upon release or after violations of parole or mandatory supervision.
M	Sex Offender	Sex offender registration and the submission of

	Registration & DNA Submission	DNA is required as a condition of parole or mandatory supervision.
N	Prohibition on Internet Access	At any time Special Condition "N" is in effect, the offender is prohibited from using the internet or any type of electronic device used for internet access.
No Contact	No Contact	At any time this condition is in effect, the offender can have no contact for a child or children of a legally recognized parent or spouse.
P	Special Needs	At any time Special Condition "P" is in effect, the offender shall participate in mental health assessments and evaluation, Intellectual Developmental Disorder assessment and evaluations, mental health/intellectual development disorder treatment or counseling, rehabilitation training, and use medication as prescribed.
R	Restitution	Payment by the offender to the victim of the offense through the Division for financial loss sustained as a result of the offense.
S	Substance Abuse	At any time this condition is in effect, unless modified or withdrawn by a parole panel, an offender shall not unlawfully use drugs, narcotics, or controlled substances or use intoxicating inhalants, or consume alcoholic beverages. The parolee will submit to urinalysis monitoring, not enter an establishment where the primary function is the sale and dispensing of alcoholic beverages, and obey all driving restrictions. Some offenders will be required to attend substance abuse treatment programs or counseling.
SAFP	Substance Abuse Felony Program	A special condition imposed by a parole panel that will serve to confine and treat an offender

		and requires the offender to participate in a post-release drug or alcohol abuse continuum of care treatment plan. The special condition may be imposed when a parole panel renders a finding following a hearing or proceeding concerning alleged violations of the terms and conditions of parole or mandatory supervision under Chapter 146 of the Board Rules for an offender who is a suitable candidate as determined by the suitability criteria.
SISP	Super Intensive Supervision Program	The parolee requires enhanced monitoring. At any time this condition is in effect, unless modified or withdrawn by the SISP panel, an offender shall: A. submit to electronic monitoring; B. comply with a daily activity schedule; C. not travel within or beyond county of residence without approval of supervising Parole Officer; D. not unlawfully use drugs, narcotics or controlled substances; E. not use intoxicating inhalants; F. not consume alcoholic beverages; G. submit to urinalysis testing; and H. obey all driving restrictions. In addition, at any time Special Condition SISP is imposed, and to the extent directed in writing by the offender's supervising Parole Officer, an offender shall: A. reside in a community residential facility (halfway house) designated by the Division and comply with all facility rules and regulations in effect during their period of residence at the facility; B. attend adult basic education program; C. attend District Reentry Center (DRC) programming; D. actively seek employment; E. not enter an establishment where the primary function is the sale and dispensing of alcoholic beverages for on-premises consumption; F. submit to alcohol use testing; G. attend substance abuse counseling sessions; H. participate in substance abuse (alcohol/narcotics) treatment program; I. attend and participate in the Special Needs Offender Program; J. take prescribed medication as

		directed; K. participate in anger management or counseling program; L. participate in family counseling program; M. not contact, or cause to be contacted, in person, by telephone, correspondence, video or audio device, third person, media, or by any electronic means, the victim, or guardian of the victim of instant offense; N. pay restitution as instructed; or O. inform any prospective employer of supervision status.
T	Electronic Monitoring	Offender will wear an electronic monitor.
V1	Avoiding Victim of Stalking Offense	This condition shall be imposed when the offender is serving a conviction for Texas Penal Code 42.072, Stalking. 1. PS I's shall review the Commitment screen to determine if the offender was convicted of the listed Texas Penal Code. 2. If the "V1" special condition is to be imposed, the PS I's shall submit a transmittal requesting a Psychological Evaluation (Special Condition P1) in accordance with Texas Government Code, Section 508.223. 3. If it is determined that the special conditions are warranted, the PS I's shall enter the appropriate special conditions (V1 and/or P1)
V2	No Contact with Victim	At any time that Special Condition "V2" is in effect, as a condition of mandatory supervision or parole, the offender not intentionally or knowingly communicate directly or indirectly with a victim of the offense, or intentionally or knowingly go near a residence, school, place of employment, or business of a victim.
X	Sex Offender Condition	At any time Special Condition "X" is in effect, the offender shall fully comply with state laws governing sex offender treatment, sex offender registration and DNA submission, internet

		access, child safety zone restrictions, as well as Board and Division policies governing sex offender conditions and supervision. There are many other components of Condition X and an offender does not need to have been convicted of a sex crime for the state of Texas to add Condition X to their parole.
Z	Not to Enter a Specified County	Special Condition "Z" is intended to prohibit an offender from entering a specified county without prior written approval by the parole panel.
General	Parole Fee for Certain Releasees	The offender is required to pay a parole supervision fee of $5.00 each month during the period of parole supervision.
General	Parole Supervision Fee	The offender is required to pay a parole supervision fee of $10.00 and an administrative fee of $8.00 to the Parole Division for each month the offender is under parole supervision.

Parole Approval and Denial Reasons

There are ten categories used by each board commissioner and board member to vote with a simple A for Approve or D for Deny. One or more categories may apply, but only one is required for approval or denial in the decision making process.

Rule 145.6 - Notification of Parole Panel Decision

An inmate considered for parole or mandatory supervision shall be notified of the Parole Panel's decision in writing.

Consideration and notification of the parole panel's decision includes any cumulative, pre-final consecutive sentence.

Upon considering a case for parole or mandatory supervision, the parole panel shall make a record of its decision and the reasons for its decision on the minute sheet of the inmate's file. Reasons for the parole panel's decision include but are not limited to the following:

I. Criminal History

A The record does not include a documented pattern of violent or assaultive arrests or convictions on the part of the inmate; or criminal history appears to be primarily restricted to non-violent offenses; or available information indicates only incarceration.

D The record indicates that the inmate has repeatedly committed criminal episodes or has a pattern of similar offenses that indicates a predisposition to commit criminal acts upon release; or the record indicates that the inmate is a leader or active participant in gang or organized criminal activity; or the record indicates a juvenile or adult arrest for felony or misdemeanor offenses.

II. Nature of the Offense

A The record indicates non-violent offenses; or instant offense indicates no tendency toward violent/assaultive behavior; or offense reveals limited potential for future assaultive type offenses.

D The record indicates that the inmate committed one or more violent criminal acts indicating a conscious disregard for the lives, safety, or property of others; or the instant offense or pattern of criminal activity has elements of brutality, violence, or conscious selection of victim's vulnerability such that the inmate poses a continuing threat to public safety;

III. Drug and Alcohol Involvement

A The record indicates limited or non-involvement with drug sales or usage; or the record indicates limited or non-involvement with alcohol consumption.

D The record indicates excessive drug or alcohol involvement that includes possession, use or delivery in the instant offense or criminal history.

IV. Institutional Adjustment

A The record indicates that the inmate has maintained a satisfactory institutional adjustment; i.e., no major disciplinary cases, loss of time or demotion in classification since the previous review.

D The record indicates that the inmate committed a major disciplinary offense during the preceding six months resulting in a loss of good conduct time or loss of status below that at which the inmate entered prison; or a pattern of disciplinary infractions since the last review indicates a disregard for the rules.

V. Adjustment During Periods of Supervision

A The record indicates successful periods of supervision on probation, parole, or mandatory supervision.

D The record indicates unsuccessful periods of supervision on previous probation, parole, or mandatory supervision that resulted in incarceration, including parole-inabsentia.

VI. Participation in TDCJ-CID Proposed or Specialized Programs

A The record indicates participation in and completion of TDCJ-CID proposed or specialized programs; or the inmate has completed one or more vocational or academic programs that should enhance chances to obtain and maintain full-time stable employment.

D The record indicates that the inmate refused to participate or intentionally failed to complete TDCJ-CID proposed program(s) made available to the inmate.

VII. Time Served

A The record indicates that length of time served by the inmate is congruent with offense severity and criminal history.

D The record indicates that length of time served by the inmate is not congruent with offense severity and criminal history.

VIII. Felony Offense (There is no 'A' vote)

D The record indicates that the inmate has been charged before a magistrate, indicted, or convicted by a court of competent jurisdiction, with a felony offense committed while incarcerated.

IX. Discretionary Mandatory Supervision - For a vote NOT to release, it is necessary to vote both D1 and D2, along with any other reasons that may apply.

A Release to Discretionary Mandatory Supervision

D D1 – The record indicates that the inmate's accrued good conduct time is not an accurate reflection of the inmate's potential for rehabilitation.

D2 – The record indicates that the inmate's release would endanger the public.

X. Gang Affiliation

A The record indicates that the offender is not a confirmed member of one of the TDCJ-CID designated security threat groups.

D The record indicates that the offender is a confirmed member of one of the TDCJ-CID designated security threat group.

XI. Other

A or D - Write an explanation

Parole Analysis

Parole Considerations and Approval Rates History

	Cases Considered	Cases Approved	Approval Rate
FY 2002	61,601	15,369	24.95%
FY 2003	59,685	16,306	27.32%
FY 2004	64,008	19,440	30.37%
FY 2005	71,207	19,582	27.50%
FY 2006	72,583	19,061	26.26%
FY 2007	74,488	22,209	29.82%
FY 2008	74,895	23,025	30.74%
FY 2009	76,607	23,182	30.26%
FY 2010	78,575	24,368	31.01%
FY 2011	78,391	24,342	31.05%
FY 2012	80,638	29,689	36.80%
FY 2013	77,619	28,077	36.17%
FY 2014	77,300	27,500	35.58%
FY 2015	82,340	28,925	37.01%
FY 2016	81,712	28,268	34.60%
FY 2017	78,974	27,595	34.94%
FY 2018	80,495	26,566	33.00%
FY 2019	78,346	26,566	35.55%
FY 2020	77,530	29,919	38.59%
FY 2021	65,488	25,190	38.47%
FY 2022	62,579	24,604	39.32%

Offender Decision Notifications Sent

	Notifications of Status Letters Sent
FY 2013	79,773
FY 2014	78,717
FY 2015	83,555
FY 2016	86,683
FY 2017	84,798
FY 2018	84,606
FY 2019	83,524
FY 2020	78,681
FY 2021	66,967
FY 2022	61,457

Parole Consideration for Consecutive Sentences (2022)

	Parole From CID	Parole in Absentia	Totals
Considered	1,079	10	1,089
Approved	287	1	288
Approval Rate	26.60%	10.00%	26.45%

Parole Approvals By Voting Options (2022)

	Voting Options	Total Votes	Percent
FI-1	Release when eligible	5,130	20.85%
FI-2	Release on a specified date	4,097	16.65%
FI-3R*	Requires the offender to complete a TDCJ rehabilitation program and be released no earlier than three months from specified date.	4,007	16.29%
FI-4R*	Transfer to TDCJ Sex Offender Education Program (SOEP). Release to parole only after program completion and not earlier than four months from specified date.	693	2.82%
FI-5	Requires the offender to complete an In-Prison Therapeutic Community (IPTC) program prior to release on parole.	3,055	12.42%
FI-6	Transfer to a DWI Program (DWI), then release to an alcohol abuse treatment program.	935	3.80%
FI-6R*	Requires the offender to complete a TDCJ rehabilitation program and be released no earlier than six months from specified date.	5,187	21.08%
FI-7R*	Transfer to the TDCJ Serious and Violent Offender Reentry Initiative (SVORI) program. Release to parole only after program completion and not earlier than seven months from the specified date.	105	0.43%
FI-9R*	Transfer to the Sex Offender Treatment Program (SOTP-9) program. Release to parole only after program completion and not earlier than nine months from the specified date.	1,028	4.18%
FI-I8R*	Transfer to the Sex Offender Treatment Program (SOTP-18). Release to parole only after program completion and not earlier than 18 months from the specified date.	79	0.32%
CUFI	Approval for parole on the current sentence in a series; offenders serving consecutive sentences are considered for parole for each individual sentence upon reaching eligibility. The offender must receive parole on or discharge the first sentence to commence	288	1.17%

	serving the next sentence in the series.		
	Total FI Votes	24,604	100%
	Total Tier Votes Only	11,099	45.11%

** Rehabilitation tier voting options include requirements that offenders complete various programs in TDCJ-CID before release on parole.*

Parole Approval Rates by Guideline Level (2022)

Guideline Score	Cases Considered	Cases Approved	Approval Rate	Recommended Approval Rate
1	154	19	12.34%	0% - 20%
2	5,306	1,498	28.23%	15%-35%
3	6,804	2,481	36.46%	25%-40%
4	21,938	7,257	33.08%	30%-45%
5	12,559	4,787	38.12%	35%-50%
6	11,614	5,911	50.90%	45%-70%
7	4,196	2,643	62.99%	65%-100%
Total with Guidelines	62,571	24,596	39.31%	

Parole Approval Rates by Offense Types (2022)

Offense Type	Cases Considered Considered	Cases Approved	Approval Rate
Violent Aggravated Sexual	10,724	4,389	40.91%
Violent Aggravated Non-Sexual	3,499	1,424	40.70%
Violent Non-Aggravated Non-Sexual	11,413	3,617	31.69%
Non-Aggravated Sexual	1,930	673	34.87%
Non-Violent	35012	14,501	41.424%
Total	62,579	24,604	39.32%

DMS Considerations and Approval Rate History

	Cases Considered	Cases Approved	Approval Rates
FY 2011	20,886	10,155	48.62%
FY 2012	20,893	12,075	57.79%
FY 2013	17,785	9,522	53.54%
FY 2014	17,968	9,141	50.87%
FY 2015	19,017	9,106	47.88%
FY 2016	20,471	9,341	45.63%
FY 2017	20,093	9,792	48.73%
FY 2018	19,077	9,136	47.89%
FY2019	18,947	9,392	49.57%
FY2020	16,867	8,136	48.24%
FY 2021	14,812	6,984	47.15%
FY 2022	14,073	6,936	49.29%

DMS Considerations and Approval Rates by Offense Types (2022)

Offense Type	Cases Considered Considered	Cases Approved	Approval Rate
Violent Aggravated Non-Sexual	18	8	44.44%
Violent Aggravated Sexual	1	0	0.00%
Violent Non-Aggravated Non-Sexual	3,627	1,528	42.13%
Non-Aggravated Sexual	272	118	43.38%
Non-Violent	10,155	5,282	52.01%
Total	14,073	6,936	49.29%

DMS Decisions By Board Members & Parole Commissioners (2022)

Particulars	Total Parole Votes	Total Approved	Approval Rate	Denial Rate
Adams, R.	400	197	49.25%	50.75%
Aiello, R.	330	173	52.42%	47.58%
Brito, E.	1,545	562	36.38%	63.62%
Eck-Massingill, L.	1,984	861	42.89%	57.11%
Evans, I.	1,635	902	55.17%	44.83%
Farley, M.	1,263	626	49.56%	50.44%
Fox, T.	1,882	980	52.07%	47.93%
Gonzalez, R.	1,594	853	53.51%	46.49%
Gutierrez, D.	111	54	58.03%	51.35%
Jernigan, D.	126	58	48.65%	53.97%
Jones, C.	1,169	644	46.03%	44.91%
Kiel, J.	945	532	56.30%	43.70%
LaFavers, J..	1,185	527	44.47%	55.53%
Long, B.	887	476	53.66%	46.34%
Long, T.	1,192	514	43.12%	56.88%
Marton, J.	1,581	602	38.08%	61.92%
Moberley, M.	1,507	886	58.79%	41.21%
Molina, L.	1,595	712	44.64%	55.36%
Ramirez, A.	1,783	859	48.18%	51.82%
Robertson, E.	1,439	782	54.34%	45.66%
Saliagas, W.	954	417	43.71%	56.29%
Speier, C.	1,450	869	59.93%	40.07%
Tejada, R.	2,214	1,013	45.75%	54.25%
TOTALS	28,771	14,089	48.97%	51.03%

MRIS Considerations and Approval Rates (Total)

	Screened	Presented	Approved
FY 2009	1,318	337	59
FY 2010	1,443	457	102
FY 2011	1,807	349	100
FY 2012	1,857	491	72
FY 2013	1,362	359	69
FY 2014	1,113	318	67
FY 2015	1,738	213	85
FY 2016	2,273	176	86
FY 2017	2,263	207	94
FY 2018	2,122	169	63
FY 2019	2,803	196	76
FY 2020	2,858	201	61
FY 2021	2,508	222	48
FY 2022	2,670	320	58

Medically Recommended Intensive Supervision (MRIS) Approvals

	Terminally Ill	Physically Handicapped	Long Term Care	Elderly	Mentally Ill	Mentally Retarded
FY 2009	34	0	1	24	0	0
FY 2010	54	0	1	46	1	0
FY 2011	49	3	4	44	0	0
FY 2012	40	2	0	21	0	0
FY 2013	48	2	0	19	0	0
FY 2014	50	1	0	16	0	0
FY 2015	52	2	31	0	0	0
FY 2016	55	0	31	0	0	0
FY 2017	69	0	25	0	0	0
FY 2018	52	0	11	0	0	0
FY 2019	59	0	17	0	0	0
FY 2020	40	0	21	0	0	0
FY 2021	33	0	15	0	0	0
FY 2022	35	0	16	7	0	0

Parole Panel Votes After Approval for Special Review (2022)

	Special Review Voting Options	Number	Percent
FI-1	Parole when eligible	90	32.03%
FI-2	Parole on a specified date	20	7.12%
FI-3R*	Transfer to a TDCJ rehabilitation program, such as Changes/Life Skills, no earlier than a specified date at least three months with release on parole after completion.	14	4.98%
FI-4R*	Transfer to a Sex Offender Education Program (SOEP) no earlier than a specified date for at least four months from specified date.	2	0.71%
FI-5	Transfer to an In-Prison Therapeutic Community Program (IPTC), with release to an aftercare component.	13	4.63%
FI-6	Transfer to a DWI Program (DWI), then release to an alcohol abuse treatment program.	0	0.00%
FI-6R*	Requires the offender to complete a TDCJ rehabilitation program (PRTC, PRSAP) and be released no earlier than six months from specified date.	15	5.34%
FI-7R*	Transfer to the TDCJ Serious and Violent Offender Reentry Initiative (SVORI) program. Release to parole only after program completion and not earlier than seven months from the specified date.	0	0.00%
FI-9R*	Transfer to the Sex Offender Treatment Program (SOTP-9) program. Release to parole only after program completion and not earlier than nine months from the specified date.	6	2.14%
FI-I8R*	Transfer to the Sex Offender Treatment Program (SOTP-18, Innerchange). Release to parole only after program completion and not earlier than 18 months from the specified date.	0	0.00%
NR	Deny parole and set time for next parole consideration. (Set-Off)	71	25.27%
CU/NR	Deny favorable action and set next review in consecutive sentence case.	5	1.78%

CU/FI	Approval for parole on the current sentence in a series; offenders serving consecutive sentences are considered for parole for each individual sentence upon reaching eligibility. The offender must receive parole on or discharge the first sentence to commence serving the next sentence in the series.	0	0.00%
CU/SA	Deny, Serve All	1	0.36%
SA	Required to Serve All. Deny parole with no regular subsequent review, requiring offender to serve balance of sentence if discharge date occurs in less than three years.	13	4.63%
RMS	Release to Mandatory Supervision	12	4.27%
DMS	Deny Mandatory Supervision	19	6.76%
	Total	281	100%

SISP Panel Considerations (2022)

A special panel for Super Intensive Supervision Program (SISP) considers offenders known to have:

- Committed or threatened to commit an act resulting in a victim; caused bodily injury or serious bodily injury; or placed an individual in danger of bodily injury or serious bodily injury; or

- Had problematic institutional adjustment, such that their accrued good conduct time is not an accurate reflection of their potential for rehabilitation and their release would endanger the public; or identified by TDCJ as a member of an organized prison gang.

	Parole	MS	Totals
Considerations	6,361	1,214	7,575
Imposed	1,045	190	1,235
Percent Imposed	16.43%	15.65%	16.30%

Parole and DMS Considerations & Approval Rates History

	Parole Cases Voted	Parole Cases Approved	Parole Approval Rate	DMS Cases Voted	DMS Cases Approved	DMS Approval Rate
FY 2002	61,601	15,369	24.95%	15,577	8,945	57.42%
FY 2003	59,685	16,306	27.32%	18,014	10,917	60.60%
FY 2004	64,008	19.440	30.37%	18,478	10,737	58.11%
FY 2005	71,207	19,582	27.50%	13,765	7,206	52.35%
FY 2006	72,583	19,061	26.26%	17,025	8,876	52.14%
FY 2007	74,488	22,209	29.82%	18,131	9,437	52.05%
FY 2008	74,895	23,025	30.74%	17,811	8,900	49.97%
FY 2009	76,607	23,182	30.26%	18,554	8,957	48.28%
FY 2010	78,575	24,368	21.01%	18,938	9,409	49.68%
FY 2011	78,391	24,342	31.05%	20,866	10,155	48.62%
FY 2012	80,638	29,689	36.80%	20,893	12,075	57.79%
FY 2013	77,619	28,077	36.17%	17,785	9,522	53.54%
FY 2014	77,299	27,499	35.57%	17,968	9,141	50.87%
FY 2015	82,340	28,925	37.01%	19,017	9,106	47.88%
FY 2016	81,712	28,268	34.60%	20,471	9,341	45.63%
FY 2017	78,974	27,595	34.94%	20,093	9,792	48.73%
FY 2018	80,495	26,566	33.00%	19,077	9,136	47.89%
FY 2019	78,346	26,566	35.55%	18,947	9,392	49.57%
FY 2020	77,530	29,919	38.59%	16,867	8,136	48.24%
FY 2021	65,488	25,190	38.47%	14,872	6,984	47.15%
FY 2022	62,579	24,604	39.32%	14,073	6,936	49.29%

Parole Considerations by Board Member & Commissioners (2022)

Member	Total Votes	Number Approved	Approval Rate	Denial Rate
Adams, R.	2,529	983	38.87%	61.13%
Aiello, R.	1,309	547	41.79%	58.21%
Brito, E.	5,981	2,059	34.43%	65.57%
Eck-Massingill, L.	6,826	3,151	46.16%	53.84%
Evans, I.	7,642	3,179	41.60%	58.40%
Farley, M.	6,385	3.095	48.47%	51.53%
Fox, T.	7,455	2,799	37.55%	62.45%
Gonzalez, R.	7,657	3,195	41.73%	58.27%
Gutierrez, D.	1,500	1,092	72.80%	27.20%
Jernigan, D.	1,358	544	40.06%	59.94%
Jones, C..	7,875	4,092	51.96%	48.04%
Kiel, J.	5,190	1,807	34.82%	65.18%
LaFavers, J.	6,318	2,770	43.84%	56.16%
Long, B.	6,801	2,707	41.18%	58.87%
Long, T.	6,595	2,768	41.97%	58.03%
Marton, J.	6,205	2,018	32.52%	67.48%
Moberley, M.	6,411	2,795	43.60%	56.40%
Molina, L.	7,761	2,859	36.84%	63.16%
Ramirez, A.	6,624	2,290	34.57%	65.43%
Robertson, E.	7,510	3,022	40.24%	59.76%
Sallagas, W.	5,217	1,687	32.34%	67.66%

Speier, C.	5,025	1,845	36.72%	63.28%
Tejada, R.	7,849	3,595	45.67%	54.33%
Totals	134,023	54,979	41.02%	58.98%

Amarillo Parole Board Release Statics by PGS

Level	Cases Considered	Cases Approved	Approval Rate	Recommended Approval Rate	Denial Rate
1	74	14	18.92%	0%-20%	81.06%
2	2,305	693	30.07%	15%-35%	69.93%
3	2,799	1,107	39.55%	25%-40%	60.45%
4	6,918	2,410	34.84%	30%-45%	65.16%
5	3,298	1,194	36.20%	35%-50%	63.80%
6	2,441	1,106	45.31%	45%-70%	54.69%
7	669	323	48.28%	65%-70%	51.72%
Total	18,504	6,847	37.00%		63.00%

Angleton Parole Board Release Statics by PGS

Level	Cases Considered	Cases Approved	Approval Rate	Recommended Approval Rate	Denial Rate
1	28	6	21.43%	0%-20%	78.57%
2	1,394	457	32.78%	15%-35%	67.22%
3	2,081	857	41.18%	25%-40%	58.82%
4	7,321	2.391	32.66%	30%-45%	67.34%
5	4.066	1,488	36.60%	35%-50%	63.40%
6	4,735	2,561	54.09%	45%-70%	45.91%
7	2,085	1,409	67.58%	65%-70%	32.42%
Total	21,710	9,169	42.23%		57.77%

Austin Parole Board Release Statics by PGS

Level	Cases Considered	Cases Approved	Approval Rate	Recommended Approval Rate	Denial Rate
1	42	6	13.95%	0%-20%	83.72%
2	1,637	554	33.84%	15%-35%	64.81%
3	2,788	1,282	45.98%	25%-40%	51.90%
4	7,765	2,840	36.57%	30%-45%	59.61%
5	4,371	1,661	38.00%	35%-50%	58.04%
6	4,389	2,104	47.94%	45%-70%	48.23%
7	1.650	1,000	60.61%	65%-70%	36.79%
Total	22,643	9,447	41.72%		54.91%

Gatesville Parole Board Release Statics by PGS

Level	Cases Considered	Cases Approved	Approval Rate	Recommended Approval Rate	Denial Rate
1	26	5	19.23%	0%-20%	80.77%
2	975	438	44.92%	15%-35%	55.08%
3	1,792	1,015	56.64%	25%-40%	43.36%
4	4,958	2,035	41.04%	30%-45%	58.96%
5	3,045	1,182	38.82%	35%-50%	61.18%
6	3,794	2,069	54.53%	45%-70%	45.47%
7	1,585	1,084	68.39%	65%-70%	31.61%
Total	16,175	7,828	48.40%		51.60%

Huntsville Parole Board Release Statics by PGS

Level	Cases Considered	Cases Approved	Approval Rate	Recommended Approval Rate	Denial Rate
1	48	5	10.42%	0%-20%	77.08%
2	1,912	578	30.23%	15%-35%	60.41%
3	2,822	1,382	48.97%	25%-40%	45.68%
4	6,693	2,656	39.68%	30%-45%	51.05%
5	3,369	1,580	46.90%	35%-50%	42.77%
6	2,610	1,546	59.23%	45%-70%	33.22%
7	903	640	70.87%	65%-70%	24.14%
Total	18,357	8,387	45.69%		45.89%

Palestine Parole Board Release Statics by PGS

Level	Cases Considered	Cases Approved	Approval Rate	Recommended Approval Rate	Denial Rate
1	58	1	1.72%	0%-20%	98.28%
2	1,761	346	19.65%	15%-35%	80.35%
3	2,559	954	37.28%	25%-40%	62.72%
4	6,063	1,794	29.59%	30%-45%	70.41%
5	3,093	1,200	38.80%	35%-50%	61.20%
6	2,763	1,402	50.74%	45%-70%	49.26%
7	911	594	65.20%	65%-70%	34.80%
Total	17,208	6,291	36.56%		63.44%

San Antonio Parole Board Release Statics by PGS

Level	Cases Considered	Cases Approved	Approval Rate	Recommended Approval Rate	Denial Rate
1	46	7	15.22%	0%-20%	84.78%
2	1,692	552	30.85%	15%-35%	69.15%
3	2,519	1,076	42.72%	25%-40%	57.28%
4	7,063	2,349	33.26%	30%-45%	66.74%
5	4,296	1,445	33.64%	35%-50%	66.36%
6	2,996	1,276	42.59%	45%-70%	57.41%
7	798	319	39.97%	65%-70%	60.03%
Total	19,410	6,994	36.03%		63.97%

The Key to Effective Parole Packet

The key to creating an effective parole packet is planning and organization.

When To Submit a Parole Package

While no inmate can be released prior to their statutory parole eligibility date, current Parole Board policy defines the parole "review period" as being "a period greater than two months but less than six months prior to the month of the next scheduled review." That is the period during which the Board asks that any written materials be submitted to the Board. The Board votes most parole cases within a month or so of the scheduled parole eligibility date or next review date; however, some cases are not voted until months after the parole review date. The Board has also been known to vote cases as early as two months prior to the month of scheduled review.

With that being said, parole packages should mailed and placed in the offender's file **at least five months prior to the scheduled review date**. More than a few inmates have found themselves preparing to submit materials to the Parole Board for consideration as they vote their case only to find out their case has already been voted – and denied.

Purpose of the Parole Package

The purpose of the parole package is to introduce the offender to the Parole Board. It should show the offender in a positive way and demonstrate that the offender can be a productive member of society when released.

The voting members of the Parole Board will have the offender's case file. In the file will be a lot of negative information about the offender. It will include:

- a criminal history report,
- information from the prosecutor,
- information from the trial,
- a victim impact statement,
- all victim statements and transcripts from the victim on why the offender should ot be released,
- information from the arresting officers

This negative information needs to be offset by positive information in the parole package.

Instructions for Completing a Parole Package

The awarding of parole to an offender in Texas often appears to be completely random. Two individuals, each with nearly identical cases and history, can receive wildly different results.

Unfortunately, the decision on who makes parole can be based on something as simple as whether the voting members of the parole board "have a bad day".

The volume of cases voted on in any given month is tremendous and some estimates are that each file is subjected to an average review of 3-5 minutes.

It is this tremendous volume that makes it so important for the potential parolee to make an effort to distinguish their file (in a good way) from the hundred, or thousands of others under review.

The most important thing that can be done to improve the chances of parole is to influence the basic human nature of the voters by "humanizing" the potential parolee.

> "Humanize**: 1 a**: to represent as human: attribute human qualities to **b**: to adapt to human nature or use. **2**: to make humane." - Merriam-Webster Online Dictionary

The first way to humanize the potential parolee is through the use of photographs. Typically, the only visual representations of the person contained in the parole file are "mug shots" or photos taken when the offender first enters the prison system. These are taken within hours of their head being shaved (in the case of males) and typically after long periods without sunshine or adequate rest, resulting in a photograph that makes the person look like someone who shouldn't be allowed to walk the streets.

The example Parole Package that is part of this book has places for a number of photographs along with captions. The photograph on the cover page should be of the potential parolee alone, and be the best possible photograph you have available. The others in the package should show the person at work or home, interacting with other people including family members. The "caption" below each photo should explain who is in the picture along with what was happening.

Be sure the photographs ***do not*** show anyone, particularly the potential parolee, engaging in or conducting activity the voters may feel is inappropriate. It would not be wise to include photographs of anyone with drug paraphernalia, alcohol, tobacco, or wearing any clothing depicting these. With computers as they are today a few minutes with a software package can remove or cover up any offensive objects. If you don't feel comfortable doing this yourself, almost any print or copy shop can provide you a reference to an individual or company who can "photo shop" pictures into an acceptable format at a reasonable cost.

Parts of the Parole Package

Introductory Letter

The Parole Package should start with a introductory letter, as shown on the example on in the next section. The introductory letter briefly states who the parole package is for, what documents are enclosed and a short statement. The letter is used to introduce the offender to the voting members. The letter should be from the offender and addressed to the members of the parole board.
The introductory letter should be just one page long.

Cover Page

The next page of the parole package should be the cover page for the Parole Package. The information on this page should be brief, just the name, identification number, and a photograph of the offender. It is designed solely to catch the attention of the voter and encourage them to look further in the package, thus simplicity is the key.

Table of Contents

The next page of the package should contain a Table of Contents with the items being identified by page number and/or an exhibit number. The key here is often a simple yet interesting synopsis of the contents along with the "key" to finding the item quickly if it catches the board member's attention.

Parole Plan (Post-Prison Plan)

This section of the parole package contains the plans for when the offender is released.

It is the offender's responsibility to provide an appropriate release plan. An offender should call upon friends and relatives to help arrange a place to live, a job, a means of transportation, and moral support. If the source of an offender's trouble is related to the environment to which the offender intends to return, he or she is advised to live somewhere else. If there are no resources in the community to help the offender, the Parole Division's Review and Release Processing Section can assist in making a halfway house placement upon release approval. In this case, the offender should contact an IPO for assistance.

Offenders whose crimes were alcohol or drug-related should look for a location where counseling is available for those problems. Additionally, eligible offenders can expedite their job searches by securing certified birth certificates and replacement Social Security cards through the TDCJ-Reentry & Integration Division prior to release.

A parole or mandatory release plan includes the name, address and phone number(s) of the person with whom an offender plans to reside following release to supervision. The offender should provide as many release plans as available when interviewed by the Parole Officer. He or she should also inform the Parole Officer about any changes in the plan that occur after the interview and prior to release. A District Parole Officer (DPO) must verify the plan before the offender can be released.

The offender's parole plan should be included in the parole package.

As an example:

"Upon parole I plan to return to my home at 100 Your Street, Your Town, Texas, where I will reside with my wife, Jane, and my children, Riley and Lillian.

As shown on the letter of support from my employer, Elizabeth Martin, I will resume my position as Cook for Waffle House.

In addition to my job as Cook, I intend to enroll in college part-time.

At home, I have not only the support of my family, but friends as well, as shown by the attached letters of support. My sister lives within twenty minutes from my house.

My wife, Jane, is employed at Sears Company as a sales assistant. She has worked for her employer for four years, and as shown in her letter of support, is fully prepared to support me in my parole.

Also living with us, are my two children, Riley and Lillian who are both in elementary school."

Try to include as much information as you can because it shows that you are serious about your parole; that you have a safe place to live; that you have employment and you have a support system on the outside.

Parole Guideline Score

Many believe the Parole Package should contain the information from the Parole Guideline Score worksheet which consists of the Risk Assessment Scoring and Offense Severity Class. If this information is favorable then by all means use it. However, if the Parole Guideline Score is low, the use of it may be counter-productive.

Educational and Work History

In the form of a resume, include a brief description of all education received prior to incarceration and while incarcerated, whether it be college, GED, or vocational courses, along with the description of the courses as well as all certificates and diplomas. This is thought to be particularly strong evidence for parole as statistics show education lowers the chances of someone returning to prison. In addition, education demonstrates not only an ability to follow a plan but also that an effort is being made to improve one's position in life.

On the same page as the educational history list the description of any work done while in prison. This is beneficial so that the parole board knows the offender has additional skills to rely on in the event the anticipated job does not work out. A one page resume of job history from the free world as well as from prison may assist the parole board in determining whether an offender has marketable job skills.

Make sure to highlight the educational and work you have done in prison. This includes vocational certificates, degrees, and any skills you developed.

Place this information in the form of a resume similar to the one on the next page.

(SAMPLE)

John M. Doe
123 Anywhere Street
Houston, Texas 77338
713-222-2222

Previous Employment:

Gurney Unit, Palestine, Texas 2020-2023
Cook -Prepare food, clean kitchen.

Ellis Unit, Huntsville, Texas 2019-2020
Mechanic - Responsible for vehicle repair and other small motor repair.

Waffle House, Houston, Texas 2017-2019
Grill Cook - Responsible for cooking on the grill, maintain cleanliness in kitchen, follow safety and sanitation procedures, keep food orders flowing

The Kettle Restaurant, Houston, Texas 2015-2017
Line Cook - Learn new recipes, cook, maintain cleanliness in kitchen, follow safety and sanitation procedures, keep food orders flowing

McDonald's Corporation, Houston, Texas 2014-2015
Crew Member - Greet customers, clean area, sweep, follow safety and sanitation procedures, ensure items are well stocked, work in different sections as needed.

Education:

2022, - 100+ hours Life Skills
2020, - Automotive Technology Certification while at Ellis Unit
2019, - Automotive Certifications - Brake Repair at Ellis Unit
2015 - GED, Aldine High School

Skills:

Auto mechanics, brake repair, cook

Certifications and Degrees

You want to highlight the educational and vocation programs you completed. Include copies of all certificates, certifications and other awards received while in prison. Also include any certifications or degrees obtained prior to incarceration.

Also include information about participation in therapeutic programs, all jobs held while incarcerated and any voluntary activities. Emphasize any leadership roles while incarcerated. Basically, include any significant achievements made while in prison.

Support Letters

When an offender is eligible for parole, a letter of support to the Parole Board can help them make parole.

Support letters are extremely important. They are so important that in early 2019, the Texas Board of Pardons and Parole modified the factors used in their parole decision-making process to include support letters. The Parole Panel reviews the offender's support letters before or during the parole review process.

Letters of support can be from family, friends or employers. They should be from individuals who know the offender personally and explain how they know the offender, how they will support the offender when the offender is released, and why they feel parole is appropriate in this particular case.

A support letter is evidence that the offender will have a network of family and friends to provide financial, emotional, and other support when the offender is released. Support letters should be brief, just one page in length.

The goal of a support letter is to show the offender in a good light when the voting member of the parole board reads the offender's prison file. The file will contain a lot of negative information such as a criminal history report, information from the arrest, information from the trial, letters and correspondence from the victims, and the victim impact statement. The support letter will be used to offset this negative information.

Who can write a support letter?

- Family, close friends, and loved ones can write support letters.
- Other relatives who are close to the offender can write support letters.

- Business people and other community members can write support letters.
- Potential employers, counselors, teachers, fellow students, and religious mentors can write support letters.
- People who have known the inmate while in prison such as Prisoner's Corrections Counselor, supervisor from work detail, prison chaplains, and volunteers can write support letters.

Support Letter Salutation

The letter of support should be addressed to:

TDCJ- Parole Division
Attention: Correspondence
P.O. Box 13401,
Capitol Station
Austin, Texas 78711

This is the address to the main office in Austin.

You should start the letter by addressing the parole board members. Feel free to use any of these greetings.

Dear Parole Board Members,
To the Honorable Members of the Parole Board,

Do NOT open the letter with:

To Whom It May Concern,
Dear Sirs,
Dear Gentlemen,

There are female voting members and any gender-specific salutation might offend them.

Contents to Include in the Support Letter

The support letters should include details that demonstrate the offender has a strong support system in place. The letter should be written on letterhead stationery.

A letter of support should include four paragraphs with the following information:

First paragraph:

- Include the inmate's name, TDC number, occupation, and age in the first paragraph.
- If the inmate has worked in an occupation for several years, it is important to state how many years the offender worked in this role.

Second paragraph:

- How you have known the offender and your relationship to the offender.
- How the offender has improved. Did the offender complete any classes, obtain a GED, court mandated therapy, anger management program, or any other self-improvement course?
- Why you believe the offender will not commit a crime again.

Third paragraph:

- How the offender has improved in attitude, behaviors, and any efforts to improve while in prison.
- What help you can provide the offender when released on parole such as mentorship, transportation, housing, or employment.
- The offender's good qualities which can counter balance against the negative items contained in the offender's parole file.

Fourth paragraph/conclusion:

- Sign the letter with your full name, address, and contact information.

The letter of support should follow the outline above. However, some people can write a personal or emotional support letter as long as it contains the information above.

Do not include an emotional appeal on releasing the offender. Just state the facts and why, if released, you believe the offender will be a productive member of society. The parole board is now swayed by emotion. They are not there to make a moral judgment about how awful the crime was or how the family needs the offender at home. The voting members will review the evidence and look to see if they think there is a risk the offender will re-offend if released on parole.

It is generally thought that 3-5 support letters are enough and any more may dilute the effect. If you choose to have more than four then the page of excerpts discussed earlier is particularly important.

If you have a number of support letters, make a page of excerpts which includes a simple one or two line statement from the support letters that are particularly strong. Be sure and identify which letter it is taken from by name so if the parole board wants to read further the letter will be easy to find.

Offender Support Letter

One of the support letters should be from the offender. It should tell their side of "the story", accepting responsibility for their crime, and explaining why and how they have rehabilitated.

Since the voting members only have negative information about the offender, this letter should demonstrate that the offender is committed to doing what is right once released from prison.

The letter should address the offender's criminal history. The Board members have a record of the offender's criminal history and convictions so the offender needs to address what they did, their state of mind, and the outcome of the case. Do not go into details, just a brief overview. For example:

> *"On September 1, 2010 I was convicted of a DUI. I was not working and had been out to celebrate a friend's birthday. I was arrested on July 5, 2010, pled guilty and received a 3 year sentence. I deeply regret drinking and driving that day and have enrolled in an alcohol rehabilitation program."*

Offenders should address their convictions and express remorse.

> *"I realize that selling drugs is illegal and that drugs destroy lives and families. At the time I was hanging out with the wrong people and I did not have the energy or patience to get a low-paying job or to save money to buy the things I wanted. I now realize that was wrong. I do not need those people around me. When I was selling drugs and robbing stores I did not see my victims as people. And I am ashamed of that."*

Statements of accepting responsibility and how the offender has changed should be included.

> *"I accept full responsibility for my actions. I realize that I made poor choices and while incarcerated I have learned how to make better, more positive choices in the future. "*

Include brief information about where you plan to live if you are paroled.

Pictures

The final section should contain pictures of the offender with their family. These pictures are design to humanize the offender so they are not just a number. Include pictures of the offender interacting with their family but make sure you do not use any pictures which could be offensive or include activities which are illegal.

The Parole Package should be typed and carefully checked for spelling and grammatical errors. The copy sent to be placed in the parole file should be bound or placed in a folder and kept clean until it is mailed.

If the first attempt at parole is unsuccessful the package can be updated as additional materials become available.

A sample parole package is available for you to review in the next section.

Parole Package - Completion and Mailing

Following the instructions on the prior pages in this package, complete the material with a word processor or typewriter. Legible hand writing is acceptable but not recommended.

Assemble the Parole Package in this order:

1. Introductory Letter
2. Cover Page (with picture)
3. Table of Contents
4. Parole Plan
5. Risk Assessment Security and Offense Severity Class (if not negative)
6. Short Essay about activities while Incarcerated, educational history and work experience
7. Copies of certificates, degrees, etc.
8. Work history or resume
9. Excerpts from Support Letters
10. Support Letter from Offender
11. Support Letters from Friends, Family and Others
12. Pictures

Assemble all papers including photographs, certificates, support letters, etc. and mail the package via U.S. Mail (preferably certified mail, return receipt requested) to:

TDCJ- Parole Division
Attention: Correspondence
P.O. Box 13401,
Capitol Station
Austin, Texas 78711

In addition, if the time is within six months of the parole vote, then send a copy of the completed parole package to the Parole Board office assigned to the unit. The address of each Parole Office and their assigned units can be found in Appendix 4.

(Sample Introductory Letter)

John D. Doe
TDC #01234567
Gurney Unit
1385 FM 3328
Tennessee Colony, TX 76067
July 2, 2023

TDCJ- Parole Division
Attention: Correspondence
P.O. Box 13401
Capitol Station
Austin, Texas 78711-3401

To the Honorable Members of the Parole Board,

Enclosed please find the parole packet for John D. Doe, TDC # 01234567. I would appreciate your review of this packet prior to voting on my parole.

The packet contains letters of support, an outline of my parole plan, as well as other information I believe you will find useful in your review.

I consider myself, overall, to be a very fortunate person who has made a serious mistake. I would ask that you please take the time to read the support letters as they truly show I have more support and opportunities than is typical in this situation.

Sincerely,

John D. Doe

Parole Package

For

John D. Doe

TDC # 01234567

**current photo

**We are using photos from www.free digital photos.net for these examples, be sure to insert photos and captions in the appropriate places.

Table of Contents

Parole Plan

Upon parole, I plan to return to my home at 100 Your Street, Your Town, Texas, where I will reside with my wife, Jane, and my children, Riley (age 6) and Lillian (age 3). We currently own a small three-bedroom house in a quiet neighborhood.

As shown on the letter of support from my former employer, Elizabeth Martin, I will resume my position as Cook for Waffle House. Ms. Martin has assured me there will be no conflicts with my schedule and parole commitments.

In addition to my job as Cook, I intend to enroll in classes at a local junior college part-time.

At home, I have not only the support of my family, but friends as well, as shown by the attached letters of support. My sister lives within twenty minutes from my house.

My wife, Jane, is employed at Sears Company as a sales assistant. She has worked for her employer for six years, and as shown in her letter of support, is fully prepared to support me in my parole.

Example of Presentation of Parole Guideline Level, Risk Assessment Security and Offense Severity Level

Parole Guideline Level for JOHN D. DOE
TDC # 01234567

Question	Select One	Your Score
Does the commitment offense include an UUMV, Burglary Of A Habitation, Burglary of a Motor Vehicle, or Forgery charge?	No = 0 Points Yes = 1 Point	0
Is there a history of supervisory release revocations for felony offenses?	No probation, parole or mandatory supervision revocations = 0 Points One Revocation = 1 Point More than one revocation = 3 Points	0
Does the offender have prior incarcerations?	None = 0 Points One or two prior incarcerations = 1 Point Three or more prior incarcerations = 3 Points	0
Does the offender's employment history include six months of continuous full-time employment or school attendance in the two years before incarceration?	Yes = 0 Points No - 1 Point	0
What was the offenders age at first admission to a juvenile or adult correctional facility?	26 or older = 0 Points 18 to 25 = 1 Point 17 or Under = 2 Points	0
Total Static Points		0

Question	Select One	Your Score
What is the Offender's Current Age?	Under 25 years old = 3 Points 25-34 years old = 2 Points 35-44 years old = 1 Point Over 45 = 0 Points	1
Is the offender a confirmed member of a security threat group (Gang)?	Active STG (Gang) Member = 1 Points No Gang "Tag" = 0 Points	0
Were there any education, vocational, or certified on-the-job training programs completed during the present incarceration?	Yes = 0 Points No = 1 Points	0
Is there any prison disciplinary conduct in the last eighteen months?	None = 0 Points Demoted below entry level OR good time lost = 1 Point Zero balance of good time = 2 Points	0
What is the offender's current prison custody level?	Minimum Out (outside trusty S-2) = 0 Points Minimum In (inside trusty S-3) = 1 Point Medium, close custody or Ad. Seg. = 2 Points	0
Total Dynamic Points		1

Total Static Points	0
Total Dynamic Points	1
Your Total Score	1

Offense Severity Level	L (Low)

Male Risk Levels

Offense Severity Class	Risk Level: Highest (16)	Risk Level: High (9-15)	Risk Level: Moderate (4-8)	Risk Level: Low (3 or less)
Highest	1	2	2	3
High	2	3	4	4
Moderate	2	3	5	6
Low	3	4	6	7

John M. Doe
123 Anywhere Street
Houston, Texas 77338
713-222-2222

Previous Employment:

Gurney Unit, Palestine, Texas 2020-2023
Cook -Prepare food, clean kitchen.

Ellis Unit, Huntsville, Texas 2019-2020
Mechanic - Responsible for vehicle repair and other small motor repair.

Waffle House, Houston, Texas 2017-2019
Grill Cook - Responsible for cooking on the grill, maintain cleanliness in kitchen, follow safety and sanitation procedures, keep food orders flowing

The Kettle Restaurant, Houston, Texas 2015-2017
Line Cook - Learn new recipes, cook, maintain cleanliness in kitchen, follow safety and sanitation procedures, keep food orders flowing

McDonald's Corporation, Houston, Texas 2014-2015
Crew Member - Greet customers, clean area, sweep, follow safety and sanitation procedures, ensure items are well stocked, work in different sections as needed.

Education:

2022, - 100+ hours Life Skills
2020, - Automotive Technology Certification while at Ellis Unit
2019, - Automotive Certifications - Brake Repair at Ellis Unit
2015 - GED, Aldine High School

Skills:

Auto mechanics, brake repair, cook

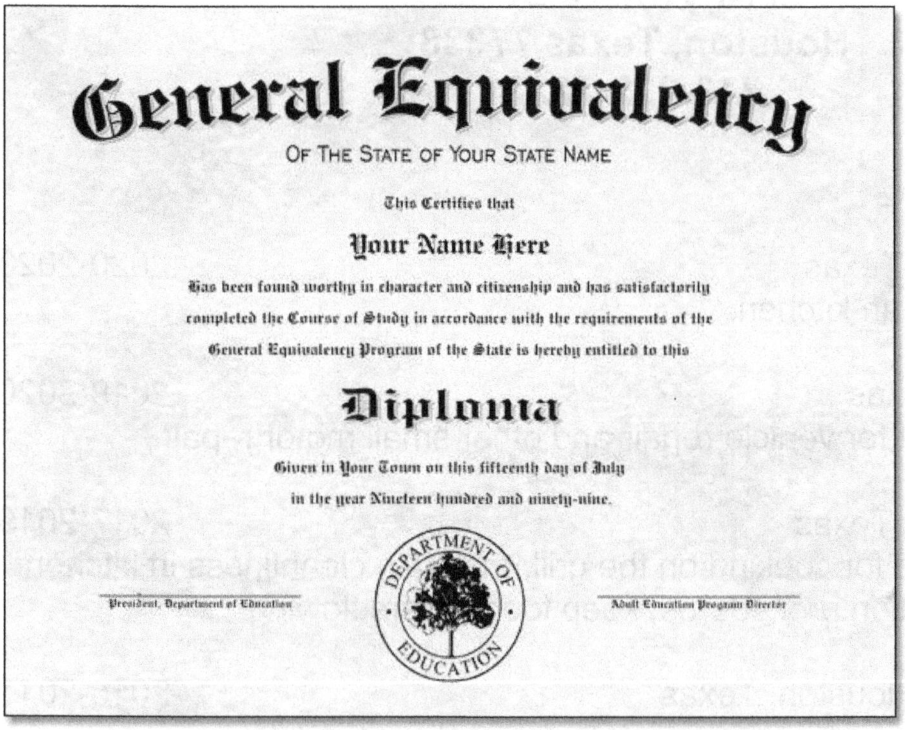
General Equivalency

OF THE STATE OF YOUR STATE NAME

This Certifies that

Your Name Here

Has been found worthy in character and citizenship and has satisfactorily completed the Course of Study in accordance with the requirements of the General Equivalency Program of the State is hereby entitled to this

Diploma

Given in Your Town on this fifteenth day of July in the year Nineteen hundred and ninety-nine.

President, Department of Education

DEPARTMENT OF EDUCATION

Adult Education Program Director

Excerpts from Support Letters

Volunteer Work

Elizabeth Martin, Assistant Manager, Waffle House.
"Mr. Doe has been of invaluable assistance to many who are in need. He frequently donates his time to helping at the food bank."

Employment Prospect

Elizabeth Martin, Assistant Manager, Waffle House.
"I am offering John back his position as cook. His skills in this area are greater than anyone I have ever seen."

Past Work Performance

Elizabeth Martin, Assistant Manager, Waffle House.
"I know well, for I have seen with my own eyes, how devoted he can be for someone that might otherwise be regarded as the least among us.

John D. Doe
TDCJ # 01234567
123 Anywhere Street
Houston, Texas 77338
July 2, 2023

Honorable Members of The Parole Board
Texas Board Of Pardons and Parole
P.O. Box 13401
Capital Station
Austin, Texas 78711-3401

Re. John D. Doe TDC # 01234567

Dear Honorable Members of The Parole Board,

I am writing this support letter in the hope of being approved for parole. I have accumulated over 100 % of my time. I have not lost any good time or work time and I have completed all required programs.

I have learned in the classes and through self-reflection what brought me to be in prison. I take full responsibility for the crime I committed. I know that I would not have been able to improve myself without the help and structure I have had while incarcerated. The time I have spent in prison has been a positive experience which has given me the opportunity to learn the steps to take to never return. I have a greater awareness of crimes and how it affects everyone, and I am prepared to do whatever it takes to continue with my life and succeed in my recovery and rehabilitation.

My goal on release from prison is to continue with my life and be the best husband, father and son to my family. I want to be a law abiding citizen and provide for my family. I am very fortunate that I have a large support system in place. They all encouraged me to learn all I can about while here. They have told me that I can count on them for support when I need it after I am released from prison and return home.

Prior to incarceration, I was successfully employed as a cook. I plan to return to my prior job upon release.

In conclusion, I know that with all I have learned from my incarceration and the support I have from my family and friends I will be able to make a positive transition back into the free world never to return again to prison.

I thank you for your time and consideration for this review for my parole.

Sincerely,

John D. Doe #01234567

Jake Marin
555 Texas Ave.
Houston, Texas 77338
July 1, 2023

Honorable Members of the Parole Board
Texas Board of Pardons and Parole
P.O. Box 13401
Capital Station
Austin, Texas 78711-3401

Re. John D. Doe
TDC # 01234567

Dear Honorable Members of the Parole Board,

I am 37 years old and employed as an Assistant Manager at Waffle House where I have worked for eight years.

I have known John Doe for seven years as a coworker and friend. Despite his mistakes, I know John to be a good person because he cares about his family and the customers who eat at Waffle House.

I believe that John will be able to be a useful and a law-abiding member of society.

While John has been in prison he has made numerous efforts to improve himself. He wrote me several times requesting training material to ensure he is better qualified for his position at Waffle House.

After John returns home, I will be available to him as a boss, friend and mentor. He can rely on my guidance and support to help him transition to life on the outside.

Sincerely,

Jake Marin

Pictures

**John and Riley

**John and Riley fishing on vacation

**John, Riley and Samantha at Riley's 3rd birthday party.

**We are using photos from www.free digital photos.net for these examples, be sure to insert photos and captions in the appropriate places.

Appendix 1

How the Parole Process Works

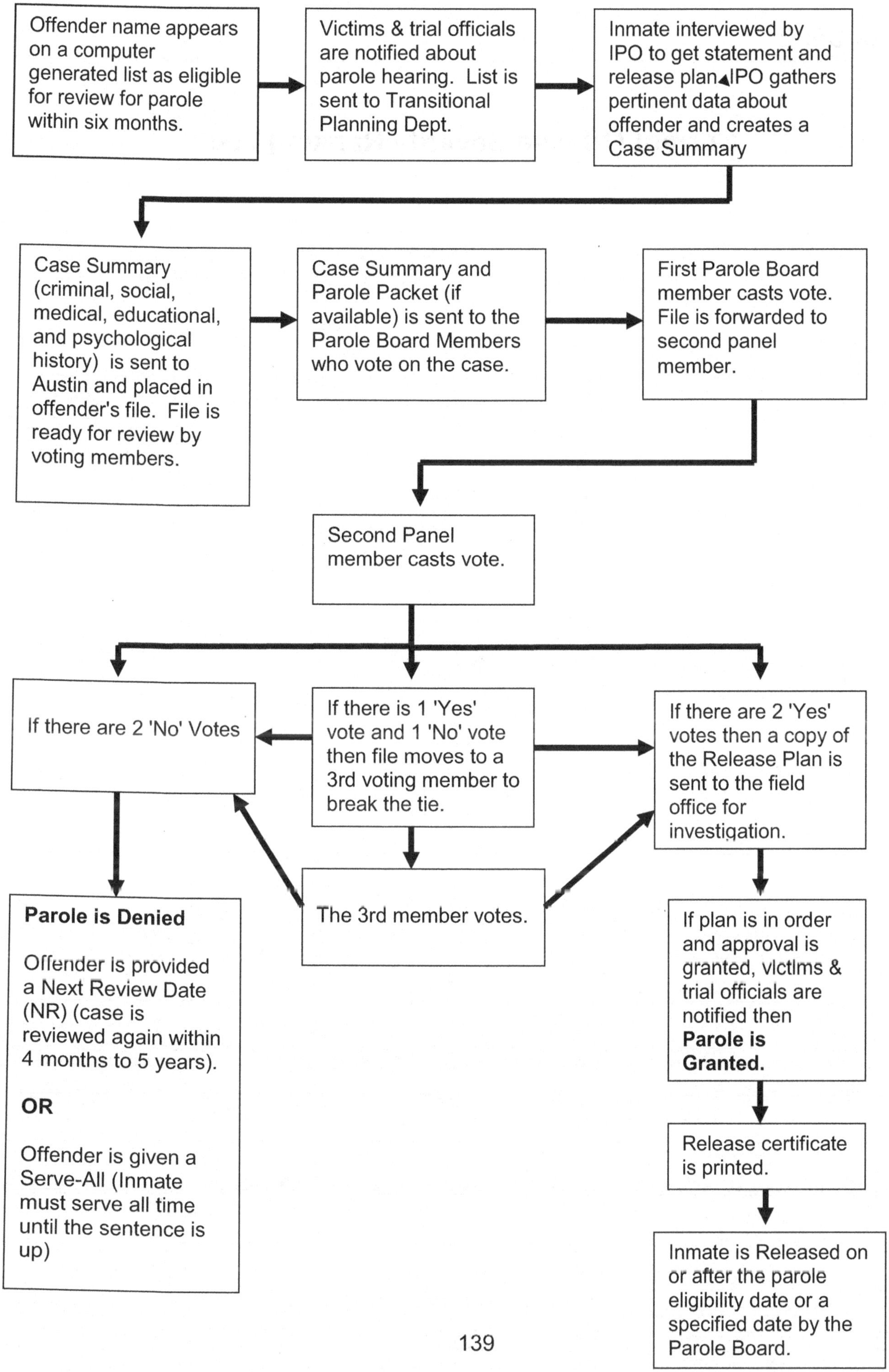
Offender name appears on a computer generated list as eligible for review for parole within six months.
Victims & trial officials are notified about parole hearing. List is sent to Transitional Planning Dept.
Inmate interviewed by IPO to get statement and release plan. IPO gathers pertinent data about offender and creates a Case Summary
Case Summary (criminal, social, medical, educational, and psychological history) is sent to Austin and placed in offender's file. File is ready for review by voting members.
Case Summary and Parole Packet (if available) is sent to the Parole Board Members who vote on the case.
First Parole Board member casts vote. File is forwarded to second panel member.
Second Panel member casts vote.
If there are 2 'No' Votes
If there is 1 'Yes' vote and 1 'No' vote then file moves to a 3rd voting member to break the tie.
If there are 2 'Yes' votes then a copy of the Release Plan is sent to the field office for investigation.
The 3rd member votes.
Parole is Denied
Offender is provided a Next Review Date (NR) (case is reviewed again within 4 months to 5 years).
OR
Offender is given a Serve-All (Inmate must serve all time until the sentence is up)
If plan is in order and approval is granted, victims & trial officials are notified then Parole is Granted.
Release certificate is printed.
Inmate is Released on or after the parole eligibility date or a specified date by the Parole Board.

Appendix 2

Current Offense Severity Ranking List

Current Offense Severity Ranking List

NCIC CODE	OFFENSE DESCRIPTION	RANK
00010000	STATED CHARGE NOT CLEAR	L
00020000	ARREST DATA NOT RECEIVED	L
01000000	SOVEREIGNTY	L
01010000	SOVEREIGNTY-TREASON	L
01020000	SOVEREIGNTY-TREASON MISPRISON	L
01030000	SOVEREIGNTY-ESPIONAGE	L
01040000	SOVEREIGNTY-SABOTAGE	L
01050000	SOVEREIGNTY-SEDITION	L
01060000	SOVEREIGNTY-SELECTIVE SERVICE	L
01990000	SOVEREIGNTY-OTHER	L
02000000	MILITARY	L
02010000	MILITARY-DESERTION	L
02990000	MILITARY-OTHER	L
03000000	IMMIGRATION	L
03010000	IMMIGRATION-ILLEGAL ENTRY	L
03020000	IMMIGRATION-FALSE CITIZENSHIP	L
03030000	IMMIGRATION-SMUGGLE ALIENS	L
03990000	IMMIGRATION-OTHER	L
09000000	HOMICIDE	H
09000001	MURDER W/INT	H+
09000002	MURDER INTENDS SBI CAUSING DEATH	H
09000003	MURDER WHILE COMMITTING FELONY	H+
09000004	CAPITAL MURDER POLICE OFFICER OR FIREMAN	H+
09000005	CAPITAL MURDER WHILE COMMITTING CITED OFFENSES	H+
09000006	CAPITAL MURDER REMUNERATION	H+
09000007	CAPITAL MURDER ESCAPING PENAL INSTITUTION	H+
09000008	CAPITAL MURDER IN PENAL INSTITUTION	H+
09000009	CAPITAL MURDER MULTIPLE	H+
09000010	VOLUNTARY MANSLAUGHTER	H
09000011	INVOLUNTARY MANSLAUGHTER	M
09000013	CAPITAL MURDER INDIVIDUAL UNDER AGE SIX	H+
09000015	CAPITAL MURDER PENAL INSTIT COMBINATION	H+
09000016	CAPITAL MURDER WHILE INCARC FOR MURDER	H+
09000017	CAPITAL MURDER WHILE INCARC FOR LIFE/99YRS	H+
09010000	HOMICIDE-WILLFUL KILL-FAMILY-GUN	H+
09020000	HOMICIDE-WILLFUL KILL-FAMILY	H+
09030000	HOMICIDE-WILLFUL KILL-NONFAMILY GUN	H+
09040000	HOMICIDE-WILLFUL KILL-NONFAMILY	H+
09050000	HOMICIDE-WILLFUL KILL-PUB OFF-GUN	H+
09060000	HOMICIDE-WILLFUL KILL-PUB OFF	H+
09070000	HOMICIDE-WILLFUL KILL-POL OFF-GUN	H+
09080000	HOMICIDE-WILLFUL KILL-POL OFF	H+

NCIC CODE	OFFENSE DESCRIPTION	RANK
09090000	HOMICIDE-NEGLIG MANSL-VEH	M
09100000	HOMICIDE-NEGLIG MANSL	M
09110000	HOMICIDE-WILLFUL KILL-GUN	H+
09120000	HOMICIDE-WILLFUL KILL	H+
09130000	HOMICIDE-CAPITAL MURDER	H+
09140000	HOMICIDE-ATT/ASSLT TO CAP MUR	H
09150000	HOMICIDE-MURDER - SB 45 CASES ONLY	H+
09150000	HOMICIDE-MURDER - NON-SB 45 CASES	H
09160000	HOMICIDE-ATTEMP/ASSLT TO COMMIT MURDER	H
09170000	HOMICIDE-CONSP, SOLIC, TO CAP MURDER	H+
09180000	HOMICIDE-VOL MANSLAUGHTER/ATT VOL	H
09190000	HOMICIDE-INVOL MANSLAUGHTER/ATT INVOL	M
09990000	HOMICIDE-OTHER	H
09990001	MURDER INTENTIONALLY CAUSE DEATH	H+
09990002	MURDER INTENDS SBI CAUSING DEATH	H
09990003	MURDER WHILE COMMITTING FELONY	H+
09990004	MURDER INTENTIONALLY CAUSE DEATH/PASSION	H
09990005	MURDER INTENDS SBI CAUSING DEATH/PASSION	H
09990006	MURDER WHILE COMMITTING FELONY/PASSION	H
09990007	CAPITAL MURDER POLICE OFFICER/FIREMAN	H+
09990008	CAPITAL MURDER IN COMM OF CITED OFFENSES	H+
09990009	CAPITAL MURDER REMUNERATION	H+
09990010	CAPITAL MURDER ESCAPING PENAL INSTITUTION	H+
09990011	CAPITAL MURDER IN PENAL INSTITUTION	H+
09990012	CAPITAL MURDER PENAL INSTIT COMBINATION	H+
09990013	CAPITAL MURDER WHILE INCARC FOR MURDER	H+
09990014	CAPITAL MURDER WHILE INCARC FOR LIFE/99YRS	H+
09990015	CAPITAL MURDER MULTIPLE	H+
09990016	CAPITAL MURDER INDIVIDUAL UNDER AGE SIX	H+
09990017	MANSLAUGHTER	H
09990018	CRIMINAL NEGLIGENT HOMICIDE	L
09990018	CRIMINAL NEGLIGENT HOMICIDE	M
09990019	MURDER	H
09990020	CAPITAL MURDER OF A PEACE OFFICER OR FIREMAN	H+
09990021	MURDER UNDER INFLUENCE OF SUDDEN PASSION	H
09990022	CAPITAL MURDER BY TERROR THREAT/OTHER FELONY	H+
09990023	CAPITAL MURDER WHILE REMUNERATION	H+
09990024	CAPITAL MURDER PERSON WHILE ESCAPING/ATTEMPT	H+
09990025	CAPITAL MURDER ANOTHER PERSON IN PRISON	H+
09990026	CAPITAL MURDER OF MULTIPLE PERSONS	H+
09990027	CAPITAL MURDER PERSON UNDER SIX YEARS OF AGE	H+
09990028	CAPITAL MURDER FOR RETALIATION JUDGE/JUSTICE	H+

NCIC CODE	OFFENSE DESCRIPTION	RANK
10000000	KIDNAPPING	H
10000001	AGG KIDNAPPING REL VICTIM ALIVE	H+
10000002	AGREEMENT TO ABDUCT FROM CUSTODY	L
10000003	KIDNAPPING	H
10000004	AGG KIDNAPPING VICTIM NOT HELD	H
10010000	KIDNAP MINOR FOR RANSOM	H+
10020000	KIDNAP ADULT FOR RANSOM	H+
10030000	KIDNAP MINOR TO SEXUALLY ASSLT	H+
10040000	KIDNAP ADULT TO SEXUALLY ASSLT	H+
10050000	KIDNAP MINOR	H
10060000	KIDNAP ADULT	H
10070000	KIDNAP HOSTAGE FOR ESCAPE	H+
10080000	ABDUCT-NO RANSOM OR ASSLT	H
10090000	KIDNAP-HIJACK AIRCRAFT	H+
10100000	AGGRAVATED KIDNAPPING	H+
10110000	KIDNAPPING	H
10120000	KIDNAPPING-FALSE IMPRISONMENT	M
10130000	KIDNAPPING-ATT/AGG/CONSP TO COMMIT	H
10990000	KIDNAPPING-OTHER	H
10990001	KIDNAPPING	H
10990001	ATTEMPTED KIDNAPPING	L
10990002	AGREEMENT TO ABDUCT FROM CUSTODY	L
10990002	AGREEMENT TO ABDUCT FROM CUSTODY	L
10990003	AGG KIDNAPPING RELEASE VICTIM SAFEPLACE	H
10990004	AGG KIDNAPPING	H+
10990005	AGG KIDNAPPING W/DEADLY WEAPON	H+
10990006	AGG KIDNAPPING REL VICTIM SAFE PLACE	H
10990007	AGG KIDNAPPING FOR RANSOM/REWARD	H+
10990008	AGG KIDNAPPING FOR RANSOM/REWARD SAFE RELEASE	H
10990009	AGG KIDNAPPING USE AS SHIELD/HOSTAGE	H+
10990010	AGG KIDNAPPING USE AS SHIELD/HOSTAGE SAFE REL	H
10990011	AGG KIDNAPPING FACILITATE	H+
10990012	AGG KIDNAPPING FACILITATE SAFE RELEASE	H
10990013	AGG KIDNAPPING BI/SEXUAL ABUSE	H+
10990014	AGG KIDNAPPING BI/SEXUAL ABUSE SAFE RELEASE	H
10990015	AGG KIDNAPPING TERRORIZE	H+
10990016	AGG KIDNAPPING TERRORIZE SAFE RELEASE	H
10990017	AGG KIDNAPPING INTERFERE PERFORMANCE	H+
10990018	AGG KIDNAPPING INTERFERE PERFORMANCE SAFE REL	H
11000000	SEXUAL ASSAULT	H
11000001	AGG SEXUAL ASSLT CHILD	H+
11000002	SEXUAL ASSLT ANOTHER PERSON	H

NCIC CODE	OFFENSE DESCRIPTION	RANK
11000003	SEXUAL ASSLT CHILD	H
11000006	AGG SEXUAL ASSLT ANOTHER PERSON	H+
11000007	SEXUAL EXPLOIT MEN HLTH SERV PROVIDER	M
11000008	SEXUAL EXPLOIT MEN HLTH SERV PROVIDER ENH	H
11010000	RAPE-GUN	H+
11020000	RAPE	H
11030000	RAPE-STRONGARM	H
11040000	SEX ASSLT-SODOMY-BOY-GUN	H+
11050000	SEX ASSLT-SODOMY-MAN-GUN	H+
11060000	SEX ASSLT-SODOMY-GIRL-GUN	H+
11070000	SEX ASSLT-SODOMY-WOMAN-GUN	H+
11080000	SEX ASSLT-SODOMY-BOY	H
11090000	SEX ASSLT-SODOMY-MAN	H
11100000	SEX ASSLT-SODOMY-GIRL	H
11110000	SEX ASSLT-SODOMY-WOMAN	H
11120000	SEX ASSLT-SODOMY-BOY-STRONGARM	H
11130000	SEX ASSLT-SODOMY-MAN-STRONGARM	H
11140000	SEX ASSLT-SODOMY-GIRL-STRONGARM	H
11150000	SEX ASSLT-SODOMY-WOMAN-STRONGARM	H
11160000	SEXUAL ASSAULT/STATUTORY RAPE	M
11170000	SEX ASSLT-CARNAL ABUSE	H
11180000	SEXUAL ASSLT/RAPE AGG/SEX ABUSE	H+
11190000	SEXUAL ASSLT/RAPE OF CHILD	H
11200000	SEXUAL ASSLT/ATTEMPTED RAPE	H
11210000	SEXUAL ASSLT/ATTEMPTED RAPE OF CHILD	H
11220000	SEXUAL ASSLT/AGGR RAPE OF CHILD	H+
11990000	SEXUAL ASSAULT-OTHER	H
11990001	SEXUAL ASSAULT	H
11990001	SEXUAL ASSAULT	H
11990002	SEXUAL ASSAULT CHILD	H
11990003	AGG SEXUAL ASSAULT	H+
11990004	AGG SEXUAL ASSAULT CHILD	H+
11990005	AGG SEXUAL ASSAULT 65 YEARS OR OLDER	H+
11990006	AGG SEXUAL ASSAULT OF ELDERLY/DISABLED PERSON	H+
11990008	IMPROPER RELATIONSHIP BETWEEN EDUCATOR/STUDENT	M
11990009	SEXUAL ASSLT PROH/PURPORT SPOUSE	H
11990010	SEXUAL ASSLT PROH/PURPORT SPOUSE UNDER 14YOA	H
11990011	SEXUAL ASSLT BIGAMY	H
11990012	SEX ABUSE OF CHILD CONTINUOUS: VICTIM UNDER 14	H+
11990013	SEXUAL CONT/INTERCOURSE W/PERSON TYC/ST FAC	H
12000000	ROBBERY	H
12000001	AGG ROBBERY	H+

NCIC CODE	OFFENSE DESCRIPTION	RANK
12000002	ROBBERY	H
12010000	ROBBERY-BUSINESS-GUN	H+
12020000	ROBBERY-BUSINESS	H
12030000	ROBBERY-BUSINESS-STRONGARM	H
12040000	ROBBERY-STREET-GUN	H+
12050000	ROBBERY-STREET	H
12060000	ROBBERY-STREET-STRONGARM	H
12070000	ROBBERY-RESID-GUN	H+
12080000	ROBBERY-RESID	H
12090000	ROBBERY-RESID-STRONGARM	H
12100000	FORCIBLE PURSE SNATCHING	H
12110000	ROBBERY-BANKING-TYPE INST	H
12120000	ROBBERY, NO WEAPON	H
12130000	ROBBERY, WITH WEAPON	H+
12140000	ROBBERY, ATTEMPTED	H
12150000	ROBBERY, CONSPIRACY TO COMMIT	H
12990000	ROBBERY-OTHER	H
12990001	ROBBERY	H
12990002	AGG ROBBERY	H+
13000000	ASSAULT	H
13000001	AGG ASSLT CAUSES BI COURT PROCEEDING PARTICIP	H
13000002	AGG ASSLT CAUSES SBI	H+
13000003	AGG ASSLT THREATEN CITED BOARD MEMBER/EMPL/PO	H
13000004	AGG ASSLT W/DEADLY WEAPON	H+
13000005	AGG ASSLT W/DEADLY WPN CITED BOARD MEM/EMPL/PO	H+
13000011	ASSLT FAMILY MEMBER-MORE THAN TWO TIMES	M
13000013	ASSLT CAUSES BI PATIENT EXCEPT TYC/TDC	H
13000014	ASSLT CAUSES BI PATIENT MEDICAL/PSYCH INSTIT	H
13000017	ASSLT TEACHER/ADMIN EMPL PUB SCHOOL 3RD	H
13000020	COERCION OF PUB SERV/VOTER THREAT OF FELONY	M
13000023	INJURY CHILD RECKLESSLY SBI	M
13000026	INJURY ELDERLY RECKLESSLY SBI	M
13000029	INJURY INVALID RECKLESSLY SBI	H
13000030	INJURY CHILD BI	M
13000031	INJURY CHILD SBI	H+
13000032	INJURY ELDERLY BI	M
13000033	INJURY ELDERLY SBI	H
13000034	INJURY NVALID BI	H
13000035	INJURY NVALID SBI	H+
13000036	RETALIATION	M
13000037	RETALIATION AGAINST VOTER	M
13000038	SECURE BY COERSION CONTRACT COIN-OP MACH	L

NCIC CODE	OFFENSE DESCRIPTION	RANK
13010000	AGGRAV ASSLT-FAMILY-GUN	H+
13020000	AGGRAV ASSLT-FAMILY	H
13030000	AGGRAV ASSLT-FAMILY-STRONGARM	H
13040000	AGGRAV ASSLT-NONFAMILY-GUN	H+
13050000	AGGRAV ASSLT-NONFAMILY	H
13060000	AGGRAV ASSLT-NONFAMILY-STRONGARM	H
13070000	AGGRAV ASSLT-PUB OFF-GUN	H+
13080000	AGGRAV ASSLT-PUB OFF	H+
13090000	AGGRAV ASSLT-PUB OFF-STRONGARM	H+
13100000	AGGRAV ASSLT-POL OFF-GUN	H+
13100001	DEADLY ASSLT W/ SBI PEACE OFFICER/CITED EMPL	H+
13100002	DEADLY ASSLT W/ SBI COURT PROCEEDING PARTICIP	H+
13100003	DEADLY ASSLT W/ SBI COMMUNITY SUPERVISION EMPL	H+
13100004	DEADLY ASSLT W/ SBI EMPL OF TEXAS YOUTH COMMIS	H+
13110000	AGGRAV ASSLT-POL OFF	H+
13120000	AGGRAV ASSLT-POL OFF-STRONGARM	H+
13130000	SIMPLE ASSLT	L
13140000	AGGRAV ASSLT-GUN	H+
13140001	AGG ASSAULT MV DISCH FIREARM AT HAB/BLDG/VEH	H+
13140002	AGG ASSAULT MV DISCH FRARM RKLS AT OCCUP H/B/V	H+
13140003	AGG ASSAULT MV DISCH FIREARM AT H/B/V SBI	H+
13150000	AGGRAV ASSLT	H
13150001	AGG ASSAULT BY/AGAINST PUB SERV/WITNESS/INFORM	H+
13150002	AGG ASSAULT AGAINST PUB SERVANT	H+
13150003	AGG ASSAULT AGAINST WITNESS/INFORMANT	H+
13150004	AGG ASSAULT CAUSES SERIOUS BODILY INJ	H+
13150005	AGG ASSAULT W/DEADLY WEAPON	H+
13150006	AGG ASSAULT AGAINST SECURITY OFFICER	H+
13150007	AGG ASSAULT DATE/FAMILY/HOUSE W/WEAPON	H+
13150008	AGG ASSAULT IN RETALIATION	H+
13150009	AGG ASSAULT AGAINST SECURITY OFFICER	H+
13150010	AGG ASSAULT BY PUB SERVANT	H+
13150011	AGG ASSAULT AGAINST PUB SERVANT	H+
13160000	INTIMIDATION	M
13160001	CORRUP INFLU OUTCOME HORSE/DOG RACE	L
13160002	CORRUP INFLU OUTCOME HORSE/DOG RACE ENH	M
13160007	STALKING ENH	M
13160009	STALKING W/PREV CONVIC	M
13160010	STALKING	M
13160011	STALKING W/PREV CONVIC	M
13170000	ASSAULT	H
13180000	ASSAULT ON PEACE OFFICER	H

NCIC CODE	OFFENSE DESCRIPTION	RANK
13190000	ASSAULT-INJURY TO CHILD	M
13200000	ASSAULT-INJURY TO ELDERLY PERSON	M
13210000	ASSAULT-RETALIATION	H
13220000	ASSAULT-MUTILATION	H
13990000	ASSAULT-OTHER	H
13990001	ASSLT CAUSES BODILY INJ	L
13990002	INJURY CHILD SBI/MENTAL	H+
13990003	INJURY CHILD MENTAL INJ	H+
13990004	RECKLESS INJ TO A CHILD SBI	M
13990005	RECKLESS INJ TO A CHILD MENTAL INJ	M
13990006	INJURY CHILD W/INT BODILY INJ	M
13990007	RECKLESS INJ TO A CHILD BODILY INJ	L
13990007	RECKLESS INJ TO A CHILD BODILY INJ	L
13990008	INJURY TO CHILD NEGLIGENCE	L
13990008	INJURY TO CHILD NEGLIGENCE	L
13990009	INJURY ELDERLY PERSON SBI/MENTAL	H
13990010	INJURY ELDERLY MENTAL INJ	H
13990011	RECKLESS INJ TO ELDERLY SBI	M
13990012	RECKLESS INJ TO ELDERLY MENTAL INJ	M
13990013	INJURY ELDERLY PERSON W/INT BODILY INJ	M
13990014	RECKLESS INJ TO ELDERLY BODILY INJ	L
13990014	RECKLESS INJ TO ELDERLY BODILY INJ	L
13990015	INJURY ELDERLY CRIMINAL NEG	L
13990015	INJURY ELDERLY CRIMINAL NEG	L
13990016	INJURY DISABLED PERSON SBI/MENTAL	H
13990017	INJURY DISABLED MENTAL INJ	H
13990018	RECKLESS INJ TO DISABLED SBI	M
13990019	RECKLESS INJ TO DISABLED MENTAL INJ	M
13990020	INJURY DISABLED PERSON W/INT BODILY INJ	M
13990021	RECKLESS INJ TO DISABLED BODILY INJ	L
13990021	RECKLESS INJ TO DISABLED BODILY INJ	L
13990022	INJURY DISABLED CRIMINAL NEG	L
13990022	INJURY DISABLED CRIMINAL NEG	L
13990024	INTOXICATED ASSAULT W/VEHICLE SBI	H
13990024	ATT INTOXICATED ASSLT W/VEH SBI	L
13990025	INTOXICATED MANSLAUGHTER W/ VEHICLE	H
13990026	OBSTRUCTION OR RETALIATION	M
13990026	ATT RETALIATION	L
13990027	COERCION OF PUB SERV/VOTER THREAT OF FELONY	M
13990028	ASSLT CAUSES BODILY INJ FAMILY MEMBER +2	M
13990028	ASSLT CAUSES BODILY INJ FAMILY MEMBER +2	M
13990029	ASSLT PUBLIC SERVANT	H

NCIC CODE	OFFENSE DESCRIPTION	RANK
13990029	ASSLT PUBLIC SERVANT	L
13990032	INJURY DISABLED PERSON RECKLESS SBI/MENTAL	M
13990033	INJURY ELDERLY PERSON RECKLESS SBI/MENTAL	M
13990034	INJ ELDERLY PERSON RECKLESS/CRIMINAL NEGL	L
13990035	INJURY CHILD RECKLESS SBI/MENTAL	M
13990036	INJURY DISABLED PERSON RECKLESS/CRIMINAL NEGLE	L
13990037	ASSLT CAUSES BODILY INJURY FAMILY MEMBER ENH	M
13990040	OBSTRUCTION OR RETALIATION AGAINST JUROR	M
13990041	INJ CHILD/ELDERLY/DISABLED W/INT SBI/MENTAL	H+
13990042	INJ CHILD/ELDERLY/DISABLED RECKLESS SBI/MENTAL	H
13990043	INJ CHILD/ELDERLY/DISABLED W/INT BODILY INJ	M
13990044	INJ CHILD/ELDERLY/DISABLED RECKLESS BODILY INJ	L
13990045	INJ CHILD/ELDERLY/DISABLED CRIMINAL NEGLIGENCE	L
13990046	RETALIATION AGAINST VOTER	M
13990047	ASSAULT ON SECURITY OFFICER	H
13990048	ASSAULT CAUSES BODILY INJ FAMILY VIOLENCE ENH	M
13990051	ASSAULT AGAINST PERSON CONTRACTING W/GOVERN	H
13990052	ASSAULT AGAINST GOVERNMENT CONTRACTOR/EMPLOYEE	H
13990053	ASSAULT BY/AGAINST PUB SERVANT W/WEAPON	H
13990054	ASSAULT CAUSES BI CONVICTED ANOTHER STATE	M
13990055	ASSAULT CAUSES BI DATE/FAMILY/HOUSE W/PREV	M
13990056	ASSAULT CAUSES BI DATE/FAMILY/HOUSE W/WPN	H
13990057	ASSAULT CAUSES BI RETALIATION W/GOVERN	H
13990058	ASSAULT CAUSES BI RETALIATION W/WEAPON	H
13990059	ASSAULT CAUSES BODILY INJ DATE/FAMILY/HOUSE	M
13990061	ASSAULT ON SECURITY OFFICER	H
13990062	ASSAULT ON SECURITY OFFICER W/WPN	H
13990063	ASSAULT PUBLIC SERVANT	H
13990064	OWNER/OPER/EMP GROUP/NURSE W/INT BOD INJ/EXPLO	M
13990065	OWNER/OPERATOR/EMP GROUP/NURSE NEGLIGENT/OMISS	L
13990066	OWNER/OPER/EMP GRP/NURSE NEGLIGENT	L
13990067	OWNER/OPER/EMP GRP/NURSE RECKLESS	M
13990068	OWNER/OPER/EMP GRP/NURSE RECKLESS	L
13990069	OWNER/OPER/EMP GRP/NURSE W/INT VIOL	H
13990070	ASSAULT EMS PERSONNEL PROV SERV	H
13990071	ASSAULT BI FAM/HOUSE MEM 2+ W/IN 12 MONTHS	M
13990072	ASSAULT W/PREV CONV	M
13990073	ASSAULT INT/RECK IMPEDE BREATH/CIRCULATION	M
13990074	ASSAULT FAMILY/HOUSEHOLD MEMBER	M
13990075	ASSAULT FAMILY/HOUSEHOLD MEMBER W/PREV CONV	M
13990076	ASSAULT FAM/HOUSE MEM IMPEDE BREATH/CIRCULAT	M
13990077	INT BOD INJ CHILD/ELDER/DISABLED STATE FAC EMP	H

NCIC CODE	OFFENSE DESCRIPTION	RANK
14000000	ABORTION	M
14010000	ABORTIONAL ACT ON OTHER	M
14020000	ABORTIONAL ACT ON SELF	M
14030000	SUBMISSION TO ABORTIONAL ACT	M
14040000	ABORTIFACIENT	M
14990000	ABORTION-OTHER	M
16020002	TERRORISTIC THREAT CAUSE IMPAIR PUB SERVICE	M
16020004	TERRORISTIC THREAT IMPAIR PUBLIC/GOV SERVICE	M
16020005	TERROR THREAT CAUSES PECUNIARY LOSS >$1500	L
20000000	ARSON	H
20000001	ARSON	H
20000002	ARSON BODILY INJ OR DEATH	H+
20010000	ARSON-BUSINESS-ENDANGERED LIFE	H+
20020000	ARSON-RESID-ENDANGERED LIFE	H+
20030000	ARSON-BUSINESS-DEFRAUD INSURER	H
20040000	ARSON-RESID-DEFRAUD INSURER	H
20050000	ARSON-BUSINESS	H
20060000	ARSON-RESID	H
20070000	BURNING OF	H
20080000	ARSON-PUB BLDG-ENDANGERED LIFE	H+
20090000	ARSON-PUB BLDG	H
20100000	ARSON-ATTEMPTED/CONSP/COMMIT	H
20110000	ARSON (NO IDENTIFIER)	H
20990000	ARSON-OTHER	H
20990001	ARSON	H
20990002	ARSON BODILY INJ OR DEATH	H+
20990003	ARSON BODILY INJ/DEATH/PLACE OF WORSHIP	H+
20990004	ARSON CAUSING BODILY INJURY/DEATH	H+
20990005	ARSON INTEND DAMAGE HABITAT/PLACE OF WORSHIP	H+
20990006	ARSON OF BLDG/HABIT/VEH W/INT INJ OR DAMAGE	H
20990007	ARSON W/MAN OR ATT MAN CONT SUB CAUSE BI/DEATH	H
20990008	ARSON W/MAN OR ATT MAN CONT SUB	L
20990009	ARSON OF BLDG/HABIT/VEH RECKLESS CAUSE DAMAGE	L
21000000	EXTORTION	M
21010000	EXTORT-THREAT INJURE PERSON	M
21020000	EXTORT-THREAT DAMAGE PROP	M
21030000	EXTORT-THREAT INJURE REPUTATION	M
21040000	EXTORT-THREAT ACCUSE PERSON OF CRIME	M
21050000	EXTORT-THREAT OF INFORMING OF VIO	M
21990000	EXTORTION	M
22000000	BURGLARY	M
22000001	BURGLARY OF HABITATION	M

NCIC CODE	OFFENSE DESCRIPTION	RANK
22000002	BURGLARY OF BUILDING	L
22000003	BURGLARY OF BUILDING-ARMED W/EXPLOSIVES OR DW	H
22000004	BURGLARY HAB W/EXPLOSIVES OR DW INJ OR ATT INJ	H
22000006	BURGLARY OF VEHICLE	L
22010000	BURGL-SAFE-VAULT	M
22020000	BURGL-FORCED ENTRY-RESID	M
22030000	BURGL-FORCED ENTRY-NONRESID	L
22040000	BURGL-NO FORCED ENTRY-RESID	M
22050000	BURGL-NO FORCED ENTRY-NONRESID	L
22060000	BURGL-TOOLS-POSSESS	L
22060005	UNL USE OF CRIMINAL INSTRUMENT	L
22060006	UNL USE OF CRIMINAL INSTRUMENT	L
22060007	MAN SELL INSTALLS/SETUP/USE CRIMINAL INSTRUM	L
22060008	POSS UNL USE OF CRIMINAL INSTRUMENT	L
22060008	POSS UNL USE OF CRIMINAL INSTRUMENT	L
22060009	UNL USE OF CRIMINAL INSTRUMENT	L
22060009	UNL USE OF CRIMINAL INSTRUMENT	L
22070000	BURGL-BANKING-TYPE INST	M
22080000	BURGLARY	M
22090000	BURGLARY OF HABITATION	M
22100000	BURGLARY WITH INTENT TO COMMIT SEX	H+
22110000	BURGLARY OF HABITATION WITH WEAPON	H
22120000	BURGLARY OF BUILDING	L
22130000	BURGLARY OF BUILDING WITH WEAPON	M
22140000	BURGLARY OF MOTOR VEHICLE	L
22150000	BURGLARY/ATTEMP OF HABITATION	M
22160000	BURGLARY/ATTEMP OF BUILDING	L
22170000	BURGLARY/ATTEMP OF MOTOR VEHICLE	L
22990000	BURGLARY-OTHER	M
22990001	BURGLARY OF BUILDING	L
22990001	BURGLARY OF BUILDING	L
22990002	BURGLARY OF HABITATION	M
22990003	BURGLARY HABITATION INTEND OTHER FELONY	H+
22990004	BURGLARY OF VEHICLE	L
22990006	BURGLARY OF RAIL CAR	L
22990007	BURGLARY HABITATION INTEND SEX OFFENSE	H+
22990008	BURGLARY OF VEHICLES W/PREV 2 OR MORE CONV	L
23000000	LARCENY	L
23000001	UNL USE OF HUMAN SERVICE FUNDS	L
23000003	TAKE CULTUR SPECIES AQUACULT FACIL OVER $750	L
23000006	APPROPRIATION PROCEEDS SALES BY COMMS MERCHANT	L
23000008	UNL CONVERSION MUTUAL ASSESSMENT	L

NCIC CODE	OFFENSE DESCRIPTION	RANK
23000009	MISAPP OF SPECIAL FUNDS	L
23000010	UNL DIVERSION OF FUNDS	L
23000012	FAIL TO REMIT ANY FEES COLLECTED	L
23000024	THEFT >= $200 BUT < $750 PUB SERV	L
23000025	THEFT >= $200 BUT < $750 BY CHECK PUB SERV	L
23000026	THEFT < $750 TWO OR MORE CONV ANY THEFT GRADE	L
23000027	THEFT >= $750 BUT < $20K OR LVSTCK < $20K	L
23000028	THEFT >= $750 BUT < $20K/LVSTK < $20K BY CHECK	L
23000029	THEFT >= $750 BUT < $20K/LVSTK < $20K PUB SERV	L
23000030	THEFT >=$750 <$20K/LVSTK < $20K BY CHK PUB SER	L
23000031	THEFT >= $20K BUT < $100K	M
23000032	THEFT >= $20K BUT < $100K BY CHECK	M
23000033	THEFT >= $20K BUT < $100K PUB SERV	M
23000034	THEFT >= $20K BUT < $100K BY CHECK PUB SERV	M
23000035	THEFT < $100K THREAT OF FELONY	M
23000036	THEFT < $100K BY CHECK THREAT OF FELONY	M
23000037	THEFT < $100K THREAT OF FELONY PUB SERV	M
23000038	THEFT < $100K BY CHECK THREAT OF FELON PUB SER	M
23000039	THEFT < $100K PETRO/NAT GAS PROD/EQUIP PUB SER	M
23000040	THEFT < $100K PETROL/NAT GAS PROD/EQUIP	M
23000041	THEFT >=$100K	M
23000042	THEFT >=$100K THREAT OF FELONY	M
23000043	THEFT >=$100K BY CHECK	M
23000044	THEFT >= $100K BY CHECK THREAT OF FELONY	M
23000045	THEFT >=$100K PUB SERV	M
23000046	THEFT >=$100K THREAT OF FELONY PUB SERV	M
23000047	THEFT >=$100K BY CHECK PUB SERV	M
23000048	THEFT >=$100K BY CHECK THREAT OF FELON PUB SER	M
23000051	THEFT FIREARM < $400 PUB SERV	L
23000052	THEFT FIREARM < $400 BY CHECK PUB SERV	L
23000053	THEFT FIREARMS TWO OR MORE	L
23000054	THEFT FIREARMS BY CHECK TWO OR MORE	L
23000055	THEFT FIREARMS PUB SERV TWO OR MORE	L
23000056	THEFT FIREARMS BY CHECK PUB SERV TWO OR MORE	L
23000057	THEFT FIREARM > $400	L
23000058	THEFT FIREARM > $400 BY CHECK	L
23000059	THEFT FIREARM > $400 PUB SERV	L
23000060	THEFT FIREARM > $400 BY CHECK PUB SERV	L
23000061	THEFT FROM HUMAN CORPSE OR GRAVE	L
23000062	THEFT FROM HUMAN CORPSE OR GRAVE PUB SERV	M
23000073	THEFT OF SERV >= $200 BUT < $750 PUB SERV	L
23000074	THEFT OF SERV >= $200 < $750 BY CHECK PUB SERV	L

NCIC CODE	OFFENSE DESCRIPTION	RANK
23000075	THEFT OF SERV >= $750 BUT < $20K	L
23000076	THEFT OF SERV >= $750 BUT < $20K BY CHECK	L
23000077	THEFT OF SERV >= $750 BUT < $20K PUB SERV	L
23000078	THEFT OF SERV >= $750 < $20K BY CHECK PUB SERV	L
23000079	THEFT OF SERV >= $20K	M
23000080	THEFT OF SERV >= $20K BY CHECK	M
23000081	THEFT OF SERV >= $20K PUB SERV	M
23000082	THEFT OF SERV >= $20K BY CHECK PUB SERV	M
23000083	THEFT OF TRADE SECRETS PUB SERV	L
23000084	THEFT OF TRADE SECRETS	L
23000086	TAMPER WITH ID NUMBERS CITED PROPTY	L
23000093	OFFICIAL MISCOND $750<$20K	L
23000094	THEFT >$200K PUB SERV/GOV CONTRACTOR	M
23000095	MISAPP $ COMMITTED FOUNDATION SCHOOL FUND	L
23000096	SELL UNREGISTERED SECURITIES	L
23000102	THEFT OYSTERS FROM PRIVATE BED 3RD	L
23000103	MISAPP FUNDS FROM PUB RETIRE SYST MEM SALARY	L
23000104	MISAPP FUNDS FROM TEACH RETIRE SYST MEM SALARY	L
23000105	MISAPP FUNDS JRS MEM SALARY >=$750 BUT <$20	L
23000106	MISAPP FUNDS JRS MEM SALARY $200-$750 PUB SERV	L
23000107	MISAPP FUND JRS MEM SALARY>=$20K<$100K PUB SER	M
23000110	MISAPP FUND JRS MEM SALARY >= $100K PUB SERV	M
23000112	MISAPP FUNDS JRS MEM SALARY $750-$20K PUB SERV	L
23000114	MISAPP FUNDS JRS MEM SALARY >=$20K BUT <$100K	M
23000116	PUBLIC SERV/JRS ACCPT $ NOT DED/SALARY>=$20K<$	M
23000119	JURORS ACCEPT $ NOT DEDUCT/SALARY >=$750 <$20K	L
23000120	JURORS ACCEPT $ NOT DEDUCT/SALARY >=$100K	M
23000121	JURORS ACCEPT $ NOT DEDUCT/SALARY >=$20K <$100	M
23000123	PUBLIC SERV/JRS ACCPT $ NOT DEDUCT/SALARY $200	L
23000126	PUBLIC SERV/JRS ACCPT $ NOT DEDUCT/SALARY $750	L
23000127	PUBLIC SERV/JRS ACCPT $ NOT DED/SALARY >=$100K	M
23000128	THEFT FROM PERSON	L
23010000	POCKETPICKING	L
23020000	PURSE SNATCHING-NO FORCE	L
23030000	SHOPLIFTING	L
23040000	LARC-PARTS FROM VEH	L
23050000	LARC-FROM AUTO	L
23060000	LARC-FROM SHIPMENT	L
23070000	LARC-FROM COIN MACHINE	L
23080000	LARC-FROM BLDG	L
23090000	LARC-FROM YARDS	L
23100000	LARC-FROM MAILS	L

NCIC CODE	OFFENSE DESCRIPTION	RANK
23110000	LARC-FROM BANKING-TYPE INST	L
23110001	CURRENCY EXCHANGE VIOL	L
23110002	CURRENCY EXCHANGE/TRANSPORT VIOLATION	L
23120000	LARC-FROM INTERSTATE SHIPMENT	L
23130000	OBSTRUCT CORRESPONDENCE	L
23140000	THEFT OF US GOVT PROP	L
23150000	LARC ON GOVT RESERV	L
23160000	LARC-POSTAL	L
23170000	LARCENY-THEFT, OF CREDIT CARD	L
23180000	LARCENY-THEFT, ATTEMPTED	L
23190000	LARCENY-THEFT OF PERSON	L
23200000	LARCENY-THEFT BY RECEIVING	L
23210000	LARCENY-THEFT OF PROPERTY	L
23220000	LARCENY-THEFT OF SERVICE	L
23250000	LARCENY-THEFT OF LIVESTOCK	L
23270000	LARCENY-THEFT THROUGH BAD CHECK	L
23280000	LARCENY-THEFT THROUGH WELFARE FRAUD	L
23990000	LARCENY-THEFT OTHER	L
23990004	THEFT PROP >=$1500 < $20K	L
23990004	THEFT PROP >=$1500 < $20K	L
23990005	THEFT LIVESTOCK <$20K	L
23990005	THEFT LIVESTOCK <$20K	L
23990006	THEFT PROP GRAVE/HUMAN CORPSE	L
23990006	THEFT PROP GRAVE/HUMAN CORPSE	L
23990007	THEFT FROM HUMAN CORPSE OR GRAVE	L
23990007	THEFT FROM HUMAN CORPSE OR GRAVE	L
23990008	THEFT OF FIREARM	L
23990008	THEFT OF FIREARM	L
23990009	THEFT PROP <$1500 2/MORE PREV CONV	L
23990009	THEFT PROP <$1500 2/MORE PREV CONV	L
23990010	ATT THEFT >=$20K <=$100K	L
23990010	THEFT PROP >=$20K <$100K	M
23990011	THEFT PROP >=$100K <$200K	M
23990013	THEFT PROP >=$200K	H
23990017	THEFT >=$500 <$1,500 PUB SERV	L
23990017	THEFT >=$500 <$1,500 PUB SERV	L
23990018	THEFT >=$1,500 <$20K PUB SERV	L
23990019	THEFT LIVESTOCK <$20K PUB SERV	L
23990020	THEFT FROM PERSON PUB SERV	L
23990021	THEFT FROM HUMAN CORPSE OR GRAVE PUB SERV	M
23990022	THEFT FIREARM PUB SERV	L
23990023	THEFT <$1,500 2 OR MORE CONV ANY THEFT PS	L

NCIC CODE	OFFENSE DESCRIPTION	RANK
23990024	THEFT >=$20K <$100K PUB SERV	M
23990025	THEFT >=$100K <$200K PUB SERV	M
23990026	THEFT >=$200K PUB SERV	H
23990029	THEFT OF SERV >=$1,500<$20K	L
23990029	THEFT OF SERV >=$1,500<$20K	L
23990030	THEFT OF SERV >=$20K<$100K	M
23990031	THEFT OF SERV >=$100K<$200K	M
23990032	THEFT OF SERV >$200K	H
23990035	THEFT >=$1,500 <$20K BY CHECK	L
23990035	THEFT STOLEN PROP >=$1500 <$20K BY CHECK	L
23990036	THEFT LIVESTOCK <$20K BY CHECK	L
23990036	THEFT LIVESTOCK <$20K BY CHECK	L
23990037	THEFT FIREARM BY CHECK	L
23990037	THEFT FIREARM BY CHECK	L
23990038	THEFT >=$20K <$100K BY CHECK	M
23990039	THEFT STOLEN PROP >=$100K <$200K BY CHECK	M
23990040	THEFT STOLEN PROP >=$200 BY CHECK	M
23990043	THEFT >=$500 <$1,500 BY CHECK PUB SERV	L
23990043	THEFT >=$500 <$1,500 BY CHECK PUB SERV	L
23990044	THEFT >=$1,500 <$20K BY CHECK PUB SERV	L
23990045	THEFT LIVESTOCK <$20K BY CHECK PUB SERV	L
23990046	THEFT FROM PERSON BY CHECK PUB SERV	L
23990048	THEFT FIREARM BY CHECK PUB SERV	L
23990049	THEFT >=$20K <$100K BY CHECK PUB SERV	M
23990050	THEFT >=$100K <$200K BY CHECK PUB SERV	M
23990051	THEFT >=$200K BY CHECK PUB SERV	H
23990054	THEFT OF SERV >=$1,500 <$20K BY CHECK	L
23990054	THEFT OF SERV >=$1,500 <$20K BY CHECK	L
23990055	THEFT OF SERV >=$20k <$100K BY CHECK	M
23990056	THEFT OF SERV >=$100K <$200K BY CHECK	M
23990057	THEFT OF SERV >$200K BY CHECK	H
23990061	ABUSE OF OFFICIAL CAPACITY>=$1,500<$20K	L
23990061	ABUSE OF OFFICIAL CAPACITY>=$1,500<$20K	L
23990062	ABUSE OF OFFICIAL CAPACITY>=$20K<$100K	M
23990063	ABUSE OF OFFICIAL CAPACITY>=$100K<$200K	M
23990064	ABUSE OF OFFICIAL CAPACITY>=$200K	H
23990065	THEFT OF TRADE SECRETS	L
23990068	THEFT LIVESTOCK >=$1500<20K	L
23990068	THEFT LIVESTOCK >=$1500<20K	L
23990071	THEFT LIVESTOCK <$100K	M
23990085	THEFT PROP >$500 <$1500 PUB SERV/ELDERLY	L
23990087	THEFT PROP >$1500 <$20K PUB SERV/ELDERLY	L

NCIC CODE	OFFENSE DESCRIPTION	RANK
23990088	THEFT PROP <$20K PUB SERV/ELDERLY	L
23990089	THEFT PROP HUMAN CORPSE/GRAVE PUB SERV/ELD	M
23990090	THEFT PERSON PUB SERV/GOVT CONTRACTOR	L
23990091	THEFT OF FIREARM PUB SERV/ELDERLY	L
23990092	THEFT PROP >=$20K <$100K PUB SERV/ELDERLY	M
23990093	THEFT PROP >=100K<200K PUB SERV/ELDERLY	M
23990094	THEFT >$200k PUB SEV/GOVT CTRATOR	M
23990096	PUBLIC TELECOMMUNICATION ACCESS DEVICE ENH	L
23990097	MAN POSS/DEL UNL TELECOMMUNICATION DEVICE	L
23990101	THEFT TELECOMMUNICATION SER >=$1,500<$20K	L
23990102	THEFT TELECOMMUNICATION SER<$1,500 W/2PREV CON	L
23990103	THEFT TELECOMMUNICATION SER >=$20K<$100K	M
23990104	THEFT TELECOMMUNICATION SER >=$100K<$200K	M
23990105	THEFT TELECOMMUNICATION SER >=$200K	H
23990109	UNAUTH TELECOMMUNICATION >=$1,500<$20K	L
23990110	UNAUTH TELECOMMUNICATION <$1,500 W/2 PREV CONV	L
23990111	UNAUTH TELECOMMUNICATION >=$20K<$100K	M
23990112	UNAUTH TELECOMMUNICATION >=$100K<$200K	M
23990113	UNAUTH TELECOMMUNICATION >=$200K	H
23990114	THEFT PROP <$1500 2+ CONV PB SERV/ELDER	L
23990122	THEFT OYSTERS FROM PRIVATE BED 3RD	L
23990124	THEFT OF ELECTION BALLOT OR CARRIER ENVELOPE	L
23990126	THEFT <10 HEAD LIVESTOCK <$20K	L
23990127	THEFT <100 HEAD LIVESTOCK <$20K	L
23990128	THEFT <10 HEAD LIVESTOCK <$100K	M
23990129	THEFT <100 HEAD LIVESTOCK <$100K	M
23990130	THEFT <10 HEAD LIVESTOCK <$100K PUB/SERV/ELDER	M
23990131	THEFT <100 HEAD LIVESTOCK <$100K PUB SERV/ELDE	M
23990132	THEFT FROM PERSON	L
23990133	ORGANIZED RETAIL THEFT>$1500<$20,000	L
23990134	ORGANIZED RETAIL THEFT=>$20,000<$100,000	M
23990135	ORGANIZED RETAIL THEFT=>$100,000<$200,000	M
23990136	ORGANIZED RETAIL THEFT=>$200,000	H
23990137	THEFT OF WIRE/CBLE50%ALUM/BRNZE/COPPER<$20,000	L
23990140	THEFT CATTLE/HORSE/EXOTIC LIVESTOCK <$100K	M
23990141	THEFT >=10 SHEEP/SWINE/GOAT <$100K	M
23990142	THEFT PROP GRAVE/HUMAN CORPSE/MILITARY MARKER	L
23990143	THEFT OF MATERIAL 50% ALUM/BRNZE/COPPER <$20K	L
23990147	THEFT OYSTERS FROM PRIVATE BED 2+PREV CONV	L
23990149	THEFT PROP GRAVE/CORPSE MILITARY MARKER ENH	M
23990150	THEFT CATTLE/HORSE/EXOTIC LIVESTOCK <$100K ENH	M
23990151	THEFT >=10 SHEEP/SWINE/GOAT <$100K ENH	M

NCIC CODE	OFFENSE DESCRIPTION	RANK
23990152	THEFT MATERIAL 50% ALUM/BRNZE/COPPER <$20K ENH	L
23990153	THEFT <10 HEAD LIVESTOCK <$20K ENH	L
23990154	THEFT OF FIREARM ENH	L
23990157	THEFT PROP $1500<$20K ENH	L
23990160	THEFT PROP $500<$1500 ENH	L
23990161	THEFT PROP >=$100K<$200K ENH	M
23990162	THEFT PROP >=$20K<$100K ENH	M
23990163	THEFT PROP <$1500 2+ CONV ENH	L
23990166	THEFT OF ELECTION BALLOT OR CARRIER ENVELOPE	L
23990167	THEFT OF ELECTION BALLOT OR CARRIER ENVE ENH	L
24000000	STOLEN VEHICLE	L
24010000	THEFT AND SALE VEH	L
24020000	THEFT AND STRIP VEH	L
24030000	THEFT AND USE VEH OTHER CRIME	L
24040000	STOLEN VEHICLE, THEFT	L
24050000	THEFT VEH BY BAILEE	L
24060000	RECEIV STOLEN VEH	L
24070000	STRIP STOLEN VEH	L
24080000	POSSESS STOLEN VEH	L
24090000	INTERSTATE TRANSP STOLEN VEH	L
24100000	AIRCRAFT THEFT	L
24110000	STOLEN VEHICLE, UNAUTHORIZED USE	L
24110001	UNAUTH USE OF MOTOR VEHICLE	L
24110003	UNAUTH USE OF VEHICLE	L
24110003	UNAUTH USE OF VEHICLE	L
24990000	STOLEN VEHICLE-OTHER	L
25000000	FORGERY	L
25000002	FORGERY COUNTERFEITING ALCOHOL BEVERAGE STAMP	L
25000005	FALSE INFORMATION OR FORGERY	L
25010000	FORGERY OF CHECKS	L
25020000	FORGERY OF	L
25020001	FORGE OIL/GAS CARGO DOCUMENT	L
25020002	FORGE FALSIFIES/ALTERS AN INVOICE	L
25020003	FORGE FALS/ALTER INVOICE/MANIFEST PETROL PROD	L
25020004	FORGERY FINANCIAL INSTRUMENT	L
25020005	FORGERY GOVT FINANCIAL INSTRUMENT	L
25020006	FORGE CONTERFEITING DRIVERS LICENSE	L
25020007	FORGE NAME PERMITS/TENDERS FOR OIL/GAS	L
25020008	FORGE NAME OF PERSON TO TENDER/PERM	L
25020009	FORGE INSTRMT INDUCE ANOTHER HANDLE OIL/GAS	L
25020010	FALSE NAME/INFO AND FORGERY	L
25020012	MAN W/INT SELL OF COUNTERFEIT INSTRUMENT	L

NCIC CODE	OFFENSE DESCRIPTION	RANK
25030000	COUNTERFEITING OF	L
25030001	COUNTERFEIT CIGARETTE STAMP	L
25030002	PLACE COUNTERF TAX PAYMT CERTIF/TAXABLE SUBST	L
25030003	PRINT/MKE/POSS FORG/COUNTERFEIT PERM	L
25030004	FORGE ALTER LOTTERY TICKET >$10K	L
25030005	FORGE ALTER LOTTERY TICKET <=$10K	L
25030006	INFLUENCE SELECTION OF LOTT WINNER <=$10K	L
25030007	INFLUENCE SELECTION OF LOTT WINNER >$10K	L
25040000	FORGERY-PASSING FORGED INSTRUMENT	L
25040007	POSS INSTRUMENT DESIGNED TO FORGE/COUNTERFEIT	L
25050000	PASS COUNTERFEITED	L
25050001	MAKE/SALE/CIRCULATE COUNTERFEIT TAX PAYMT CERT	L
25060000	FORGERY-POSSESSION FORGED INSTRUMENT	L
25070000	POSSESS COUNTERFEITED	L
25070001	COUNTERFEIT TAX PAYMENT CERTIFICATE	L
25080000	POSSESS TOOLS FOR	L
25090000	TRANSPORT FORGED	L
25100000	TRANSPORT COUNTERFEITED	L
25110000	TRANSPORT TOOLS FOR	L
25120000	FORGERY-ATTEMP TO PASS FORGED INSTRUMENT	L
25890000	FORGERY-OTHER	L
25890001	FORGERY FINANCIAL INSTRUMENT	L
25890001	FORGERY FINANCIAL INSTRUMENT	L
25890002	FORGERY GOVT/NATIONAL GOV INSTR MONEY/SECURITY	L
25890002	ATTEMPTED FORGERY GOVT FINANCIAL INST	L
25890006	FORGING PARI-MUTUEL TICKET	L
25890007	REPRODUCTION DESTRUCTION TATTOO MARK LIVESTOCK	L
25890012	FOOD STAMPS USE/ALTER/TRANSFER >=$200	L
25890014	FOOD STAMPS UNAUTH POSS >=$200	L
25890015	FOOD STAMPS W/BLANK AUTHORIZATION	L
25890019	FORGERY TO DEFRAUD OR HARM ELDERLY	L
25890020	FORGERY FINANCIAL INSTRUMENT ELDERLY	L
25890021	FORGERY GOVT/NATION INST/MONEY/SECURITY ELDER	M
25990000	COUNTERFEITING	L
25990001	COUNTERFEIT INSTRUMENT	L
25990004	TRADEMARK COUNTERFEITING >=$1,500<$20K	L
25990005	TRADEMARK COUNTERFEITING >=$20K<$100K	M
25990006	TRADEMARK COUNTERFEITING >=$100<$200K	M
25990007	TRADEMARK COUNTERFEITING >=$200K	H
25990009	FORGERY COUNTERFEITING ALCOHOL BEVERAGE STAMP	L
25990011	AIRBAGS:MAKES/SELL CNTERFEIT,INT ALT PREV CONV	L
25990012	AIRBAGS:MAKES/SELL CNTERFEIT INT ALT RESULT BI	L

NCIC CODE	OFFENSE DESCRIPTION	RANK
25990013	MAN/PRODUCE FORGED/COUNTERFEIT INST	L
25990014	MAN/PRODUCE FORGED/COUNTFEIT INST BY PUB SER	L
26000000	FRAUD	L
26000001	INVESTMENT OF MUTUAL LIFE INSURANCE FUNDS	L
26000004	PUBLIC NON-EXIST TELEPHONE # AVOID PAY ENH	L
26000007	MAKE TELECOMM EQUIP FRAUD AVOID CHARGES ENH	L
26000008	REPRODUCTION/DESTRUCTUCTION TATTOO MARK LIVEST	L
26000009	PUBLIC GRAIN WAREHOUSE FRAUD	L
26000010	FRAUDULENTLY ISSUING WEIGHT TICKET/RECEIPT	L
26000011	CHANGE SCALE WEIGHT TICKET/RECEIPT AFTER ISSUE	L
26000013	SIGN FAL STATEMENT/CERTIFICATE TAX ASSESSOR	L
26000014	UNL SIGN STATEMNT DIESEL FUEL PURCH TAX FREE	L
26000016	VETERANS LAND BOARD FAL STATEMENT	L
26000017	PURCHASE SALE/RESALE VETERANS LAND	L
26000018	DEFRAUDING VETERAN AND STATE	L
26000019	MISAPP TRUST FUND >=$500 DEFRAUD	L
26000021	CORP FILES FRAUD TAX REPORT	L
26000026	FRAUD REWARD OF BINGO PRIZES	L
26000038	DECEPTIVE CERTIFIED VITAL STATISTIC RECORDS	L
26000039	DECEPTIVE CERTIFIED VITAL STATISTIC RECORDS	L
26000040	DECEPTIVE USE OF VITAL STATISTIC RECORDS	L
26000041	FRAUD OBTAIN/REC VITAL STAT RECORDS	L
26000051	CONCEAL CREDIT UNION BOOK/RECORD	L
26000052	DEFAMATION OF FINANCIAL CONDITION CREDIT UNION	L
26000057	HINDER SECURED CREDITORS >=$10K	L
26000059	FRAUD TRANSFER OF A MOTOR VEHICLE >=$20K	M
26000060	FRAUD TRANSFER OF A MOTOR VEHICLE <$20K	L
26000068	MISAPP FIDUC/FINANCIAL INSTIT PROP >=$200<$10K	L
26000069	MISAPP FIDUC OR FINAN INSTIT PROP >=$10K<$100K	M
26000070	MISAPP FIDUC OR FINANCIAL INSTIT PROP >$100K	M
26000071	SECURE EXECUTION OF DOCUMENT BY DECEPTION	L
26000073	FRAUD DESTRUCT/REMOVAL/CON OF WRITING	L
26000076	FRAUD OBTAIN OR DENY WORKERS COMP>= $750<$10K	L
26000077	FRAUD OBTAIN OR DENY WORKERS COMP >=$10K	L
26000079	FRAUD OBTAIN WORKERS COMP INSURANCE COVERAGE	L
26000081	FOOD STAMPS USE/ALTER/TRANSFER >=$200	L
26000083	FOOD STAMPS UNAUTH POSS >=$200	L
26000084	FOOD STAMPS W/BLANK AUTHORIZATION	L
26000085	EMPLOY LIMIT OF LIABILITY OF ANY ONE BORROWER	L
26000086	LOAN TO AND TRANSACTIONS W/ OFFICER/DIRECTOR	L
26000087	LOAN OF TRUST FUNDS TO OFFICER/DIRECTOR/EMPL	L
26000088	SLANDER OR LIBEL OF BANKS	L

NCIC CODE	OFFENSE DESCRIPTION	RANK
26000089	FALSE STATEMENT FOR DISABLED ASSISTANCE PROGRA	L
26000090	AGENT ISSUE FRAUDULENT BILL OF LADING	L
26000091	AGENT ISSUE DUPLICATE ORDER BILL OF LADING	L
26000092	INDUCE ISS OF FRAUD BILL OF LADING	L
26000093	NEGOTIATING FRAUD BILL OF LADING	L
26000096	WAREHOUSEMAN ISSUE WAREHOUSE RECEIPT W/O GOODS	L
26000097	WAREHOUSEMAN ISSUE DUPLICATE WAREHOUSE RECEIPT	L
26000101	BARRATRY ECONOMIC BENEFIT	L
26000102	BARRATRY ENH	L
26000105	UNAUTH USE DPS NAME/INSIGNIA/DIVIS NAME BY MAI	L
26000116	SUBMIT INCORR INFO TO CENTRAL EDUC AGENCY	L
26000117	CLAIM LOTT PRIZE BY FRAUD <$200 ENH	L
26000119	CLAIM LOTT PRIZE BY FRAUD <= $10K	L
26000120	CLAIM LOTT PRIZE BY FRAUD >$10K	L
26000121	ILLEGAL CLAIM OF LOTT PRIZE FROM ANOTHER	L
26000122	ILLEGAL CLAIM OF LOTT PRIZE FORM ANOTHER >$10K	L
26000123	SCHOOL DIST TREAS FRAUD TAKE/MISAPPLY $	L
26000125	ALTER OF TEACHER CERTIFICATE	L
26000132	BLUE SKY LAW SECURITIES FRAUD	L
26000133	FRAUD SELL SECURITIES >=$100K	M
26000134	FRAUD SELL SECURITIES >= $10K < $100K	M
26000135	FRAUD SELL SECURITIES <$10K	L
26000136	EMPLOY DEVICE/SCHEME DEF SECURITY >=$100K	M
26000137	EMPLOY DEVICE/SCHEME DEF SECURITY >=$10K<$100K	M
26000138	EMPLOY DEVICE/SCHEME DEF SECURITY <$10K	L
26000139	FRAUD SECURITY BUS PRACTICE >=$10K <$100K	M
26000140	FRAUD SECURITY BUS PRACTICE >=$100K	M
26000141	FRAUD SECURITY BUS PRACTICE W/ SECURITY <$10K	L
26000151	PENSION PAYMENT/AFFIDAVIT/WARRANT	L
26000154	ALTER NUMBER ON VEH/PART TO CHANGE IDENTITY	L
26000159	FRAUD FRESHWATER FISH TOURN PRIZE >=$10K	L
26000161	FRAUD FRESHWATER FISH TOURN PRIZE >$10K PARTIC	L
26000168	TEXAS UNIFORM FACSIMILE SIGNATURE	L
26000177	SLANDER AGAINST SAVINGS AND LOAN ASSOC	L
26000178	PROCURE BY FRAUD OIL/GAS PERM	L
26000180	FRAUD MISREPRESENTATION TO SECURE LICENSE	L
26000193	MONEY LAUNDERING >= $3,000 <$20K	L
26000194	MONEY LAUNDERING >= $20K < $100K	M
26000195	MONEY LAUNDERING >= $100K	M
26000199	INSURANCE CLAIM FRAUD >=$750 <$20K	L
26000200	INSURANCE CLAIM FRAUD <$750 ENH	L
26000201	INSURANCE CLAIM FRAUD >=$20K <$100K	M

NCIC CODE	OFFENSE DESCRIPTION	RANK
26000202	INSURANCE CLAIM FRAUD >$100K	M
26000203	INSURANCE CLAIM FRAUD <$100K ENH	M
26000204	INSURANCE CLAIM FRAUD <$100K RISK DEATH/SBI	M
26000205	INSURANCE CLAIM FRAUD<$20K HLTH PRACT	L
26000206	INSURANCE CLAIM FRAUD>=$20K<$100K HLTH PRACT	M
26000207	INSURANCE CLAIM FRAUD>$100K HLTH PRACT	M
26000208	INSURANCE CLAIM FRAUD<$100K HLTH PRACT ENH	M
26000209	INSURANCE CLAIM FRAUD<$100K HLTH PRACT DTH/SBI	M
26000212	BARRATRY ILL INVEST/EMPLOYMENT	L
26000216	HINDER SECURED CREDITORS REMOVE PROPERTY	L
26000218	FRAUD TELECOMMUNICATION SERVICE	L
26000219	FRAUD TELECOMMUNICATION SERVICE 2ND	L
26000220	MAKE TELECOMM EQUIP FRAUD AUDIO CHARGES ENH	L
26010000	FRAUD-CONFIDENCE GAME	L
26020000	FRAUD-SWINDLE	L
26020001	ILLEGAL RECRUITMENT OF ATHLETE ACCEPT BENEFIT	L
26020003	RIGGING PUB EXHIBITED CONTEST W/ BET OR WAGER	L
26020006	ILLEGAL RECRUIT OF ATHLETE >=$1,500<$20K	L
26020006	ILLEGAL RECRUIT OF ATHLETE >=$1,500<$20K	L
26020007	ILLEGAL RECRUIT OF ATHLETE >=$20K<$100K	M
26020008	ILLEGAL RECRUIT OF ATHLETE >=$100K<$200K	M
26020009	ILLEGAL RECRUIT OF ATHLETE >=$200K	H
26020011	INVESTMENT OF MUTUAL LIFE INSURANCE FUNDS	L
26020012	INVESTMENT OF MUTUAL LIFE INSURANCE FUNDS	L
26030000	MAIL FRAUD	L
26030003	PRINT/MAKE/POSSESS FORG/COUNTERFEIT PERMIT	L
26040000	FRAUD-IMPERSONATION	L
26040002	PURPORTS TO ACT AS VOTER AGENT	L
26040006	IMPERSONATE PUB SERVANT- PEACE OFFICER	M
26040014	PRACT DENTIST UNDER NAME OTHER THAN OWN ENH	L
26040018	IMPERSONATE ADOPTEE W/INTENT/REC INFO FROM REG	L
26040019	IMPERSONATE ADOPT REGISTRY EMPL OBTAIN CONFID	L
26040026	FALSE HOLD ONESELF OUT AS A LAWYER	L
26040028	UNAUTH PRACTICE OF LAW W/PREV CONVIC	L
26040029	IMPERSONATE W/INT TO SECURE ADOPTION INFO	L
26040030	IMPERSONATE W/INT GAIN INFO REG ADMIN/AGEN/EMP	L
26040034	IMPERSONATE PUBLIC SERVANT	M
26040038	FRAUD USE/POSS OF IDENTIFYING INFO	L
26040038	FRAUD USE/POSS OF IDENTIFYING INFO	L
26040039	FRAUD PLACEMENT OF FACSIMILE SIGNATURE/SEAL	L
26040042	FRAUD USE/POSS IDENTIFYING INFO # ITEMS < 5	L
26040043	FRAUD USE/POSS IDENTIFYING INFO # ITEMS 5<10	L

NCIC CODE	OFFENSE DESCRIPTION	RANK
26040044	FRAUD USE/POSS IDENTIFYING INFO # ITEMS 10<50	L
26040045	FRAUD USE/POSS IDENTIFYING INFO #ITEMS 50/MORE	M
26040046	FRAUD USE/POSS IDENT # ITEMS <5 ELDERLY	L
26040047	FRAUD USE/POSS IDENT # ITEMS 5>10 ELDERLY	M
26040048	FRAUD USE/POSS IDENT INFO # ITEMS 10<50 ELDER	M
26050000	FRAUD-CREDIT CARD ABUSE	L
26050001	CREDIT CARD ABUSE	L
26050004	DEBIT CARD ABUSE	L
26050005	CREDIT CARD ABUSE	L
26050005	CREDIT CARD ABUSE	L
26050006	DEBIT CARD ABUSE	L
26050006	DEBIT CARD ABUSE	L
26050009	CREDIT CARD TRANS LAUNDERING >=$1,500<$20K	L
26050009	CREDIT CARD TRANS LAUNDERING >=$1,500<$20K	L
26050010	CREDIT CARD TRANS LAUNDERING >=$20K<$100K	M
26050011	CREDIT CARD TRANS LAUNDERING >=$100K<$200K	M
26050012	CREDIT CARD TRANS LAUNDERING >=$200K	H
26050014	CREDIT CARD OR DEBIT CARD ABUSE	L
26050015	CREDIT CARD OR DEBIT CARD ABUSE ELDERLY	L
26060000	FRAUD-INSUFF FUNDS CHECK	L
26060002	OFFICER/EMPLOYEE CERTIF OF CHECK W/O FUNDS	L
26070000	FRAUD-FALSE STATEMENT	L
26070001	FALSE STATEMENT ON ALCOHOL BEVERAGE LICENSE	L
26070004	FALSE REPORT TO RAILROAD COMMISSION	L
26070007	SOLICIT FAL STATEMENT ON VOTER REGISTR APPLIC	L
26070010	FALSE REPORT TO INSURANCE BOARD	L
26070011	MOTOR FUEL TAXES	L
26070012	MAKE/DEL FAL TAX REPORT INFO	L
26070013	MAKE FAL STATEMENT IN CLAIM FOR TAX REFFERAL	L
26070014	FILE FALSE RETURN W/COMPTROLLER	L
26070015	MAKE FAL ENTRY IN RECRDS REQ BY TAX CODE	L
26070016	BOOK RECORDS ON TOBACCO PRODUCTS	L
26070018	FALSE STATEMENT OR MISAPP BY MUTUAL COMPANY	L
26070020	FALSE MISLEADING OR DECEPTIVE ADVERTISING ENH	L
26070021	ACCOUNTANT FOR CORP ENTER FAL INF/TAX REPORT	L
26070024	FALSE STATEMENT UNDER TEXAS RACING ACT	L
26070027	FALSE RECORD FOR/ON BIRTH/DEATH CERTIFICATE	L
26070028	FALSE APPLICATION DELAYED BIRTH/DEATH CERTIF	L
26070029	FALSE APPLIC CERTIFIED COPY OF VITAL RECORD	L
26070030	FALSE STATEMENT CERTIFICATE/RECORD OR REPORT	L
26070031	SUPPLY CREATE FAL RECORD	L
26070035	ACT W/INSURANCE AGENT WHOLESALE LIC REVOKED	L

NCIC CODE	OFFENSE DESCRIPTION	RANK
26070037	FALSE STATEMENT TO STATE BOARD OF INSURANCE	L
26070038	FALSE ENTRY IN CREDIT UNION RECORDS	L
26070039	FALSE DOCUMENT/ANSWER IN CREDIT UNION INVESTIG	L
26070041	FALSE CLEANUP/PREVENT DISCHARGE/SPILL REPORT	L
26070042	FALSE ENTRY IN PETROL PROD STORAGE RECORD	L
26070043	TRANSP PETROL PROD W/ FAL CARGO MANIFEST	L
26070044	MAKE/DEL FAL PETROL PROD STORAGE REPORT	L
26070049	BANK EMPLOYEE/DIRECTORS FAL ENTRY/STATEMENT	L
26070051	FALSE STATEMENT BY INSUR OFFICER OF FOREIGN CO	L
26070052	FALSE CLAIM AGAINST STATE COMPTROLLER	L
26070054	OIL SPILL PREVENTION/RESPONSE ACT	L
26070055	FALSE REP/FAIL TO GIVE REPORT MEAT/POULTRY ACT	L
26070056	FALSE OF FINGERPRINTS/PHOTOGRAPHS	L
26070057	FALSE MAKING INCORRECT RECORD BIRTH/DEATH	L
26070058	MIDWIFE FALSIFICATION OF DOCUMENTS	L
26070061	FALSE STATEMENT CHEM LAB APARATUS RECD/REPORT	L
26070064	FURNISH FAL INFO UNDER TEXAS CS ACT CS SCHED I	L
26070065	FURNISH FAL INFO UNDER TEXAS CS ACT CS SCHED I	L
26070066	FALSE STATEMENT IN REPORT TO STATE BANKING COM	L
26070067	FALSE STATEMENT TO ADOPTION REGISTRY	L
26070068	FALSE FOUNDATION SCH PROG RECORD/BUDGET	L
26070075	FALSE STATEMENT SECURITIES <$10K	L
26070076	FALSE STATEMENT SECURITIES >=$10K <$100K	M
26070077	FALSE STATEMENT SECURITIES >=$100K	M
26070078	MAKE FAL STATEMENT COAL MINING CERTIFICATE	L
26070079	FALSE APPL PURCH CONTRACT DISADVANT BUSINESS	L
26070080	FALSE STATEMENT RETAIL DEALERS LICENSE	L
26070081	FALSE STATEMENT RETAIL DISTRIBUTOR LICENSE	L
26070082	FALSE STATEMENT MANUFACTURE LICENSE	L
26070083	FALSE STMT TO SECURE BOND REGISTRATION	L
26070087	CONVERSION ERS FUNDS CONFISCATE/FALSE STMT	L
26070088	FALSE/CONVERT RECORDS TEACHER RETIRE SYSTEM	L
26070092	PROCURING TENDER/PERMIT FOR OIL/GAS	L
26070093	FALSE APPLICATION/REPORT/DOCUMENT	L
26070101	INSURANCE FRAUD >=$1,500<$20K	L
26070101	INSURANCE FRAUD >=$1,500<$20K	L
26070102	INSURANCE FRAUD >=$20K<$100K	M
26070103	INSURANCE FRAUD >=$100K<$200K	M
26070104	INSURANCE FRAUD >=$200K	H
26070105	INSUR CLAIM FRAUD <$200k RISK DEATH OR INJ	M
26070107	FAL STATE OF CHILD SUPP PAYMENT	L
26070108	FALSE STATEMENT W/OPERATING REGISTRY ADOPTION	L

NCIC CODE	OFFENSE DESCRIPTION	RANK
26070111	FAL STMT UNDER TX RACING ACT/COMMISSION ACTION	L
26070112	FAL STATEMENT UNDER TX RACING ACT	L
26070116	FALSE STATEMENT/DOC/DISTR CREDIT UNION RECORDS	L
26070117	FAL DOC/ANSWER IN CREDIT UNION INVESTING	L
26070120	FAL STMT CHEM LAB APARATUS RECD/REPORT	L
26070121	FALSE STMT CHEM LAB APP RECD/REPORT ENH	L
26070122	BOOK RECORDS ON CIGARETTE TAX	L
26070123	BINGO ENABELING ACT	L
26070126	FALSIFICATION FINGERPRINTS/PHOTOS	L
26070129	BINGO REGULATIONS AWARD FRAUD PRIZES	L
26070131	FAL STMT CHEM LAB APARATUS RECD/REPORT ENH	L
26070133	GRAIN WAREHOUSE FRAUD	L
26070134	FRAUD ISSUING A SCALE WEIGHT TICKET	L
26070135	CHANGE RECEIPT OR SCALE WGT TICKET	L
26070136	SIGN FAL STATEMENT/CERTIFICATE	L
26070139	FALSE STATEMENT FOR PROPERTY/CREDIT $1500<$20K	L
26070140	FALSE STATEMENT FOR PROPERTY/CREDIT $20K<$100K	M
26070141	FALSE STATEMENT FOR PROPERTY/CREDIT$100K<$200K	M
26070142	FALSE STATEMENT FOR PROPERTY/CREDIT $200K	H
26070144	PRIVATE INVESTIGATORS/SECURITY AGENCIES ACT	L
26070145	UNL CONVERSION MUTUAL ASSESSMENT	L
26070146	UNL DIVERSION OF FUNDS	L
26070149	VETERANS LAND BOARD FAL STATEMENT	L
26070150	PURCHASE SALE RESALE VETERANS LAND	L
26070151	DEFRAUDING VETERAN AND STATE	L
26070157	SUPPORT SERVICES FOR DISABLED PERSON VIOL	L
26070158	AGENT ISSUE FRAUDULENT BILL OF LADING	L
26070159	AGENT ISSUE DUPLICATE ORDER BILL OF LADING	L
26070160	INDUCE ISSUANCE OF FRAUD BILL OF LADING	L
26070161	NEGOTIATING FRAUDULENT BILL OF LADING	L
26070164	WAREHOUSEMAN ISSUE WAREHOUSE RECEIPT W/O GOOD	L
26070165	WAREHOUSEMAN ISSUE DUPLICATE WAREHOUSE RECEIPT	L
26070169	UNAUTH USE DPS NAME/INSIGNIA/DIV NAME BY MAIL	L
26070174	FRAUD FRESHWATER FISH TOURN PRIZE >=$10K	L
26070176	TEXAS UNIFORM FACSIMILE SIGNATURE	L
26070179	PENSION PAYMENT/AFFIDAVIT/WARRANT	L
26070180	INVESTMENT ADVISER OR REPRESENTATIVE W/O REGIS	L
26070183	UNINCORPORATED BUS/PROF SERV W/FALSE STATEMENT	L
26070184	UNINCORPORATED BUS/PROF SERV W/FALSE STATEMENT	L
26070185	UNINCORPORATED BUS/PROF SERV W/FALSE STATEMENT	L
26070195	FALSE REPORT CHILD CARE/FAM HOME COMPL ENH	L
26070196	INSURANCE FRAUD RISKING BODILY INJ/DEATH	M

NCIC CODE	OFFENSE DESCRIPTION	RANK
26070197	INSURANCE FRAUD >=$100K<$200K	M
26070198	INSURANCE FRAUD >=$1500<$20K	L
26070199	INSURANCE FRAUD >=$200K	H
26070200	INSURANCE FRAUD >=$20K<$100K	M
26070204	INSURANCE FRAUD W/INT TO DEFRAUD/DECEIVE	L
26070207	MEDICAID FRAUD =>$100K<$200K	M
26070208	MEDICAID FRAUD =>$1500 < $20K	L
26070209	MEDICAID FRAUD =>$200K	H
26070210	MEDICAID FRAUD =>$20K<$100K	M
26070214	REGULATE MONEY SERV BUSINESSES FAL STMT	L
26070218	SIGN FALSE DOCUMENT W/INT DEFRAUD/HARM ANOTHER	L
26070220	UNLAWFUL CONVERSION OF MUTUAL ASSESSMENT	L
26070221	UNLAWFUL DIVERSION OF FUNDS	L
26070222	FRAUD PLACEMENT OF FACSIMILE SIGNATURE OR SEAL	L
26070224	FALSE STATEMENT RETAIL DEALERS LICENSE	L
26070226	MEDICAID FRAUD OBST INVEST BY/AG $1500<$20,000	L
26070228	DISP/PROV FALSE INFO/STMT METL RECYC PREV CONV	L
26070231	WAREHOUSEMAN ISSUE WAREHOUSE RECEIPT W/O GOODS	L
26070232	WAREHOUSEMAN ISSUE DUPLICATE WAREHOUSE RECEIPT	L
26070235	AGENT ISSUE FRAUDULENT BILL OF LADING	L
26070236	AGENT ISSUE DUPLICATE ORDER BILL OF LADING	L
26070237	INDUCE ISSUANCE OF FRAUDULENT BILL OF LADING	L
26070238	NEGOTIATE/TRANSFER FRAUDULENT BILL OF LADING	L
26070239	MEDICAID FRAUD AMT UNKNOWN/OBST ATY GEN INVEST	L
26080000	FRAUD BY WIRE	L
26100000	FRAUD-SECURITIES	L
26120000	FRAUD-MISAPPLICATION FIDUCIARY FUNDS	L
26130000	FRAUD-HINDER SECURED CREDITORS	L
26150000	FRAUD-PRACTICING WITHOUT LICENSE	L
26180000	FRAUD-UNLAWFUL USE OF CRIMINAL INSTRMNT	L
26990000	FRAUD-OTHER	L
26990001	BARRATRY	L
26990002	BARRATRY ILL INVEST/EMPLOYMENT	L
26990004	WORKERS LIEN	L
26990007	BARRATRY ECONOMIC BENEFIT	L
26990008	BARRATRY-LIC PROFES FINANCE /INVEST FUNDS	L
26990010	BARRATRY ILL OBTAIN EMPLOYMENT W/PREV CONVIC	L
26990013	ILLEGAL CLAIM LOTTERY PRIZE FROM ANOTHER >$10K	L
26990014	ILLEGAL CLAIM LOTTERY PRIZE FROM ANOTHER	L
26990015	HINDER SECUR CREDITORS>=$1,500<$20K	L
26990015	HINDER SECUR CREDITORS>=$1,500<$20K	L
26990016	HINDER SECUR CREDITORS>=$20K<$100K	M

NCIC CODE	OFFENSE DESCRIPTION	RANK
26990017	HINDER SECUR CREDITORS>=$100K<$200K	M
26990018	HINDER SECUR CREDITORS>=$200K	H
26990021	HINDER SECUR CREDIT PROCEEDS>=$1,500<$20K	L
26990021	HINDER SECUR CREDIT PROCEEDS>=$1,500<$20K	L
26990022	HINDER SECUR CREDIT PROCEEDS>=$20K<$100K	M
26990023	HINDER SECUR CREDIT PROCEEDS>=$100K<$200K	M
26990024	HINDER SECUR CREDIT PROCEEDS>=$200K	H
26990025	FRAUD TRANSFER OF A MOTOR VEHICLE<$20K	L
26990025	FRAUD TRANSFER OF A MOTOR VEHICLE<$20K	L
26990026	FRAUD TRANSFER OF A MOTOR VEHICLE>=$20K	M
26990031	MISAPP FIDUC/FINAN PROP >=$1,500<$20K	L
26990031	MISAPP FIDUC/FINAN PROP >=$1,500<$20K	L
26990032	MISAPP FIDUC/FINAN PROPERTY >=$20K<$100K	M
26990033	MISAPP FIDUC/FINAN PROP >=$100K<$200K	M
26990034	MISAPP FIDUC/FINAN PROP >=$200K	H
26990037	SECURE EXECUTION DOC DECEPT >=$1,500<$20K	L
26990037	SECURE EXECUTION DOC DECEPT >=$1,500<$20K	L
26990038	SECURE EXECUTION DOC DECEPT >=$20K<$100K	M
26990039	SECURE EXECUTION DOC DECEPT >=$100K<$200K	M
26990040	SECURE EXECUTION DOC DECEPTION >=$200K	H
26990042	FRAUD DESTRUCT/REMOVAL/CONCEALMENT WRITING ENH	L
26990042	FRAUD DESTRUCT/REMOVAL/CONCEALMENT WRITING ENH	L
26990044	CLAIM LOTTERY PRIZE BY FRAUD >$200<=$10K	L
26990045	CLAIM LOTT PRIZE BY FRAUD <=$10K	L
26990046	CLAIM LOTTERY PRIZE BY FRAUD >$10K	L
26990051	MONEY LAUNDERING >= $3,000 <$20K	L
26990052	MONEY LAUNDERING >= $20K<$100K	M
26990053	MONEY LAUNDERING >= $100K	M
26990056	FAL STATEMENT VEH REGISTRATION ACT	L
26990057	PLACE SERIAL NUMBER W/INT TO CHANGE IDENTITY	L
26990060	PYRAMID PROMOTIONAL SCHEME	L
26990060	PYRAMID PROMOTIONAL SCHEME	L
26990063	FRAUD OBTAIN/DENY BENEFITS => $1,500	L
26990063	FRAUD OBTAIN/DENY BENEFITS => $1,500	L
26990065	FRAUD OBTAIN WORKERS COMP INS COVER =>$1,500	L
26990065	FRAUD OBTAIN WORKERS COMP INS COVER =>$1,500	L
26990067	SECURE EXEC DOC BY DECEPTIONPUB SERV	L
26990070	SIMULATING LEGAL PROCESS W/PREV CONVIC	L
26990071	FRAUD FINANCE STATEMENT/FORGED	L
26990072	FRAUD FINANCE STATEMENT/FORGED 2+ PREV CONVIC	L
26990074	FRAUD FINANCE STMT/FALSE/GROUNDLESS/INTENT	L
26990076	RECORD OF FRAUDULENT COURT 2+ PREV CONVIC	L

NCIC CODE	OFFENSE DESCRIPTION	RANK
26990079	TRUSTEE KNOWINGLY W/INT DEFRAUD PURCHASE TIMBE	L
26990080	FICTITIOUS COUNTERFEIT INSP/INS DOC TO MAKE/PO	L
26990081	FICTITIOUS COUNTERFEIT INSP/INS DOC W/INT FRAU	L
26990084	UNL MEDICAID PROGRAM BENEFIT>=$1500 <$20K	L
26990085	UNL MEDICAID PROGRAM BENEFIT>=$20K <$100K	M
26990086	UNL MEDICAID PROGRAM BENEFIT>=$100K <$200K	M
26990087	UNL MEDICAID PROGRAN BENEFIT>=$200K	H
26990089	TRADEMARK SERVICE MARK REG W/INT DEFRAUD/HARM	L
26990094	CON CREDIT UNION BOOK/RECORD	L
26990095	DEFAMATION OF FINANCIAL CONDITION CREDIT UNION	L
26990096	SLANDER OR LIBEL OF BANKS	L
26990097	CRIMINAL SLANDER AGAINST SAVINGS AND LOAN ASSO	L
26990098	FALSE OR FORGERY STATMENT VEHICLE REGISTRATION	L
26990100	WILLFUL/FRAUD REPORT ON FRANCHISE TAX	L
26990102	FALSE NAME/INFO/FORGERY VEHICLE REGISTRATION	L
26990105	REPRESENT AS ATTORNEY W/PREV CONVIC	L
26990106	TIMBER PURCHASE AS TRUSTEEW/INT TO DEFRAUD	L
26990107	UNL USE OF FUNDS FOR HUMAN SERVICES	L
26990108	APPROPRIATION PROCEEDS SALES BY COMMS MERCHANT	L
26990110	MISAPP OF SPECIAL FUNDS	L
26990116	MISAPP TRUST FUND >=$500 DEFRAUD	L
26990119	FRAUD SELL SECURITIES	L
26990120	FRAUD SELL SECURITIES >=$100K	M
26990121	FRAUD SELL SECURITIES >= $10K< $100K	M
26990122	FRAUD SELL SECURITIES <$10K	L
26990123	EMPLOY DEVICE SCHEME DEF SECURITY >=$100K	M
26990124	EMPLOY DEVICE SCHEME DEF SECURITY >=$10K<$100K	M
26990125	EMPLOY DEVICE SCHEME DEF SECURITY <$10K	L
26990126	FRAUD SECURITY BUS PRACTICE >=$10K <$100K	M
26990127	FRAUD SECURITY BUS PRACTICE >=$100K	M
26990128	FRAUD SECURITY BUS PRACTICE W/ SECURITY <$10K	L
26990132	FRAUD TELECOMMUNICATION SERVICE 2ND	L
26990137	PREVENTION DETECTION OF FRAUD MEDICAL ASSIST	L
26990141	BARRATRY ILL OBTAIN EMPLOYMENT	L
26990142	MISAPP FIDUCIARY/FINANCE PROPERTY ELDERLY	L
26990143	SECURE EXECUTION BY DECEPTION ELDERLY	L
26990146	CLAIM LOTTERY PRIZE FRAUD >$10K	L
26990147	CLAIM LOTTERY PRIZE FRAUD >$200<=$10K	L
26990150	CLAIM LOTTERY PRIZE W/PREV CONV	L
26990152	MONEY LAUNDERING >=$100K<$200K	M
26990153	MONEY LAUNDERING >=$1500 <$20K	L
26990154	MONEY LAUNDERING >=$200K	H

NCIC CODE	OFFENSE DESCRIPTION	RANK
26990155	MONEY LAUNDERING >=$20K<$100K	M
26990161	SECURITIES W/O REGISTRATION	L
26990162	UNAUTHORIZED INSURANCE BUSINESS	L
26990165	SECURE EXECUTION DOC BY DECEPTION PUB SERVANT	L
26990167	TEMPORARY TAG FOR DIST TO UNAUTH PERSON	L
26990168	ORGANIZED CRIM ACTIVITY - TEMPORARY TAG	L
26990170	TAMPER W/GOVERN RECORD LIC/SEAL DEFRAUD/HARM	L
26990171	TAMPER W/GOV SCHOOL RECORD LIC/SEAL/PERM	L
26990174	NONREPAIRABLE MOTOR VEHICLE W/2+ PREV CONV	L
27000000	EMBEZZLEMENT	L
27000001	EMBEZZLEMENT UNAUTH ISS FAL ENTRY	L
27010000	EMBEZZLE-BUSINESS PROP	L
27020000	EMBEZZLE-INTERSTATE SHIPMENT	L
27030000	EMBEZZLE-BANKING-TYPE INST	L
27030001	EMPLOY EMBEZZ/ABSTRACT/MISAPPL BANK FUNDS	L
27040000	EMBEZZLE-PUBLIC PROP	L
27050000	EMBEZZLE-POSTAL	L
27990000	EMBEZZLEMENT	L
28000000	STOLEN PROPERTY	L
28000001	PURCHASE SALE TRANSP TATTOO LIVESTOCK W/O CONS	L
28000004	UNAUTH DUPLICATION RECORDING >100 RCRD W/I 180	L
28000006	LIVE PFM>=1000 RCRD/>=65 AUDIOV RCRD W/I 180d	L
28000007	RCRD LVE PFM<1000 RCRD<65 AUDVS RCRD W/I 180d	L
28010000	SALE OF STOLEN PROP	L
28010001	UNAUTH RCRD/LIVE>100 RCRD/>7 AUD RCRD W/I 180D	L
28010002	SALE>=1000 LVE RCRD/>=65 AUDIOVS RCRD W/I 180d	L
28010003	LABELING RECORD >7 RCRD W/I 180D	L
28010004	SELL/POSS UNLABELED RCRD <65 W/I 180D	L
28010004	SALE POSS UNLABELED RCRD <65 RCRD W/I 180d	L
28010007	UNAUTH DUPLIC RECORDING >100 RCRD W/I 180D	L
28010009	UNAUTH OPER RECORD DEVICE THEATER W/PREV CONV	L
28010010	UNAUTH OPER RECORD DEVICE THEATER W/2PREV CONV	L
28010011	SELL STOLEN REGULATED MATERIALS	L
28010012	SELL STOLEN REGULATED MATERIALS W/PREV CONV	L
28020000	TRANSPORT INTERSTATE STOLEN PROP	L
28030000	RECEIV STOLEN PROP	L
28030001	STEALING RECEIVING STOLEN GRAIN	L
28040000	POSSESS STOLEN PROP	L
28050000	CANCEAL STOLEN PROP	L
28990000	STOLEN PROPERTY	L
28990001	PURCHASE SALE TRANSP TATTOO LIVESTOCK W/O CONS	L
28990002	UNAUTH DUPLICATION RECORDING >100 W/I 180D	L

NCIC CODE	OFFENSE DESCRIPTION	RANK
28990004	UNAUTH RECORDING >100 LIVE/>7 AV W/I 180D	L
28990007	UNAUTH OPER RECORD DEVICE THEATER W/PREV CONV	L
28990008	UNAUTH OP RECORD DEVICE THEATER W/2+ PREV CONV	L
28990009	LABELING UNAUTH RECORDING >7 W/I 180D	L
28990136	STEALING GRAIN OR RECEIVING STOLEN GRAIN	L
28990138	PURCHASE STOLEN REGULATED MATERIAL W/PREV CONV	L
29000000	DAMAGE PROPERTY	L
29000001	DESTRUCT OF WATER WORKS	L
29000004	MUTILATE/DESTRUCT TAX BOOK RECORD	L
29000005	DESTRUCT MUTILATE/CON TAX BOOK OR RECORD	L
29000009	VANDALIZE CAVE W/PREV CONV	L
29000010	DISTURBING NATURAL CONDITION ANY CAVE ENH	L
29000012	DESTRUCT OF PETROL PRODUCT STORAGE RECORD	L
29000015	CRIMINAL MISCH $750<$20K	L
29000016	CRIMINAL MISCH IMPAIR INTERUPT PUB SERVICE	L
29000017	CRIMINAL MISCH >=$20K	M
29000018	CRIMINAL MISCH CHURCH/PUB BLDG/SOC PROG $20<$2	L
29000019	CRIMINAL MISCH CHURCH PUB BLDG SOC PROG >$20K	M
29000020	TAMPER W/LOTTERY EQUIPMENT	L
29010000	DAMAGE PROP-BUSINESS	L
29010001	TAMPER W/LOTTERY EQUIPMENT	L
29020000	DAMAGE PROP-PRIVATE	L
29030000	DAMAGE PROP-PUBLIC	L
29030001	INJURY DESTROY PIPELINE FACILITIES	M
29030002	DAMAGE DESTRUCT PUB UTILITY SERVICE	M
29030008	VANDALIZE CAVE W/PREV CONV	L
29040000	DAMAGE PROP-BUSINESS-WITH EXPLOSIVE	H
29050000	DAMAGE PROP-PRIVATE WITH EXPLOSIVE	H
29060000	DAMAGE PROP-PUBLIC-WITH EXPLOSIVE	H
29990000	DAMAGE PROPERTY	L
29990004	CRIMINAL MISCHIEF >=$1,500<$20K	L
29990004	CRIMINAL MISCHIEF >=$1,500<$20K	L
29990005	CRIMINAL MISCHIEF >=$20K<$100K	M
29990006	CRIMINAL MISCHIEF >=$100K<$200K	M
29990007	CRIMINAL MISCHIEF >=$200K	H
29990008	CRIMINAL MISCH CHURCH/CEMETERY/ PUB BLDG <$20K	L
29990008	CRIMINAL MISCH CHURCH/CEMETERY/ PUB BLDG <$20K	L
29990011	GRAFFITI PECUNIARY LOSS <$20K	L
29990012	GRAFFITI PECUNIARY LOSS <$100K	M
29990013	GRAFFITI PECUNIARY LOSS <$200K	M
29990014	GRAFFITI PECUNIARY LOSS >$200K	H
29990015	GRAFFITI WORSHIP/BURIAL/PUBLIC MONUMENT/SCHOOL	L

NCIC CODE	OFFENSE DESCRIPTION	RANK
29990017	CRIMINAL MISCH <$1500 HAB DAMAGE FIREARM/EXPLO	L
29990018	DESTRUCTION OF WATER WORKS	M
29990020	CRIMINAL MISCHIEF <$1500 DAMAGE HABITAT/ANIMAL	L
29990021	CRIMINAL MISCHIEF $1500 < $20K DESTROY SCHOOL	L
29990022	CRIMINAL MISCHIEF DAMAGE/DESTR WORSHIP/SCHOOL	L
29990023	CRIMINAL MISCHIEF FOR MAD COW DISEASE	H
29990025	CRIM MISCHIEF TRANS/COMM EQUIP/DEV <$100,000	M
29990026	DESTROY/INTERFERE/SABOTAGE UTILITY FACIL/EQUIP	M
29990028	CRIMINAL MISCHIEF IMP/INT PUB SERVICE <$20,000	L
29990029	CRIMINAL MISCHIEF <$1500 HABITATION FA/EXPLOS	L
29990030	CRIMINAL MISCHIEF <$1500 LS/GAME ANIM FENCE	L
29990033	INTERFERE W/OYSTER BOUY/MARKER +2 PREV CONV	L
30000002	HARM ACCESS COMPUTER DAMAGE >=$20K	M
30000003	HARM ACCESS COMPUTER DAMAGE $750<$20K	L
35000000	DANGEROUS DRUGS	L
35000007	UNL TRANS/RECEIPT CHEM PRECURSOR/ENH	M
35000008	SELL TRANSF/FURNISH PRECURSOR SUBSTANCE	M
35000009	SELL TRANSF/FURNISH APPARATUS TO MAN CS	M
35000010	MAN DEL POSS CONTROLLED SUBSTANCE <28G	M
35000011	AGG MAN/DEL/POSS CS >=28G BUT <200G	M
35000012	AGG MAN/DEL/POSS CS >=200 BUT <400G	M
35000013	AGG MAN/DEL/POSS CS >=400G	H
35000014	MAN DEL POSS CONT SUBST PEN GP 2 <28 GRAMS	M
35000015	AGG MAN/DEL/POSS CS >=28G BUT <400G	M
35000016	AGG MAN/DEL/POSS CS >=400G	H
35000017	MAN DEL POSS CS <200G PG 3/4	M
35000018	AGG MAN/DEL/POSS CS >=200G BUT <400G PG 3/4	M
35000019	AGG MAN/DEL/POSS CS >=400G PG 3/4	H
35000020	POSS CS PG 1 <28G UNLESS PRESCRIPTION	M
35000021	AGG POSS CS PG 1 >=28G BUT <400G	M
35000022	AGG POSS CS PG 1 >=400G	H
35000023	POSS CS PG 2 <28G	L
35000024	AGG POSS CS PG 2 >=28G BUT <400G	M
35000025	AGG POSS CS PG 2 >=400G	H
35000027	AGG POSS CS PG 3 >=200G BUT <400G	M
35000028	AGG POSS CS PG 3 >=400G	H
35000030	AGG POSS CS PG 4 >=200G BUT <400G	M
35000031	AGG POSS CS PG 4 >=400G	H
35000034	AGG MAN/DEL/POSS CS ANA SCHD 1/PG 1>=200G<400G	M
35000035	AGG MAN/DEL/POSS CS ANA SCHD 1/PG 1 >=28G<200G	M
35000036	MAN DEL POSS CS ANALOGUE SCHED 1/PG 1 <28G	M
35000037	AGG MAN/DEL/POSS CS ANALOGUE SCHD 1/PG 1 >400G	H

NCIC CODE	OFFENSE DESCRIPTION	RANK
35000038	AGG POSS CS ANALOGUE SCH 1/PG 1 400G OR MORE	H
35000039	POSS CS ANALOGUE SCH 1/PG 1 < 28G	M
35000040	AGG POSS CS ANALOGUE SCH 1/PG 1 >=28G <400G	M
35000041	MAN DEL POSS CS ANALOGUE PG 2 <28G	M
35000042	AGG MAN/DEL/POSS CS ANALOGUE PG 2 >=28G <400G	M
35000043	AGG MAN/DEL/POSS CS ANALOGUE PG 2 400G OR MORE	H
35000044	AGG POSS CS ANALOGUE PG 2 >=28G < 400G	M
35000045	AGG POSS CS ANALOGUE PG 2 400G OR MORE	H
35000046	POSS CS ANALOGUE PG 2 <28G	M
35000047	ILLEGAL EXPEND/INVEST FROM CONT SUBST/MARIJ	H
35000048	DISTR CS LISTED IN SCH 1 OR 2 W/O ORDER	M
35000049	USE FICT REGIS # IN MAN/PRESC/DISTR CS SCH 3/4	L
35000051	USE FICT REGIS # IN MAN/PRESC/DISTR CS SCH 1/2	M
35000053	USE TRIP PRESC FORM ISS TO ANOTH CS SCHED 1/2	M
35000054	USE TRIP PRESC FORM ISS TO ANOTH CS SCHED 3/4	L
35000056	POSS CS BY FRAUD CS SCHED 3/4	L
35000057	POSS CS BY FRAUD CS SCHED 1/2	M
35000060	DEL PRESCRIP NOT VALID MEDIC PURP CS SCHED 2	M
35000061	DEL PRESC NOT VALID MEDIC PURP CS SCHED 3/4/5	L
35000063	POSS PRESCRIPTION FOR CONTR SUBST SEC 2/3	M
35000064	CONVERT CS FOR USE/BENEFIT AFTER SEIZURE	L
35000065	DIVERT FOR UNL USE/CS PROP ALREADY SEIZED	L
35000068	MAN DEL SIM CS REPRESENT SUB TO BE A CS	L
35000069	MAN DEL SIM CS REPREST TO BE CS MISLEAD PERS	L
35000070	REPRESENT SIM SUBST TO BE CS TO THIRD PARTY	L
35000072	UNL POSS DANGEROUS DRUG	L
35000073	POSS DANGER DRUG FOR PURPOSE OF SELLING	L
35000075	DEL OFFER OF DELY OF DANGEROUS DRUG	L
35000076	UNL MAN DANGEROUS DRUG	L
35000108	DEL ABUSABLE GLUE/PAINT TO MINOR	L
35000111	PROH SUBSTANCE IN CORRECTIONAL FACILITY	M
35000112	REG DISPENSER COMMERCIAL CS VIOL	L
35000113	REGISTRANT/DISPEN COMMERCIAL CS VIOL ENH	L
35003333	MAN DEL SELL/POSS CONTROLLED SUBSTANCE	M
35003334	MAN DEL POSS CS/MARIJ DRUG FREE ZONE	M
35010000	HALLUCINOGEN-MANUFACT.	M
35020000	HALLUCINOGEN-DISTRIBUTE	M
35030000	HALLUCINOGEN-SALE	M
35040000	HALLUCINOGEN-POSSESS.	L
35050000	HALLUCINOGEN-OBTAIN	L
35100000	HEROIN-SALE	M
35110000	HEROIN-DISTRIBUTE	M

NCIC CODE	OFFENSE DESCRIPTION	RANK
35120000	HEROIN-POSSESS.	L
35130000	HEROIN-MANUFACT.	M
35140000	HEROIN-OBTAIN	L
35200000	MORPHINE-SALE	M
35210000	MORPHINE-DISTRIBUTE	M
35220000	MORPHINE-POSSESS.	L
35230000	MORPHINE-MANUFACT.	M
35240000	MORPHINE-OBTAIN	L
35300000	COCAINE-SALE	M
35310000	COCAINE-DISTRIBUTE	M
35320000	COCAINE-POSSESS.	L
35330000	COCAINE-MANUFACT.	M
35340000	COCAINE-OBTAIN	L
35400000	CONTROLLED SUBSTANCE-SALE	M
35410000	CONTROLLED SUBSTANCE-DISTRIBUTE	M
35420000	CONTROLLED SUBSTANCE-POSSESS.	L
35430000	CONTROLLED SUBSTANCE-OBTAIN	L
35440000	CONTROLLED SUBSTANCE-MANUFACT.	M
35500000	NARCOTIC EQUIP-POSSESS	M
35500002	POSS DEL DRUG PARA TO PLANT/PROC/STOR CS 2ND	L
35500006	POSS DEL DRUG PARA/ANOTH TO PLNT/PROC/STOR 2ND	L
35500007	POSS DEL DRUG PARA TO ANOTHER UNDER 18 YOA	L
35500017	DEL DRUG PARA PERS YOUNGER 18 YOA	L
35500017	DEL DRUG PARA PERS YOUNGER 18 YOA	L
35500019	TRANSF RECEIPT CHEMICAL LAB APPARATUS ENH	M
35500020	TRANSF RECEIPT CHEMICAL LAB APPARATUS	L
35500043	POSS DEL DRUG PARAPHERNALIA TO PERON U/18YR	L
35590148	POSS CS ANALOGUE PG 1-A >=20AU*	M
35600000	MARIJUANA-SALE	M
35610000	MARIJUANA-DISTRIBUTE	M
35620000	MARIJUANA-POSSESS.	L
35620003	POSS MARIJUANA <= 5 LBS BUT > 4 OZ	L
35620004	POSS MARIJUANA <= 50 LBS BUT > 5 LBS	M
35620005	AGG POSS MARIJ <= 200 LBS BUT > 50 LBS	M
35620006	AGG POSS MARIJ <= 2000 LBS BUT > 200 LBS	M
35620007	AGG POSS MARIJUANA > 2000 LBS	H
35620010	POSS MARIJ >4OZ<=5LBS	L
35620010	POSS MARIJ >4OZ<=5LBS	L
35620011	POSS MARIJ >5LBS<=50LBS	M
35620012	POSS MARIJ >50LBS<=2,000LBS	M
35620013	POSS MARIJ >2,000LBS	H
35620014	POSS MARIJ >4 OZ<=5LBS DRUG FREE ZONE	M

NCIC CODE	OFFENSE DESCRIPTION	RANK
35620015	POSS MARIJ >2 OZ<=4OZ DRUG FREE ZONE	L
35620015	POSS MARIJ >2 OZ<=4OZ DRUG FREE ZONE	L
35620017	POSS MARIJ >5LBS DRUG FREE ZONE	M
35630000	MARIJUANA-MANUFACT.	M
35640000	MARIJUANA-OBTAIN	L
35640001	DEL MARIJUANA <= 50 LBS BUT > 5 LBS	M
35640004	DEL MARIJUANA <= 4 OZ BUT > 1/4 OZ	L
35640005	DEL MARIJUANA <= 5 LBS BUT > 4 OZ	L
35640006	AGG DEL MARIJ < 200 LBS BUT > 50 LBS	M
35640007	AGG DEL MARIJ < 2000 LBS BUT > 200 LBS	M
35640008	AGG DEL MARIJ > 2000 LBS	H
35640009	AGG DEL CS/ MARIJ PG1/PG2/PG3 TO MINOR	M
35640012	DEL MARIJ >1/4 OZ<=5LBS	L
35640012	DEL MARIJ >1/4 OZ<=5LBS	L
35640013	DEL MARIJ >5LBS<=50LBS	M
35640014	DEL MARIJ >50LBS<=2,000LBS	M
35640015	DEL MARIJ >2,000LBS	H
35640016	DEL MARIJ TO MINOR	M
35640017	DEL MARIJ >1/4 OZ<=5LBS DRUG FREE ZONE	M
35640018	DEL MARIJ <=1/4OZ REMUN DRUG FREE ZONE	M
35640018	DEL MARIJ <=1/4OZ REMUN DRUG FREE ZONE	M
35640020	DEL MARIJ >5LBS DRUG FREE ZONE	H
35700000	AMPHETAMINE-MANUFACT.	M
35710000	AMPHETAMINE-SALE	M
35720000	AMPHETAMINE-POSSESS.	L
35730000	AMPHETAMINE-DISTRIBUTE	M
35740000	AMPHETAMINE-OBTAIN	L
35800000	ILLEGAL INVESTMENT	H
35840000	DANGEROUS DRUGS-ILLEGAL INVESTMENT	M
35990000	DRUG OFFENSE-OTHER	M
35990001	MAN DEL CS PG 1 <1G	L
35990001	MAN DEL CS PG 1 <1G	L
35990002	MAN DEL CS PG 1 >=1G<4G	M
35990003	MAN DEL CS PG 1 >=4G<200G	M
35990004	MAN DEL CS PG 1 >=200G <400G	M
35990005	MAN DEL CS PG 1 >=400G	H
35990006	MAN DEL CS PG 2 < 1G	L
35990006	MAN DEL CS PG 2 < 1G	L
35990007	MAN DEL CS PG 2 >=1G<4G	M
35990008	MAN DEL CS PG 2 >=4G<400G	M
35990009	MAN DEL CS PG 2 >=400G	H
35990010	MAN DEL CS PG 3/4 < 28G	L

NCIC CODE	OFFENSE DESCRIPTION	RANK
35990010	MAN DEL CS PG 3/4 < 28G	L
35990011	MAN DEL CS PG 3/4 >=28G <200G	M
35990012	MAN DEL CS PG 3/4 >=200G<400G	M
35990013	MAN DEL CS PG 3/4 >= 400G	H
35990014	POSS CS PG 1 <1G	L
35990014	POSS CS PG 1 <1G	L
35990015	POSS CS PG 1 >=1G<4G	L
35990016	POSS CS PG 1 >=4G<200G	M
35990017	POSS CS PG 1 >=200G<400G	M
35990018	POSS CS PG 1 >=400G	H
35990019	POSS CS PG 2 < 1G	L
35990019	POSS CS PG 2 < 1G	L
35990020	POSS CS PG 2 >= 1G<4G	L
35990021	POSS CS PG 2 >= 4G<400G	M
35990022	POSS CS PG 2 >= 400G	H
35990024	POSS CS PG 3 >= 28G<200G	L
35990025	POSS CS PG 3 >=200G<400G	M
35990026	POSS CS PG 3 >= 400G	H
35990028	POSS CS PG 4 >=28G<200G	L
35990029	POSS CS PG 4 >=200G<400G	M
35990030	POSS CS PG 4 >= 400G	H
35990033	DEL CS TO MINOR	M
35990034	MAN DEL CS PG 1 <1G ANALOGUE	L
35990034	MAN DEL CS PG 1 <1G ANALOGUE	L
35990035	MAN DEL CS PG 1 >=1G<4G ANALOGUE	L
35990036	MAN DEL CS PG 1 >=4G<200G ANALOGUE	M
35990037	MAN DEL CS PG 1 >=200G<400G ANALOGUE	M
35990038	MAN DEL CS PG 1 >=400G ANALOGUE	H
35990040	POSS CS PG 1 <1G ANALOGUE	L
35990040	POSS CS PG 1 <1G ANALOGUE	L
35990041	POSS CS PG 1 >= 1G<4G ANALOGUE	L
35990042	POSS CS PG 1 >=4G<200G ANALOGUE	M
35990043	POSS CS PG 1 >=200G<400G ANALOGUE	M
35990044	POSS CS PG 1 >=400G ANALOGUE	H
35990045	MAN DEL CS PG 2 < 1G ANALOGUE	L
35990045	MAN DEL CS PG 2 < 1G ANALOGUE	L
35990046	MAN DEL CS PG 2 >= 1G < 4G ANALOGUE	L
35990047	MAN DEL CS PG 2 >= 4G <400G ANALOGUE	M
35990048	MAN DEL CS PG 2 >= 400G ANALOGUE	H
35990049	POSS CS PG 2 <1G ANALOGUE	L
35990049	POSS CS PG 2 <1G ANALOGUE	L
35990050	POSS CS PG 2 >= 1G<4G ANALOGUE	L

NCIC CODE	OFFENSE DESCRIPTION	RANK
35990051	POSS CS PG 2 >= 4G<400G ANALOGUE	M
35990052	POSS CS PG 2 >= 400G ANALOGUE	H
35990056	ILLEGAL EXPEND/INVEST DRUG MONEY	H
35990057	UNAUTH DISCLOUSURE INFO FROM TRIPLET PERSCRIPT	L
35990057	UNAUTH DISCLOUSURE INFO FROM TRIPLET PERSCRIPT	L
35990058	COMM MATTERS REGISTRANT/DISPENSER	L
35990058	COMM MATTERS REGISTRANT/DISPENSER	L
35990059	FRAUD REGISTRANT ORDER FORM SCH I/II	M
35990060	FRAUD REGISTRANT ORDER FORM SCH III/IV	L
35990064	FRAUD DEL PRESCRIPT NOT MEDICAL PURPOSE	M
35990065	FRAUD DEL PRESCRIPT NOT MEDIC PURP SCH II	M
35990066	FRAUD DEL PRESCRIPT NOT MEDIC PURP SCH III/IV/	L
35990067	FRAUD POSS CS PRESCRIPT	L
35990067	FRAUD POSS CS PRESCRIPT	L
35990068	FRAUD POSS CS PRESCRIPT SCH II/III	L
35990068	FRAUD POSS CS PRESCRIPT SCH II/III	L
35990070	DIVERSION OF CS PROPERTY OR PLANT	L
35990070	DIVERSION OF CS PROPERTY OR PLANT	L
35990073	UNL DEL/MAN W/INT SIMULATED CS	L
35990073	UNL DEL/MAN W/INT SIMULATED CS	L
35990074	MAN DEL SIM CS REPREST TO BE CS MISLEAD PERS	L
35990074	MAN DEL SIM CS REPREST TO BE CS MISLEAD PERS	L
35990075	REPRESENT SIM SUBST TO BE CS TO THIRD PARTY	L
35990075	REPRESENT SIM SUBST TO BE CS TO THIRD PARTY	L
35990076	UNL POSS DANGEROUS DRUG	L
35990077	POSS DANGER DRUG FOR PURPOSE OF SELLING	M
35990078	DEL OFFER DEL OF DANGEROUS DRUG	L
35990078	DEL OFFER DEL OF DANGEROUS DRUG	L
35990079	MAN DANGEROUS DRUG	L
35990079	MAN DANGEROUS DRUG	L
35990087	OBTAIN DANGER DRUG BY FRAUD TELEPHONE CALL ENH	L
35990109	DEL ABUSABLE GLUE/AEROSOL PAINT TO MINOR	L
35990109	DEL ABUSABLE GLUE/AEROSOL PAINT TO MINOR	L
35990112	PROH SUBSTANCE IN CORRECTIONAL FACILITY	M
35990112	ATT PROH SUBSTANCE IN CORRECTIONAL FACILITY	L
35990115	FRAUD CS REGISTRATION NUMBER SCH I/II	M
35990116	FRAUD CS REGISTRATION NUMBER SCH III/IV	L
35990118	FRAUD TRIPLET PRESCRIPTION FORM SCH I/II	M
35990119	FRAUD TRIPLET PRESCRIPTION FORM SCH III/IV	L
35990121	POSS CS BY FRAUD SCH I/II	M
35990122	POSS CS BY FRAUD SCH III/IV	L
35990122	ATTEMPTED POSS CS BY FRAUD SCH III/IV	L

NCIC CODE	OFFENSE DESCRIPTION	RANK
35990124	MAN DEL CS PG 1 <1G DRUG FREE ZONE	M
35990125	MAN DEL CS PG 2 <1G DRUG FREE ZONE	M
35990126	MAN/DEL CS PG 3/4 < 28 G	L
35990126	MAN DEL CS PG 3/4 <28G DRUG FREE ZONE	M
35990127	POSS CS PG 1 <1G DRUG FREE ZONE	L
35990128	POSS CS PG 2 <1G DRUG FREE ZONE	L
35990129	POSS CS PG 3 <28G DRUG FREE ZONE	L
35990129	POSS CS PG 3 <28G DRUG FREE ZONE	L
35990130	MAN DEL CS NOT IN PG DRUG FREE ZONE	L
35990130	MAN DEL CS NOT IN PG DRUG FREE ZONE	L
35990134	MAN DEL CS PG 1A <20 AU	L
35990135	MAN DEL CS PG 1A >=20<80AU	L
35990136	MAN DEL CS PG 1A >=80<4,000AU	M
35990137	MAN DEL CS PG 1A >=4000AU	H
35990138	POSS CS PG 1A <20AU	L
35990139	POSS CS PG 1A >=20<80AU	L
35990140	POSS CS PG 1A >=80<4,000AU	M
35990141	POSS CS PG 1A >=4000<8,000AU	H
35990142	POSS CS PG 1A >=8000AU	H+
35990143	MAN DEL CS PG 1A <20AU ANALOGUE	L
35990144	MANDEL CS PG 1A >=20AU ANALOGUE	L
35990145	MAN DEL CS ANALOGUE PG 1A >=80<4,000AU	M
35990146	MAN DEL CS ANALOGUE PG 1A >=4,000	H
35990147	POSS CS PG 1A <20AU ANALOGUE	L
35990148	POSS CS PG 1A >=20<80AU ANALOGUE	L
35990149	POSS CS PG 1A >=80AU ANALOGUE	M
35990150	POSS CS PG 1A >=4,000AU ANALOGUE	H
35990151	POSS CS PG 1A >=8,000AU ANALOGUE	H+
35990152	TRANSF RECEIPT CHEMICAL PRECURSOR	L
35990153	TRANSF RECEIPT CHEMICAL PRECURSOR ENH	M
35990154	TRANSF PRECURSOR SUBSTANCE UNL MAN	M
35990155	TRANSF CHEMICAL LAB APPARATUS FOR UNL MAN	M
35990156	MAN DEL CS PG 1 >=1G DRUG FREE ZONE	M
35990157	MAN DEL CS PG 2 >=1G DRUG FREE ZONE	M
35990158	MAN DEL CS PG 3/4 >=28G DRUG FREE ZONE	H
35990159	POSS CS PG 1 >1G DRUG FREE ZONE	M
35990160	POSS CS PG 2 >=1G DRUG FREE ZONE	M
35990161	POSS CS PG 3 >=1G DRUG FREE ZONE	M
35990162	POSS CS PG 4 >=28G DRUG FREE ZONE	M
35990163	MAN DEL CS PG 1 >=1G DRUG FREE ZONE	M
35990164	MAN DEL CS PG 2 >=1G DRUG FREE ZONE	M
35990165	MAN DEL CS PG 3/4 >=28G DRUG FREE ZONE	H

NCIC CODE	OFFENSE DESCRIPTION	RANK
35990166	DEL MARIJ >=5 LBS DRUG FREE ZONE	H
35990167	DEL TO MINOR CS AT A BUSINESS	L
35990168	DEL TO MINOR CS ON SCHOOL PREMISES	M
35990169	DEL CS/MARIJ TO MINOR	M
35990170	FAIL TO COMPLY W/DRUG REGISTRATION LAW	L
35990172	MAN DEL CS PG 1 USE OF CHILD	M
35990173	MAN DEL CS PG 1A USE OF CHILD	M
35990174	MAN DEL CS PG 2 USE OF CHILD	M
35990175	MAN DEL CS PG 3/4 USE OF CHILD	M
35990176	DEL MARIJ W/USE OF CHILD	M
35990177	DEL CS/MARIJ TO MINOR W/USE OF CHILD	M
35990179	DEL TO MINOR VOLATILE CHEM	L
35990185	POSS TRANSP CHEM W/INT MAN CS PG 1/1A	M
35990186	POSS TRANSP CHEM W/INT MAN CS PG 2	M
35990187	POSS TRANSP CHEM W/INT MAN CS PG 3/4	L
35990190	FRAUD POSS CS/PRESCRIPTION SCH I/II	M
35990191	FRAUD POSS CS/PRESCRIPTION SCH III/IV	L
35990194	FRAUD DEL CS/PRESCRIPTION SCH II	M
35990195	FRAUD DEL CS/PRESCRIPTION SCH III/IV/V	L
35990196	FRAUD POSS CS PRESCRIPTION SCH II/III	L
35990202	ILLEGAL BARTER/EXPENDITURE OF PROPERTY/FINANCE	H
35990203	ILLEGAL BARTER/EXPEND INVEST IN MARIJ>50LBS<2K	M
35990204	AREA QUARANTINE FOR ENVIROMENTAL/TOXIC AGENT	L
35990206	MAN DEL CS PG 1A >= 80 AU <4,000 AU ANALOGUE	M
35990207	MAN DEL CS PG 1A =>4,000 AU ANALOGUE	H
35990208	PROH SUB CORR FACIL-POSS DEADLY WEAPON	H
35990209	PROH SUB CORR FACIL-ALCOHOL/DRUG/PHONE/TOBACCO	M
35990211	PROH SUB CORR FACIL-ATTEMPT	L
35990212	PROH SUB CORR FACIL-PROV DEADLY WEAPON	H
35993333	MAN DEL SELL/POSS CONTROLLED SUBSTANCE	M
35993334	MAN DEL SELL/POSS CS/MARIJ DRUG FREE ZONE	M
36000000	SEX OFFENSE	H
36000001	INCEST/PROHIBITED SEXUAL CONDUCT	H
36010000	SEX OFFENSE-AGAINST CHILD-FONDLING	H
36010001	INDECENCY W/CHILD SEXUAL CONTACT	H
36010002	INDECENCY W/A CHILD EXPOSURE	M
36010002	ATT INDECENCY W/A CHILD EXPOSES	L
36010003	SEXUAL PERFORM CHILD EMPLOY INDUCE/AUTHORIZE	H
36010004	SEXUAL PERFORM CHILD PRODUCE/DIRECT/PROMOTE	H
36020000	HOMOSEXUAL ACT WITH GIRL	H
36030000	HOMOSEXUAL ACT WITH BOY	H
36040000	INCEST WITH MINOR	H

NCIC CODE	OFFENSE DESCRIPTION	RANK
36050000	INDECENT EXPOSURE	M
36060000	BESTIALITY	M
36070000	INCEST WITH ADULT	L
36080000	SEDUCTION OF ADULT	L
36090000	HOMOSEXUAL ACT WITH WOMAN	L
36100000	HOMOSEXUAL ACT WITH MAN	L
36110000	PEEPING TOM	M
36120000	INCEST	H
36120001	FAIL TO REGISTER AS SEX OFFENDER	L
36120002	FAIL TO REGISTER AS SEX OFFENDER ENH	M
36120003	SEX OFFENDERS FAILURE TO COMPLY/CIVIL	M
36120004	SEX OFFENDERS DUTY TO REGISTER 10YRS	L
36120005	SEX OFFENDERS DUTY TO REGISTER LIFE/ANNUALLY	M
36120006	SEX OFFENDERS DUTY TO REGISTER LIFE/90 DAY	M
36120007	SEX OFFENDERS DUTY TO REGISTER W/PREV CONV	M
36130000	SODOMY	L
36140000	INDECENCY/EXPOSURE/ATT/INTENT/CONSP (SB 45 CASES	H
36140000	INDECENCY/EXPOSURE/ATT/INTENT/CONSP (NON-SB 45	M
36200002	FAIL TO REGISTER AS SEX OFFENDER ENH	M
36990000	SEX OFFENSES-OTHER	H
36990002	PROH SEXUAL CONDUCT	H
36990004	IMPROP PHOT/VISUAL RECORD TO AROUSE/GRATIFY	L
36990005	SEX OFFENDERS FAILURE TO COMPLY/CIVIL	M
36990006	SEX OFFENDERS DUTY TO REGISTER 10YRS	L
36990007	SEX OFFENDERS DUTY TO REGISTER LIFE/ANNUALLY	M
36990008	SEX OFFENDERS DUTY TO REGISTER LIFE/90 DAY	M
36990009	SEX OFFENDERS DUTY TO REGISTER W/PREV CONV	M
36990010	IMPROPER PHOTO/VISUAL RECORD TO AROUSE/GRATIFY	L
36990013	INDECENCY W/A CHILD EXPOSES	M
36990014	SEXUAL PERFORM CHILD EMPLOY INDUCE/AUTHORIZE	H
36990015	SEXUAL PERFORM CHILD PRODUCE/DIRECT/PROMOTE	H
36990016	IMPROPER PHOTO/VISUAL RECORDING W/OUT CONSENT	L
36990017	ONLINE SOLICIT MINOR TO AROUSE/GRATIFY	L
36990018	ONLINE SOLICIT MINOR TO MEET W/INT SEX/CONTACT	H
36990019	ONLINE SOLICIT MINOR UNDER 14 YOA	H
36990020	PROH SEXUAL CONDUCT WITH ANCESTOR/DESCENDANT	M
36990022	ONLINE SOLICIT MINOR	M
36990023	ONLINE SOLICIT MINOR UNDER 14	H
36990024	ONLINE SOLICIT MINOR SEX CONDUCT	H
36990025	SEXUAL PERF BY CHILD <14 YRS EMPLOY/DIR/PROMO	H+
36990026	SEXUAL PERF BY CHILD <14 YRS PRODUCE/DIR/PROMO	H
36990027	SEXUAL PERF BY CHILD EMPLOY/INDUCE/AUTHORIZE	L

NCIC CODE	OFFENSE DESCRIPTION	RANK
37000000	OBSCENE MATERIAL	L
37000002	USES MINOR IN SELL/DISTR/DISPLAY HARMF MATER	M
37010000	OBSCENE MATERIAL-MFR	M
37020000	OBSCENE MATERIAL-SELL	L
37020001	OBSCENITY WHOLESALE PROMOTION	L
37020003	SELL DISTB/DISPLAY HARMFUL ACT BY/MINOR	M
37030000	OBSCENE MATERIAL-MAILING	L
37040000	OBSCENE MATERIAL-POSSESS	L
37040001	ATTEMPT OF POSS OR PROMOTION OF CHILD PORNO	L
37040001	POSS OF CHILD PORNOGRAPHY	H
37040002	POSS W/INT TO PROMOTE CHILD PORNOGRAPHY	H
37040003	OBSCENE WHOLESALE PROMOTION	L
37040004	OBSCENE WHOLESALE PROMOTION W/DEVIANT SEX ACTS	L
37040006	OBSCENE PROMOTE/PROD/DIRECT W/DEVIANT SEX ACT	L
37050000	OBSCENE MATERIAL-DISTRIB	L
37060000	OBSCENE MATERIAL-TRANSPORT	L
37070000	OBSCENE COMMUNICATION	L
37990000	OBSCENITY	L
37990001	OBSCENE WHOLESALE PROMOTION	L
37990001	OBSCENE WHOLESALE PROMOTION	L
38000000	FAMILY OFFENSE	M
38000003	VIOL OF PROTECTIVE ORDER ENH	M
38010000	NEGLECT FAMILY	M
38010002	CHILD ABUSE/NEGLECT FALSE REPORT W/INT	L
38010003	CHILD ABUSE/NEGLECT FAL REPORT W/INT+PREV CONV	L
38020000	CRUELTY TOWARD CHILD	M
38030000	CRUELTY TOWARD WIFE	M
38040000	BIGAMY	L
38040001	BIGAMY	L
38040003	BIGAMY	L
38040004	BIGAMY PROH/PURPORT SPOUSE IS/OVER 16YOA	M
38040005	BIGAMY PROH/PURPORT SPOUSE UNDER 16YOA	H
38050000	CONTRIB DELINQ MINOR	L
38060000	NEGLECT CHILD	M
38060001	ABANDON ENDANGER CHILD IMMINENT DANGER BI	H
38060003	ABANDON ENDANGER CHILD W/O INTENT TO RETURN	M
38060005	CRIMINAL NONSUPPORT PREV CONV OR OTHER STATE	L
38060008	INTERFER W/CHILD CUSTODY	L
38060009	ABANDON ENDANGER CHILD CRIMINAL NEGLIGENCE	L
38060009	ABANDON ENDANGER CHILD CRIMINAL NEGLIGENCE	L
38060010	INTERFER W/CHILD CUSTODY	L
38060010	INTERFER W/CHILD CUSTODY	L

NCIC CODE	OFFENSE DESCRIPTION	RANK
38060011	CRIMINAL NONSUPPORT	L
38060011	CRIMINAL NONSUPPORT	L
38060012	ABANDON ENDANGER CHILD W/ INTENT TO RETURN	L
38060012	ABANDON ENDANGER CHILD W/ INTENT TO RETURN	L
38070000	NON-SUPPORT	L
38080000	NONSUPPORT OF PARENT	L
38090000	SALE OF A CHILD	H
38990000	FAMILY OFFENSE-OTHER	M
38990001	VIOL OF PROTECTIVE ORDER	M
38990003	PERPETRATOR OF CHILD RETURNS ENH	M
38990004	VIOL OF PROTECTIVE ORDER ENH	M
38990004	VIOL OF PROTECTIVE ORDER ENH	M
38990007	VIOL OF PROTECTIVE ORDER 2+ PREV CONVIC	M
38990008	VIOL OF PROTECTIVE ORDER/ASSAULT/STALKING	M
38990010	FALSE REPORT OF ABUSE/NEGLECT ENH	L
38990014	VIOL PROTECT ORDER BIAS/PREJUDICE W/2+PREV CON	M
38990015	VIOL OF PROTECTIVE ORDER BY ASSAULT/STALKING	M
38990018	VIOL BOND/PROTECTIVE ORDER 2+ PREV CONVICTIONS	M
38990019	VIOL BOND/PROTECTIVE ORDER ASSAULT/STALKING	M
38990020	FAIL TO REPORT ABUSE/NEGLECT CHILD STATE FACIL	L
38990021	FAIL TO REPORT ABUSE/NEGLECT ELD/DIS STATE FAC	L
39000000	GAMBLING	L
39000001	GAMBLING PROMOTION	L
39000002	ILLEGAL RACES COND ON CERTAIN INDIAN LAND	L
39000003	TOUTING	L
39000004	TOUTING ENH	L
39000005	TOUTING FROM OWNER/TRAINER/JOCKEY/EMPLOYEE	L
39000006	UNL USE CREDENTIAL ISSD BY RACING COMM	L
39000008	RACING ACT	L
39010000	GAMBLING	L
39020000	CARD GAME-OPERATING	L
39030000	CARD GAME-PLAYING	L
39040000	CARD GAME	L
39050000	DICE GAME-OPERATING	L
39060000	DICE GAME-PLAYING	L
39070000	DICE GAME	L
39080000	GAMGLING DEVICE-POSSESS	L
39080001	POSS GAMBLING DEVICE OR EQUIPMENT	L
39090000	GAMBLING DEVICE-TRANSPORT	L
39100000	GAMBLING DEVICE-NOT REGISTERED	L
39110000	GAMBLING DEVICE	L
39120000	GAMBLING GOODS-POSSESS	L

NCIC CODE	OFFENSE DESCRIPTION	RANK
39130000	GAMBLING GOODS-TRANSPORT	L
39140000	GAMBLING GOODS	L
39150000	LOTTERY-OPERATING	L
39160000	LOTTERY-RUNNER	L
39170000	LOTTERY-PLAYING	L
39180000	LOTTERY	L
39180006	UNAUTH PERSON I/K SELL LOTTERY TICKET	L
39180010	SELL LOTTERY TICKET UNAUTH PERSON	L
39190000	SPORTS TAMPERING	L
39190001	UNL INFLUENCE ON RACING	L
39200000	TRANSMIT WAGER INFORMATION	L
39200001	COMMUNICATION GAMBLING INFORMATION	L
39210000	ESTABLISH GAMBLING PLACE	L
39210001	KEEPING A GAMBLING PLACE	L
39220000	GAMBLING	L
39250000	GAMBLING PROMOTION	L
39990000	GAMBLING-OTHER	L
39990003	RACING ACT	L
39990009	RACING ACT	L
40000000	COMMERCIAL SEX	L
40010000	KEEPING HOUSE ILL FAME	L
40020000	PROCURE FOR PROSTITUTE	L
40020002	AGG PROMOTION OF PROSTITUTION	M
40030000	COMMERCIAL SEX-HOMOSEXUAL PROSTITUTION	L
40040000	PROSTITUTION	L
40040001	COMPELLING PROSTITUTION BY FORCE/THREAT	H
40040004	COMPELLING PROSTITUTION VICTIM UNDER 17 YOA	H
40040006	PROSTITUTION W/3RD OR MORE	L
40050000	FREQUENT HOUSE ILL FAME	L
40060000	TRNSP FEMALE INTERSTATE FOR IMMORAL PURP	L
40070000	AGGREVATED PROMOTION OF PROSTITUTION	M
40080000	COMPELLING PROSTITUTION	H
40990000	COMMERCIAL SEX	L
41000000	LIQUOR	L
41010000	LIQUOR-MFR	L
41020000	LIQUOR-SELL	L
41020030	ALCOHOLIC BEVERAGE IN DRY AREA 2+ TIMES	L
41030000	LIQUOR TRANSPORT	L
41030006	OUT-OF-STATE-WINE SHIPPER PERMIT 3RD VIOL	L
41040000	LIQUOR-POSSESS	L
41050000	MISREPRESENTING AGE-MINOR	L
41990000	LIQUOR	L

NCIC CODE	OFFENSE DESCRIPTION	RANK
42000000	DRUNKENNESS	L
42990000	DRUNKENNESS	L
48000000	OBSTRUCT POLICE	L
48000005	HINDER APPREH/PROSECUTION KNOWN FELON	H
48010000	RESISTING OFFICER	L
48010003	EVADING ARREST OR DETENTION SBI	H
48010007	RESIST ARREST SEARCH OR TRANSPORT DEADLY WPN	H
48010012	EVADING ARREST/DETENTION W/VEH	L
48010013	EVADING ARREST DET W/VEH W/PREV CONVIC OR SBI	M
48010014	EVADING ARREST/DETENTION W/VEH CAUSING DEATH	H
48010015	EVADING ARREST DETENTION W/PREV CONVICTION	L
48010016	EVADING ARREST DETENTION W/VEH	L
48020000	OBSTRUCT CRIMINAL INVEST	L
48020001	INTERFER W/POLICE SERV ANIMAL KILLING	M
48020004	INTERFER W/POLICE SERV ANIMAL INJURY	L
48030000	MAKING FALSE REPORT	L
48030001	FALSE INFORM SUPPRESSING EVIDENCE	L
48030003	REPORT SEIZURE- FALSE STATEMENT	L
48040000	EVIDENCE-DESTROYING	M
48040002	TAMPER/FABRICATE PHYSICAL EVIDENCE	L
48050000	WITNESS-DISSUADING	L
48060000	WITNESS-DECEIVING	L
48070000	REFUSING TO AID OFFICER	L
48080000	COMPOUNDING CRIME	L
48090000	UNAUTH COMMUNICATION WITH PRISONER	L
48100000	ILLEGAL ARREST	L
48110000	CROSSING POLICE LINES	L
48120000	FAILURE REPORT CRIME	L
48130000	FAILING TO MOVE ON	L
48140000	RESISTING ARREST	L
48990000	OBSTRUCT POLICE	L
48990003	HINDER APPREH/PROS KNOWN FELON SEX OFFENDER	H
48990003	ATT HINDERING APPREH/PROS KNOWN FELON	L
48990010	HINDER APPREHENSION OR PROSECUTION KNOWN FELON	H
48990011	HINDERING APPREH/PROS KNOWN FELON SEX OFFENDER	H
49000000	ESCAPE	H
49010000	ESCAPE	H
49010001	ESCAPE FROM CUST FEL ARREST OR PENAL INSTIT	H
49010003	ESCAPE FROM CUSTODY THREATEN USE OF DW	H+
49010005	IMPLEMENTS FOR ESCAPE DEADLY WEAPON	H
49010006	INTRODUCE/PROVIDE IMPLEMENTS FOR ESCAPE	M
49010008	PERM OR FACILITATING ESCAPE FELONY	M

NCIC CODE	OFFENSE DESCRIPTION	RANK
49020000	FLIGHT TO AVOID	L
49020001	EVADING ARREST/DETENTION SBI/DEATH	H+
49020002	EVADING ARREST/DET USING VEH	L
49020002	EVADING ARREST/DET USING VEH PREV CONV	M
49020003	EVADING ARREST/DETENTION SBI	H
49020004	EVADING ARREST/DETENTION CAUSE DEATH OF ANOTHE	H+
49030000	AIDING PRISONER ESCAPE	H
49030002	PERM FACILITATE ESCAPE CORRECTION FACILITY	H
49030003	PERM/FACILIT ESCAPE CONFINED CORR FACILITY	H
49030004	PERM FACILITATE ESCAPE DEADLY WEAPON	H+
49030005	PERM/FACILIT ESCAPE CONFINED SECURE INSTIT	H
49030006	IMPLEMENTS FOR ESCAPE	H
49030007	IMPLEMENTS FOR ESCAPE DEADLY WEAPON	M
49040000	HARBORING	L
49050000	ATTEMPT TO ESCAPE	M
49990000	ESCAPE-OTHER	H
49990001	ESCAPE FROM CUSTODY	L
49990002	ESCAPE WHILE ARRESTED/CONFINED FELONY	M
49990002	ATT ESCAPE WHILE ARRESTED/CONFINED	L
49990003	ESCAPE CAUSE BODILY INJ	H
49990004	ESCAPE CAUSE SBI/THREAT OF DEADLY WPN	H+
49990005	UNAUTH ABSENCE FROM COMMUNITY CORR	L
49990005	UNAUTH ABSENCE FROM COMMUNITY CORR	L
50000000	OBSTRUCT	L
50000005	TAMPER WITH WITNESS	L
50000009	PROH CONFLICTS OF INTEREST	L
50010000	BAIL-SECURED BOND	L
50020000	BAIL-PERSONAL RECOG	L
50030000	PERJURY	L
50030002	AGG PERJURY	M
50040000	PERJURY-SUBORNATION OF	M
50050000	CONTEMPT OF COURT	L
50060000	OBSTRUCTING JUSTICE	L
50060001	TAMPER W/WITNESS	L
50060001	TAMPER W/WITNESS	L
50070000	OBSTRUCTING COURT ORDER	L
50080000	MISCONDUCT-JUDIC OFFICER	L
50090000	CONTEMPT OF CONGRESS	L
50100000	CONTEMPT OF LEGISLATURE	L
50110000	PAROLE VIOLATION	L
50120000	PROB VIOLATION	L
50130000	CONDIT RELEASE VIOLATION	L

NCIC CODE	OFFENSE DESCRIPTION	RANK
50130001	UNAUTH ABSENCE COMMUNITY CORRECTION FACILITY	L
50130001	UNAUTH ABSENCE COMMUNITY CORRECTION FACILITY	L
50140000	MANDATORY RELEASE VIOLATION	L
50150000	FAILURE TO APPEAR	L
50150002	BAIL JUMPING AND FAIL TO APPEAR FELONY	L
50150004	BAIL JUMPING AND FAIL TO APPEAR FELONY	L
50150004	ATTEMPTED BAIL JUMPING	L
50200000	ABUSE OF OFFICE	L
50200020	INSPECT TOBACCO PRODUCT STORAGE/PROCUCT FACILI	L
50200038	REF TO ALLOW INSPECT OF TOBACCO PROD CARGO	L
50200046	REF TO PERM INSPECTION OF CIGARETTE FACIL	L
50200053	INSPECT CIGARETTE FACILITY	L
50990000	OBSTRUCT-OTHER	L
50990004	PROH CONFLICTS OF INTEREST	L
50990011	INSPECT TOBACCO PRODUCT STORAGE FACILITY	L
50990019	INSPECT CIGARETTE FACILITY	L
51000000	BRIBERY	L
51000001	BRIBERY	L
51000002	COERCION	L
51000003	COMM BRIBERY	L
51000005	OFFER TO PAY FOR SECURING/SOLICITING PATIENTS	L
51010000	BRIBE-GIVING	L
51010001	BRIBE PERSON ASSOCIATED W/HORSE/DOG RACE ENH	L
51010002	BRIBE PERSON ASSOCIATED W/HORSE/DOG RACE	L
51020000	BRIBE-OFFERING	L
51020001	LEGISLATIVE BRIBERY PROMISE/THREAT	L
51020002	LEGISLATIVE BRIBERY-THREAT	L
51030000	BRIBE-RECEIVING	L
51030001	ACCEPT BRIBE PERS ASSOC W/ HORSE/DOG RACE ENH	L
51030002	ACCEPT BRIBE BY PERSON ASSOC W/ HORSE/DOG RACE	L
51030003	DIRECTOR EMPLOYEE ACCEPTING BONUSES	L
51040000	BRIBE	L
51050000	CONFLICT OF INTEREST	L
51060000	GRATUITY-GIVING	L
51060001	PROH GIFT OR GRATUITY MEMBER OF GOVT AGENCY	L
51070000	GRATUITY-OFFERING	L
51080000	GRATUITY-RECEIVING	L
51090000	GRATUITY	L
51100000	KICKBACK-GIVING	L
51110000	KICKBACK-OFFERING	L
51120000	KICKBACK-RECEIVING	L
51130000	KICKBACK	L

NCIC CODE	OFFENSE DESCRIPTION	RANK
51140000	BRIBE/GIVING/OFFERING/RECEIVING	L
51990000	BRIBERY-OTHER	L
51990017	COMMERCIAL BRIBERY	L
51990017	COMMERCIAL BRIBERY	L
51990018	BRIBERY	L
51990020	COERCION	L
51990020	BRIBERY & CORRUPT INFLUENCE	L
51990021	BRIBERY & CORRUPT INFLUENCE/STEWARD/JUDGE/ECT	L
51990033	UNL CONTRIBUTION/EXPENDITURE BY COMMITTEE	L
51990034	UNL CONTRIBUTION/EXPENDITURE BY CORP/LABOR ORG	L
52000000	WEAPON OFFENSE	M
52000001	DEADLY WEAPON IN PENAL INSTITUTION	H
52000002	EXHIBIT FIREARM ANY PORTION PUB/PRIV SCHOOL	H
52000004	TAKE WEAPON OR ATTEMPT FROM PEACE OFFICER	M
52003333	WEAPONS VIOL IN WEAPON FREE ZONE	M
52010000	ALTERING IDENTIFICATION ON	L
52020000	CARRYING CONCEALED	M
52020002	UNL CARRY HANDGUN LIC HOLDER ALCH PREM/CORR FA	M
52030000	CARRYING, POSSESSION OF WEAPON	M
52030002	PROH WEAPONS	M
52030005	UNL CARRYING WEAPON ON ALCOHOL PREMISES	H
52030006	UNL CARRYING WEAPON RESTRICTED PREMISES	H
52030007	UNL POSS FIREARM BY FELON	M
52030009	PLACE WEAPONS PROHIBITED	H
52030010	PROH WEAPON	M
52030012	UNL POSS FIREARM BY FELON	M
52030012	ATT UNL POSS FIREARM BY FELON	L
52030013	DEADLY WEAPON IN PENAL INSTITUTION	H
52030014	UNL CARRYING WEAPON ON ALCOHOL PREMISES	H
52030015	EXHIBIT FIREARMS ON CAMPUS OR SCHOOL BUS	H
52030016	PROH WEAPONS/WEAPONS FREE ZONE	M
52030017	PROH WPN SWITCHBLADE/KNUCKLE WEAPONS FREE ZONE	L
52030018	UNL CARRY WEAPON/WEAPONS FREE ZONE	L
52030020	UNL POSS METAL OR BODY ARMOR BY FELON	L
52030021	TAKE WEAPON FROM AN OFFICER	L
52030022	ATTEMPT TO TAKE WEAPON FROM AN OFFICER	L
52030022	ATTEMPT TO TAKE WEAPON FROM AN OFFICER	L
52030024	UNL POSS FIREARM BY FELON	M
52040000	EXPLOSIVES-TEACHING USE	H
52050000	EXPLOSIVES-TRANSPORTING	H
52060000	EXPLOSIVES-USING	H
52070000	INCENDIARY DEVICE-POSSESS	H

NCIC CODE	OFFENSE DESCRIPTION	RANK
52080000	INCENDIARY DEVICE-USING	H
52090000	INCENDIARY DEVICE-TEACHING USE	H
52100000	LICENSING-REGISTRATION	M
52110000	EXPLOSIVES-POSSESSING	H
52110001	COMPONENTS OF EXPLOSIVES	H
52110003	COMPONENTS OF EXPLOSIVES	H
52110004	COMPONENTS OF EXPLOSIVES WEAPONS FREE ZONE	H
52120000	POSSESSION OF	M
52120001	POSS ELECTRICITY PROD DEVICE >TWO PREV CONV	L
52120004	POSS FIREARM W/O PERM ENH	M
52120006	UNL POSS FIREARM BY FELON WEAPONS FREE ZONE	H
52120006	UNL POSS FIREARM BY FELON WEAPONS FREE ZONE	H
52120007	UNL POSS FIREARM BY FELON WEAPONS FREE ZONE	H
52130000	FIRING	M
52130005	DEADLY CONDUCT DISCHARGE FIREARM	H
52130005	ATT DEADLY CONDUCT DISCH FIREARM	L
52130006	DEADLY CONDUCT DISCH FIREARM HAB/BUILD/VEH	H
52130006	ATT DEADLY COND DISCH FIREARM	L
52140000	SELLING	M
52140001	MAN SELL FISH SHOCKING DEVICE >TWO PREV CONV	L
52140004	UNL TRANSF OF CERTAIN WEAPONS	L
52140005	UNL TRANSF HANDGUN UNDER 18YOA	L
52140006	UNL TRANSF CERTAIN WEAPONS/WEAPONS FREE ZONE	L
52140007	UNL TRANSF CERTAIN WPNS U/18 WEAPONS FREE ZONE	M
52150000	THREAT TO BOMB	H
52150002	HOAX BOMB WEAPONS FREE ZONE	L
52160000	THREAT TO BURN	H
52170001	FIREARM SMUGGLING	M
52170002	FIREARM SMUGGLING 3 OR MORE FIREARMS	H
52180000	POSSESSION, USE OF BOMB	H
52190000	SALE, ILLEGAL FIREARM	H
52990000	WEAPON OFFENSE-OTHER	M
52990001	TAKE WEAPON FROM PEACE OFFICER	L
52990001	TAKE WEAPON FROM PEACE OFFICER	L
52990004	TAKE OR ATTEMPT TO TAKE WEAPON FROM AN OFFICER	L
53000000	PUBLIC PEACE	L
53000004	INTERFER W/EMERG COMMUN SBI OR LOSS >$1,000	M
53000009	STALKING ENH	M
53010000	ANARCHISM	M
53020000	RIOT-INCITING	M
53030000	RIOT-ENGAGING IN	L
53040000	RIOT-INTERFERE FIREMAN	M

NCIC CODE	OFFENSE DESCRIPTION	RANK
53050000	RIOT-INTERFERE OFFICER	M
53060000	RIOT	M
53060003	RIOT PARTICIPATION	L
53060003	RIOT PARTICIPATION	L
53060004	RIOT PARTICIPATION	M
53060005	RIOT PARTICIPATION	H
53060006	RIOT PARTICIPATION	H
53070000	ASSEMBLY-UNLAWFUL	L
53080000	FALSE FIRE ALARM	L
53080002	FALSE ALARM OR REPORT EMERGENCY	L
53080002	FALSE ALARM OR REPORT EMERGENCY	L
53090000	HARASSING COMMUNICATION	L
53090002	HARRASSMENT ENH	L
53090003	ONLINE HARRASSMENT-NAME/PERSONA TO CREATE PAGE	L
53090005	ONLINE HARASS-W/IDENT INFO SOLICIT EMS	L
53100000	DESECRATING FLAG	L
53110000	DISORD CONDUCT	L
53110005	REPEAT/HABITUAL FELONY OFFENDERS	L
53120000	DISTURB PEACE	L
53130000	CURFEW	L
53140000	LOITERING	L
53990000	PUBLIC PEACE	L
53990006	STALKING ENH	M
53990011	INTERFER W/EMERGENCY CALL W/PREV CONVIC	L
53990014	FALSE ALARM OR REPORT EMERGENCY	L
54000000	TRAFFIC OFFENSE	L
54000001	FAIL SURRENDER UNEXPIRED LIC PLATE/CERTIF ENH	L
54000016	REF STOP MOTR VEHC WHILE TRANSP TOBACCO PROD	L
54010000	HIT AND RUN/FAILURE TO STOP AND AID	M
54010001	FAIL TO STOP AND RENDER AID	M
54010001	ATTEMPTED FAIL TO STOP AND RENDER AID	L
54010003	ACCIDENT INVOLVING INJ/DEATH	H
54010003	ATT FAIL TO STOP AND RENDER AID INJ/DEATH	L
54010005	ACCIDENT INVOLVING SBI/DEATH	H
54010007	ACCIDENT INVOLVING INJURY	M
54020000	TRANSP DANGEROUS MATERIAL	M
54020004	POSS TRANSP ANHYDROUS AMMONIA	L
54020005	POSS TRANSP ANHYDROUS AMMONIA	L
54020006	POSS TRAN ANHYDROUS AMMONIA USE/TAMPER W/EQUIP	M
54030000	DRIVING UNDER INFLUENCE DRUGS	L
54040000	DWI (LIQUOR AND DRUGS)	L
54040005	DRIVING WHILE INTOXICATED 3RD	L

NCIC CODE	OFFENSE DESCRIPTION	RANK
54040006	DRIVING WHILE INTOXICATED 3RD OR MORE W/ SBI	M
54040008	OP VESSEL WHILE INTOXICATED ENH	L
54040011	DRIVING WHILE INTOXICATED 3RD OR MORE	L
54040017	DRIVING WHILE INTOX/OPEN ALCH CONT 3RD/MORE	L
54040020	DWI W/PREVIOUS INTOXICATION MANSLAUGHTER CONV	M
54040021	INTOX ASSLT CAUSE SBI PEACE OFC/FIREFIGHT/EMS	H
54050000	MOVING TRAFFIC VIOL	L
54060000	NONMOVING TRAFFIC VIOL	L
54990000	TRAFFIC OFFENSE-OTHER	L
54990003	BOATING WHILE INTOXICATED 3RD OR MORE	L
54990006	FLYING WHILE INTOXICATED 3RD OR MORE	L
54990033	RACING ON HIGHWAY W/2 PREV CONV	L
54990034	RACING ON HIGHWAY CAUSING BODILY INJURY	L
54990035	RACING ON HIGHWAY CAUSING SERIOUS BODILY INJ	M
54990045	VOLUNTARY ADOPTION REGISTRIES DISCLOSES RECORD	M
54990048	PROVIDING FAL INFO ON VOTING APPLICATION	L
54990050	DRIVING WHILE INTOXICATED W/CHILD<15YOA	L
54990054	PASSING A SCHOOL BUS W/PREV CONV	L
54990062	FLYING INTOX W/PREV INTOX MANSLAUGHTER CONV	M
54990063	BOATING INTOX W/PREV INTOX MANSLAUGHTER CONV	M
55000000	HEALTH-SAFETY	L
55000009	PESTICIDE/HERBICIDE CAUSING INJ ENH	M
55000014	AREA QUARANTINE COMMUNICABLE DISEASE	L
55000030	TRANSP INDIV W/ COMMUN DISEASE INTO TEXAS DEFR	L
55000032	TRANSP INFECT PERSON/ANIMAL INTO TEXAS W/INT H	L
55000034	TRANSP INFECTED PERS/ANIM/OBJ INTO TEXAS DEFRA	L
55010000	DRUGS-ADULTERATED	M
55020000	DRUGS-MISBRANDED	M
55030000	DRUGS	L
55040000	FOOD-ADULTERATED	L
55110000	FOOD-MISBRANDED	L
55120000	FOOD	L
55120002	SELL POSS HORSEMEAT FOR HUMAN CONSUMPTION ENH	L
55120006	TRANSF HORSEMEAT TO SELLER HUMAN CONSUMP ENH	L
55200000	COSMETICS-ADULTERATED	L
55210000	COSMETICS-MISBRANDED	L
55220000	COSMETICS	L
55990000	HEALTH-SAFETY	L
55990006	USE OF EQUIPMENT FOR ANHYDROUS AMMONIA	L
55990014	USE OF EQUIPMENT FOR ANHYDROUS AMMONIA	M
55990020	PESTICIDE HERBICIDE CAUSING INJ ENH	M
55990025	AREA QUARANTINE COMMUNICABLE DISEASE	L

NCIC CODE	OFFENSE DESCRIPTION	RANK
55990035	TRANSPORT INFECT PERSON/ANIMAL INTO TX INT HAR	L
55990055	VIOL PROH FOOD/DRUG/COSMETIC ACT ENH	L
55990066	VIOL PROH FOOD/DRUG/COSEMETIC WHOLESALE DIS	L
56000000	CIVIL RIGHTS	M
56000001	VIOL PRISONER CIVIL RIGHTS	M
56000002	VIOL PRISONER CIVIL RIGHTS DEATH	H
56000003	VIOL PRISONER CIVIL RIGHTS SBI	H
56990000	CIVIL RIGHTS	M
56990002	VIOL CIVIL RIGHTS PERSON IN CUSTODY VIOL/SEX	L
56990006	SEXUAL CONT/INTERCOURSE W/SUPERVISED PERSON	L
56990007	UNL RESTRAINT WHILE IN CUSTODY	L
57000000	INVADE PRIVACY	L
57000003	DISCLOSE CONTENTS OF WIRE/ORAL/ELEC COMM	L
57000005	DISCLOSE INFORMATION FROM ADOPTION REGISTRY	L
57000009	ILLEGAL DISCLOSE/CCH ON DEPT HUMAN RES EMPLOYE	L
57000011	ILLEGAL DISCLOSE OF CCH ON HOUSING EMPLOYEES	L
57000014	ILLEGAL DIVULGENCE PUB COMMUNICATIONS	L
57000016	ILLEGAL INTERCEPTION ENH	L
57000018	INTERC WIRE/ORAL/ELEC COMM W/O CRT ORDER	L
57000019	INTERC WIRE/ORAL/ELECTRONIC COMMUNICATION	L
57000020	MAN ASSM/POSS/SELL ELEC/MECH DEV UNL PURP	L
57000022	OBSTRUCT LAW ENF/PROS BY NOTIF OTHER OF INTERC	L
57000031	UNAUTH DISCLOSE OF INFORMATION	L
57000033	UNL ACC STORED COMM-COMMERCIAL GAIN/DESTRUCT	L
57000035	UNL MEDIA ADVERTISEMENT OR ELEC/MECH DEVICE	L
57000036	USE OF CRIMINAL VICTIM/MOTOR VEH ACCIDENT INFO	L
57000038	UNL USE PEN REGISTER/TRAP AND TRACE DEVICE	L
57000041	UNL REL/DISCLOSE CONVICTION INFO	L
57000045	USE ANY PERSON/DEVICE TO INTERCEPT COMM	L
57000046	USE CONTENTS OF WIRE/ORAL/ELEC COMM	L
57000049	DISCLOSE UNANNOUNCED INSPECTION	L
57010000	DIVULGE EAVESDROP INFO	L
57020000	DIVULGE EAVESDROP ORDER	L
57030000	DIVULGE MESSAGE CONTENTS	L
57040000	EAVESDROPPING	L
57050000	EAVESDROP EQUIP	L
57060000	OPENING SEALED COMMUNICATION	L
57060003	BREACH OF COMPUTER SECURITY <$20K	L
57060003	BREACH OF COMPUTER SECURITY <$20K	L
57060004	BREACH OF COMPUTER SECURITY >=$20K	M
57060006	COMPUTER SECURITY BREACH <$1,500 2+ PREV CONV	L
57060007	COMPUTER SECURITY BREACH >=$1,500<$20K	L

NCIC CODE	OFFENSE DESCRIPTION	RANK
57060008	COMPUTER SECURITY BREACH >=$20K<$100K	M
57060009	COMPUTER SECURITY BREACH >=$100K<$200K	M
57060010	COMPUTER SECURITY BREACH >$200K	H
57070000	TRESPASSING	L
57070006	ILLEGAL ACCESS ENCLOSURE WHERE RACES COND	L
57070009	UNL ENTER PRIVATE RESIDENCE	M
57080000	WIRETAP-FAILURE TO REPORT	L
57990000	INVADE PRIVACY	L
57990001	MAN ASSM/POSS/SELL ELEC/MECH DEV UNL PURP	L
57990001	MAN ASSM/POSS/SELL ELEC/MECH DEV UNL PURP	L
57990002	UNL MEDIA ADVMENT OR ELEC/MECH DEVICE	L
57990002	UNL MEDIA ADVMENT OR ELEC/MECH DEVICE	L
57990003	OBSTRUCT LAW ENF/PROS BY NOTIF OTHER OF INTERC	L
57990003	OBSTRUCT LAW ENF/PROS BY NOTIF OTHER OF INTERC	L
57990004	UNL USE PEN REGISTER/TRAP AND TRACE DEVICE	L
57990004	UNL USE PEN REGISTER/TRAP AND TRACE DEVICE	L
57990005	UNL ACCESS STORED COMMUNICATION BENEFIT	L
57990005	UNL ACCESS STORED COMMUNICATION BENEFIT	L
57990006	ILLEGAL DIVULGENCE PUB COMMUNICATIONS	L
57990006	ILLEGAL DIVULGENCE PUB COMMUNICATIONS/SCRAMBLE	L
57990007	INTERC WIRE/ORAL/ELECTRONIC COMMUNICATION	L
57990008	UNL INTERC/DISCLOSE W/INT ELECTRONIC COMMUNICA	L
57990009	USE CONTENTS OF WIRE/ORAL/ELEC COMM	L
57990010	INTERC WIRE/ORAL/ELEC COMM W/O CRT ORDER	L
57990013	USE ANY PERSON/DEVICE TO INTERCEPT COMM	L
57990015	UNAUTH USE/DISCLOSURE CCH INFO REMUNERATION	L
57990021	UNL INTERC/DISCLOSE W/INT ELECTRONIC COMMUNICA	L
57990025	UNL INTER/USE/DISC WIRE/ORAL ELEC COMMUNICATE	L
57990026	UNL INTER/USE/DISC WIRE/ORAL ELEC COMMUNICATE	L
57990037	USE OF CRIME VICTIM/MOTOR VEH INFO ENH	L
57990042	DISCLOSE UNANNOUNCED INSPECTION	L
57990045	VOLUNTARY ADOPTION REGISTRIES DISCLOSES RECORD	L
57990046	VOLUNTARY ADOPTION REGISTRIES IMPERSON ADMIN	M
57990047	VOLUNTARY ADOPTION REGISTRIES INPERSON ADOPTEE	M
57990049	VOLUNTARY ADOPTION REGISTRIES W/INT TO DECEIVE	L
57990050	CONFIDENTIALITY OF DNA RECORDS	L
57990051	IMPROPER USE OF VICTIM/ACCIDENT INFO 3+ CONV	L
58000000	SMUGGLING	M
58010000	SMUGGLE CONTRABAND	L
58020000	SMUGGLE CONTRABAND INTO PRISON	M
58030000	SMUGGLE TO AVOID PAYING DUTY	L
58030001	ILLEGAL TRANSPORTATION OF CIGARETTES	L

NCIC CODE	OFFENSE DESCRIPTION	RANK
58030002	TRANSPORT UNTAXED TOBACCO PRODUCTS	L
58030003	TRANSPORT CIGARETTES	L
58990000	SMUGGLING-OTHER	M
58990001	UNL TRANSP OF PERSON FOR PECUNIARY BENEFIT	L
58990002	TRAFFICKING OF PERSON	L
58990003	TRAFFICKING OF PERSON YOUNGER THAN 14 YOA	M
58990004	TRAFFICKING A PERSON CAUSING DEATH	M
58990005	TRAFFICKING OF PERSONS <18 FOR PROSTITUTION	H
59000000	ELECTION LAWS	L
59000023	ILLEGAL VOTING	M
59000035	CONTRIBUTE TO POLITCAL PARTY	L
59000036	UNL CONTRIBUTION/EXPENDITURE BY COMMITTEE	L
59000037	UNL CONTRIBUTION/EXPENDITURE BY CORP/LABOR ORG	L
59000038	UNL DEL OF VOTER CERTIFICATE	L
59000041	UNL DIVULGING VOTE	L
59000046	UNL REMOVAL OF BALLOT FROM BALLOT BOX	L
59000056	RESTRICTION ON CONTRIBUTIONS GENERAL ELECTION	L
59000059	CORP LOANS	L
59000060	POLITICAL ADVISING CAUSING INJ	L
59000063	UNL MAKE/ACCEPTING CONTRIBUTION ENH	L
59990000	ELECTION LAWS-OTHER	L
59990009	ILLEGAL VOTING	M
59990016	CONTRIBUTE TO POLITICAL PARTY	L
59990017	UNL DEL OF VOTER CERTIFICATE	L
59990020	UNL DIVULGING VOTE	L
59990025	UNL REMOVAL OF BALLOT FROM BALLOT BOX	L
59990035	RESTRICT ON CONTRIBUTIONS GENERAL ELECTION	L
59990038	CORPORATE LOANS	L
59990039	POLITICAL ADVISING CAUSING INJ	L
59990042	UNL MAKING/ACCEPTING CONTRIBUTION ENH	L
59990047	CARRIER ENVELOPE ACTION BY ASSISTING VOTER	L
59990050	METHOD OF RETURN MARKED BALLOT = OR > 20	L
59990051	METHOD OF RETURN MARKED BALLOT W/VOTERS CONSEN	M
59990053	ASSISTING VOTER VIOL EHN	L
59990055	UNL BUYING SELLING OF BALLOTING MATERIALS	L
60000000	ANTITRUST	L
60000003	ILLEGAL USE PREVIOUSLY USED/OLD CIGARETTE DESI	L
60000004	LIMIT OTHER PARTY RIGHT SECURE COIN-OP MACH	L
60000005	MONOPOLIZATION OF TRADE/COMMERCE	L
60000006	UNL PRACTICE OF TRADE OR COMMERCE	L
60000007	PREVIOUSLY USED/OLD CIGARETTE DESIGN	L
60990000	ANTITRUST-OTHER	L

NCIC CODE	OFFENSE DESCRIPTION	RANK
60990002	UNL PRACTICE OF TRADE OR COMMERCE	L
60990003	PREVIOUSLY USED/OLD CIGARETTE DESIGN	L
61000000	TAX-REVENUE	L
61000002	CORP EVADES/DEFEATS IMPOSITION/PAYMENT OF TAX	L
61000003	CORP FAILS TO FILE TAX REPORT	L
61000004	DESTRUCT BOOK OR RECORD REQUIRED BY TAX CODE	L
61000008	FAIL TO MAKE AND DELIVER RETURN REPORT	L
61000009	FAIL TO MAKE/DELIVER TAX RETURN OR REPORT	L
61000010	FAIL TO REMIT COLLECTED TAX FUNDS	L
61000011	FAIL MAKE ENTRIES IN RCRD REQ BY TAX CODE	L
61000013	MAKE/DEL INCOMPLETE TAX RECORD OR RETURN	L
61000017	POSS ITEM W/UNPAID CONTROL SUBSTANCE TAX	L
61000018	POSS TOBACCO PROD ON WHICH TAX OF > $50 IS REQ	L
61000019	REF ALLOW INSPECT RECRDS REQD BY TAX CODE	L
61000021	POSS TOBACCO PRODUCT WHICH TAX OF >$50 IS REQ	L
61010000	INCOME TAX	L
61020000	SALES TAX	L
61020001	MOTOR FUEL TAXES	L
61020003	DEALER PURCHASE OF MOTOR FUEL TO EVADE TAX	L
61020004	DEALER UNAUTHOR PURCH MOTOR FUEL TAX FREE	L
61020005	ILLEGAL SALE CIGARETTE STAMPS	L
61020006	POSS UNSTAMP CIGARETTES/QUANTITY OF >=10,000	L
61020008	SALE TAX FREE DIESEL FUEL STOR FACIL ILL PERS	L
61020009	SALE TAX FREE GASOLINE TO ILL PERSON	L
61020017	SELL CIGARETTE STAMPS	L
61020018	POSS UNSTAMP CIGARETTES/QUANTITY OF >=10K	L
61020041	COOPERATIVE AGREEMENTS W/STATES ON FUEL TAX	L
61020042	COOPERATIVE AGREEMENTS W/STATES ON FUEL TAX	M
61020043	COOPERATIVE AGREEMENTS W/STATES ON FUEL TAX X3	M
61020045	COLLECTION OF CIGARETTE TAX KNOWING VIOL	L
61030000	LIQUOR TAX	L
61990000	TAX REVENUE-OTHER	L
61990007	FAIL TO PAY TAXES COLLECT $10K < $20K	L
61990008	FAIL TO PAY TAXES COLLECT $20K < $100K	L
61990009	FAIL TO PAY TAXES COLLECT $100K OR MORE	M
61990015	FALSE ENTRY/FAIL TO ENTER IN TAX RECORDS	L
61990016	FAIL TO REMIT TAX BY DEALER $1500 < $20K	L
61990017	FAIL TO REMIT TAX BY DEALER $20K < $100K	L
61990018	FAIL TO REMIT TAX BY DEALER $100K < $200K	M
61990019	FAIL TO REMIT TAX BY DEALER $200K	H
61990023	POSS ITEM W/UNPAID CONTROL SUBSTANCE TAX	L
61990024	POSS TOBACCO PRODUCT WHICH TAX OF >$50 IS REQ	L

NCIC CODE	OFFENSE DESCRIPTION	RANK
62000000	CONSERVATION	L
62000014	OYSTER RESTRICTED AREAS 3RD	L
62000019	PROH ACTS HUNT FROM AIRCRAFT W/PREV CONVIC	L
62000044	NIGHT DREDGING OF OYSTERS 3RD	L
62000046	NIGHT DREDGING OYSTERS POLLUTED AREA ENH	L
62000094	USE AIRCRAFT HARASS WILDLIFE ENH	L
62000114	ACCIDENT BOATING DEATH/SBI	M
62010000	CONSERVATION-ANIMALS	L
62010011	INTERFER ANIMAL OR ANIMAL FACIL $750<$20K	L
62010012	INTERFER ANIMAL OR ANIMAL FACIL >=$20K	M
62010014	WOLVES POSS/TRANSP/RECEIVE IN TEXAS	L
62010034	CONTROLLED KILLING/INJ WILD ANIMAL 2ND	L
62010037	PROH ACTS HUNT FROM AIRCRAFT W/PREV CONVIC	L
62020000	CONSERVATION-FISH	L
62020008	ILLEGAL DISPOSITION OF UNFIT/UNL SHELLFISH/3RD	L
62020011	ILLEGAL SELL OF IMPROPERLY HANDLED SHELLFISH	L
62020014	ILLEGAL TRANSPORTATION SHELLFISH/3RD	L
62020017	EXOTIC HARM FISH/SHELLFISH/AQUATIC PLANTS 3RD	L
62020022	INTRODUCE FISH/SHELLFISH/PLANTS PUB WATER 3RD	L
62020030	SELL SHELLFISH W/O CERTIFICATE NUMBER 3RD	L
62020034	TAKE FISH BY ELECTRIC SHOCK 3RD	L
62020037	UNL OPERATE SHELLFISH PLANT 3RD	L
62020040	UNL TAKE SHELLFISH FROM POLLUTED AREA 3RD	L
62030000	CONSERVATION-BIRDS	L
62040000	CONSERVATION-LICENSE-STAMP	L
62040029	OYSTER LICENSE REQUIRED 3RD	L
62040032	HARVEST OYSTERS NON-COMM PURP W/O LIC 3RD	L
62040035	HARVEST OYSTERS W/O COMMERCIAL LIC 3RD	L
62040050	SALE OF SPORT OYSTERS PROHIBITED 3RD	L
62040052	USE AIRCRAFT HUNT ANIMALS W/O PERM ENH	L
62040054	USE AIRCRAFT MANAGE WILDLIFE W/O PERM ENH	L
62050000	CONSERVATION-ENVIRONMENT	L
62050002	DISCHARGE HAZ WASTE CAUSE SBI/DEATH BY ANOTHER	M
62050003	DISCHARGE HAZ WASTE FEAR/CAUSE SBI/DEATH/ANOTH	M
62050006	DISCHARGE WASTE/POLLUT CAUSING DEATH/SBI	M
62050010	ILLEGAL DUMPING W/PREV CONVIC	L
62050012	DISPOSE HAZ WASTE CAUSE SBI/DEATH	M
62050013	DISPOSE HAZ WASTE FEAR/CAUSE SBI/DEATH	M
62050015	DISPOSE OF LITTER IN CAVE 2 OR MORE CONV	L
62050028	PERSON CONDUCT DISCHARGE WASTE RESULT DEATH/SB	M
62050030	RECKLESS REL HAZ WASTE IN ENVIRONMENT BY ANOTH	L
62050031	RECKLESS REL HAZ WASTE IN ENVIRONMENT	L

NCIC CODE	OFFENSE DESCRIPTION	RANK
62050032	REL HAZ WASTE CAUSING SBI/DEATH ANOTHER	M
62050033	REL HAZ WASTE IN ENVIRON CAUSE SBI/DEATH	M
62050034	REL HAZ WASTE IN ENVIRON FEAR/CAUSE SBI	M
62050035	REL HAZ WASTE IN ENVIR SBI/DEATH BY ANOTHER	M
62050036	REL HAZARDOUS WASTE CAUSING SBI/DEATH	M
62050045	VIOL SOLID WASTE DISP ACT W/SBI/DEATH OF ANOTH	M
62050046	VIOL SOLID WASTE DISP ACT W/SBI/DEATH BY ANOTH	M
62050047	VIOL SLD WASTE DIS ACT W/SBI/DEATH RESULT	M
62050048	VIOL SOLID WASTE DISPOSE ACT W/SBI/DEATH	M
62050053	DISPOSE USED OIL ENDANGER HEALTH/ENVIRON	L
62050054	VIOL RELATING TO SOLID WASTE/ENCLOSED CONTAINE	L
62050056	VIOL RELATING TO HANDLING USED OIL	L
62050057	VIOL OF HANDLING USED OIL W/PREV CONVIC	L
62050060	TRANSPORT MEDICAL WASTE W/PREV CONVIC	L
62050061	VIOL RELATING TO HAZARDOUS WASTE W/PREV CONVIC	L
62050062	INTENT KNOW VIOL MEDICAL WASTE KNOW ENDANGER	L
62050063	INTENT KNOW VIOL MEDICAL WASTE/ENDANGERMENT	L
62050068	ILLEGAL DUMPING 1000LBS OR MORE	L
62050069	ILLEGAL DUMPING COMM WGT BARREL OR DRUM	L
62050072	ILLEGAL DUMPING W/PREV CONV	L
62050074	VIOL RELATING TO DISCHARGE/SPILL FAL RECORD	L
62050077	INT/KNOW UNAUTH DISCHARGE/KNOW ENDANGERMENT	L
62050078	VIOL RELATING TO HAZARDOUS WASTE	L
62050080	RECKLESS EMISSION OF AIR CONTAMINANT	L
62050085	FAILURE TO PROPERLY USE POLLUTION CONTROL	L
62080085	FAILURE TO PROPERLY USE POLLUTION CONTROL	L
62990000	CONSERVATION-OTHER	L
62990004	TAKE WILDLIFE RES W/O CONSENT OF OWNER 3 ENH	L
62990007	TAKE CERTAIN WILDLIFE RESOURCES W/O CONSENT	L
62990009	TAKE WILDLIFE RESOURSES W/O CONSENT 2ND	L
62990010	TAKE WILDLIFE RESOURSES W/O CONSENT 3RD	L
62990012	HUNT FROM VEHICLE ENH	L
62990014	HUNT AT NIGHT ENH	L
62990016	HUNT W/LIGHT ENH	L
62990018	RETRIEVAL AND WASTE OF GAME ENH	L
62990023	OYSTER RESTRICTED AREAS 3RD	L
62990026	NIGHT DREDGING OF OYSTERS 3RD	L
62990037	ACCIDENT BOATING DEATH/SBI	M
62990041	ATTACK ON ASSISTANCE ANIMAL-CAUSES INJURY	L
62990042	ATTACK ON ASSISTANCE ANIMAL-CAUSES DEATH	M
62990046	ATTACK ON ASSISTANCE ANIMAL W/INJURY	L
62990047	ATTACK ON ASSISTANCE ANIMAL CAUSING DEATH	M

NCIC CODE	OFFENSE DESCRIPTION	RANK
62990049	HUNT CERTAIN PARTS BIG SANDY CREEK W/PREV CONV	L
62990051	HUNTING DEER W/DOGS W/PREV CONV	L
62990055	OYSTER REGULATIONS 2+ PREV CONV	L
62990057	OYSTER RESTRICTED AREA PREV CONV	L
62990059	OYSTER NIGHT DREDGING/RESTRICTED AREA PREV CON	L
63000000	VAGRANCY	L
63990000	VAGRANCY-OTHER	L
70990000	CRIMES AGAINST PERSON	M
70990001	AIDING SUICIDE SBI	L
70990007	DISCRIMINATE DENIAL EMERGENCY SERVICE INT DEAT	M
70990011	EVADING LAW ON FREE PASSES	L
70990014	EMPLOY FAILS/PAY NEW EMPLOYEE AFTER DEMAND	L
70990015	CONTINGENT FEES ON EMPLOYEES OF LEGISLATION	L
70990020	FALSE IMPRISIONMENT EXPOSE VICTIM TO SBI	M
70990026	EXPOSING ANOTHER TO AIDS OR HIV	H
70990036	RAILROAD EMPLOYEES UNJUST DISCRIMINATION	L
70990040	UNPROFESS COND PERTAINING TO DENTIST ENH	L
70990044	AIDING SUICIDE/SBI	L
70990044	AIDING SUICIDE/SBI	L
70990046	INMATE MISUSE OF INFO GAINED THRU WORK PROG	L
70990048	HAZING CAUSING DEATH	L
70990048	HAZING CAUSING DEATH	L
70990052	UNL RESTRAINT EXPOSE TO SBI	M
70990056	FAIL TO PAY EMPLOYEE WAGES	L
70990059	UNL RESTRAINT LESS THAN 17 YRS OF AGE	L
70990060	COERCE SOLICIT/INDUCE GANG MEMBERSHIP	L
70990061	COERCION SOLICIT/INDUCE GANG MEMBERSHIP BI	L
70990062	HARASSMENT BY PERSONS IN CORRECTIONAL FACILITY	L
70990064	TEXAS HEALTH CARE INFORMATION COUNCIL VIOL	L
70990065	CIVIL COMMITMENT REQUIREMENT	L
70990071	SOLICIT MEMBERSHIP IN CRIMINAL STREET GANG	L
70990072	SOLICIT MEMBERSHIP IN CRIMINAL STREET GANG ENH	M
70990073	UNL RESTRAINT OF PUBLIC SERVANT	L
70990075	IMPROPER CONTACT W/VICTIM WHILE CONFINED	L
70990135	HARASSMENT BY PERSON IN CORRECTIONAL/DETENTION	L
70990136	INTERFER W/RIGHTS OF GUARDIAN OF WARD	L
70990140	HARRASSMENT OF PUBLIC SERVANT	L
70990141	MISREP REGARD ENTITLE TO PRACTICE MEDICINE	M
70990144	ATTACK BY DOG RESULTING IN SBI	M
70990145	ATTACK BY DOG RESULTING IN DEATH	H
70990149	HAZING CAUSES DEATH	L
71990000	PROPERTY CRIMES	M

NCIC CODE	OFFENSE DESCRIPTION	RANK
71990004	INTERFER RAILROAD PROPTY SBI	M
71990007	INTERFER RAILROAD PROPTY $750<$20K	L
71990008	INTERFER RAILROAD PROPTY >=$20K	M
71990012	INTERFER W/BUOY/MARKER 3RD	L
71990026	SALVAGE VEHICLE DEALERS ENH	L
71990030	INTERFER RAILROAD PROPERTY>=$1,500<$20K	L
71990030	INTERFER RAILROAD PROPERTY>=$1,500<$20K	L
71990031	INTERFER RAILROAD PROPERTY>=$20K<$100K	M
71990032	INTERFER RAILROAD PROPERTY>=$100K<$200K	M
71990033	INTERFER RAILROAD PROPERTY>$200K	H
71990035	THROW OBJECT/DISCH FIREARM RR EQUIP BI	M
71990044	INTERFER RAILROAD PROPERTY CAUSES BI	L
72990000	MORALS-DECENCY CRIMES	M
72990002	DESECRATION OF VENERAT OBJ/PLACE OF WORSHIP/BU	M
72990008	PURCH OR SELL HUMAN ORGANS	L
72990009	SALE OR PURCHASE OF CHILD	M
72990010	SALE OR PURCHASE OF CHILD ENH	H
72990012	SOLICIT OF CHILD TAKEN OUT OF COUNTY	M
72990017	SELL OR PURCHASE CHILD	M
72990019	ADVERTISE PLACEMENT OF CHILD W/PREV CONVIC	L
72990020	DESECRATION OF CEMETERY	M
72990024	ENTICING A CHILD W/INT FELONY	M
72990025	FEMALE GENITAL MUTILATION PROH UNDER 18YR	L
72990028	EXECUTION OF CAPIAS OR ARREST WARRANT	L
72990028	EXECUTION OF CAPIAS OR ARREST WARNT -ENH	L
72990031	SELL OR PURCHASE CHILD FOR SEXUAL PERFORMANCE	H
72990042	PARENT/GUARDIAN CONSENT FOR MARRIAGE UNDER 16	L
72990044	CONDUCT MARRIAGE CEREMONY OF A MINOR	L
73000000	PUBLIC ORDER	L
73030000	PUBLIC ORDER, CRIMINAL MISCHIEF	L
73060000	PUBLIC ORDER, TAMPERING WITH GOVT DOC	L
73990000	PUBLIC ORDER-OTHER	L
73990007	LIVESTOCK COMMISSION MERCHANT W/O BOND	L
73990017	ADV DENTIST SERV NOT LOCATED IN TEXAS ENH	L
73990040	CORP FAIL TO KEEP RECORDS REQUIRED BY TAX CODE	L
73990042	CORP VIOL RULE COMPTRLER ADMN/ENFORC/TAX CODE	L
73990050	DEPOSIT GRAIN W/O TITLE	M
73990070	DOG FIGHTING OP FACIL/RECV PECUNIARY BENEF	L
73990076	EMPLOY STOCKHOLDER DESTRUCTUCT BANK RECORDS	L
73990079	ENGAGE IN MOTOR FUEL TRANSACTION W/O PERM	L
73990081	FAIL COMPLY CHEM LAB APPARAT REC KEEP REQ ENH	L
73990103	FAIL KEEP FOR 2 YRS RCRDS REQUIRED BY TAX CODE	L

NCIC CODE	OFFENSE DESCRIPTION	RANK
73990106	FAIL TO KEEP TAX RECORDS FOR FOUR YEARS	L
73990111	CARGO MANIFEST REQUIREMENTS	L
73990153	IMPROPER IMPORT/EXPORT OF CATTLE/CARCASSES	L
73990166	MISUSE OF OFFICIAL INFORMATION	L
73990193	OP OIL TANKER W/O CARGO MANIFEST	L
73990196	OP PUB GRAIN WAREHOUSE W/O LICENSE	L
73990200	PASSAGE CONTROL PRODUCER W/O MEASURE	L
73990207	HEALTH CARE UTILIZATION REVIEW W/O CERT ENH	L
73990208	PERM RESERVE FUND APPEAL COST UNL EXPENDED	L
73990209	FREE ON DELIVERY OF CERTAIN PETROLEUM PRODUCTS	L
73990214	PRACT PROFES NURSING W/ SUSP/REVOKED LIC ENH	L
73990222	PRACT AS RN/USE LIKE TITLES W/O LIC ENH	L
73990225	PRACT DENTIST W/ REVOKED LICENSE ENH	M
73990227	PRACT DENTIST W/O LICENSE EXHIBITED ENH	L
73990230	PRACT MEDICINE IN VIOL OF MED PRACT ACT ENH	M
73990237	PROH EVASION/PREV OF ACCURATE MEASUREMENT ENH	L
73990252	SALE OF CHECKS W/O LIC	L
73990269	STORE PROC/DISPOSE HAZARD WASTE W/O PERM ENH	L
73990271	TAMPER W/LOCK/GATE/DOOR TO CAVE ENH	L
73990272	TAMPER W/OIL/GAS RIGS W/O WRITTEN AUTH	L
73990274	TAMPER W/GOVERNMENT RECORD LIC/SEAL/CERTIF/PER	L
73990276	TAMPER W/GOVERNMENT RECORD LIC/SEAL DEFRAUD/HA	L
73990277	TAMPER W/CONSUMER PRODUCT	L
73990278	TAMPER W/CONSUMER PRODUCT SBI	M
73990279	TAMPER W/CONSUMER PRODUCT THREAT	L
73990280	TAMPER FABRICATING PHYSICAL EVIDENCE	L
73990283	TRANSP/PERM HAZARD WASTE W/O PERM ENH	L
73990284	TRANSP MOTOR FUEL UNDER FAL CARGO MANIFEST	L
73990289	UNAUTH USE LATERAL ROAD ACCOUNT	L
73990292	PRACT DENTIST W/O LICENSE ENH	M
73990294	UNL TRANSF/RECEIPT CHEM LAB APPARATUS ENH	L
73990298	UNL ADVERTISE DENTIST SERVICES ENH	L
73990299	UNL DEL FROM PUB GRAIN WAREHOUSE	L
73990300	UNL DISCLOSE INFO COMMISSION OF HEALTH	L
73990316	VIOL CONTEST AND GIFT GIVEAWAY ACT 3RD	L
73990324	VIOL OIL/GAS CARGO MANIFEST REQUIREMENTS	L
73990336	FALSE STATEMENT FOR MHMR ASSISTANCE	L
73990352	FREE PASS LAW	L
73990358	HAZARDOUS LIQUID PIPELINE TRANSPORTATION	L
73990362	OP AIRCRAFT W/ ILLEGAL FUEL TANK	L
73990363	OP AIRCRAFT W/O FAA REGISTRATION	L
73990365	OP AIRCRAFT W/O PROP ID	L

NCIC CODE	OFFENSE DESCRIPTION	RANK
73990366	TAMPER W/ GOVT RECD DEFRAUD/HARM	L
73990369	MISUSE OF OFFICIAL INFORMATION	L
73990370	CRUELTY TO ANIMALS	L
73990373	DOG FIGHTING CARE/FACILITY/PROPERTY	L
73990373	DOG FIGHTING CARE/FACILITY/PROPERTY	L
73990374	OP DOG FIGHTING FACILITY	L
73990374	OP DOG FIGHTING FACILITY	L
73990375	AUTH USE OF PROP FOR DOG FIGHTING	L
73990376	TAMPER W/GOVT RECORD DEFRAUD/HARM	L
73990376	TAMPER W/GOVT RECORD DEFRAUD/HARM	L
73990380	ACT AS PHYSICIAN ASST W/O LIC	L
73990382	RACING COMM PROHIBITED CONDUCT	L
73990383	CONDUCT GREYHOUND/HORSE RACE MTG W/O LIC	L
73990384	EMPLOY FORMER RACING COMM MEMB/EMPLOYEE	L
73990387	FALSE OR FICTITIOUS WRITE STMT FARM/RANCH PROG	L
73990388	FRAUD OF BENEFITS FARM & RANCH PROGRAM	L
73990398	DISCLOSE REGISTRY/ADOPTED CHILD	L
73990404	UNL CONDUCT/PROMOTING/ADMIN BINGO GAME	L
73990405	RECKLESSLY EMIT CONTAMINANT SBI/DEATH	M
73990406	INTENTION/KNOW EMIT CONTAMINATE SBI/DEATH	M
73990408	UNAUTH INSURANCE PROHIBITED	L
73990410	DENTAL TECHNICIAN/LABORATORY	L
73990411	UNLIC PERSON MAKING DENTAL PROSTHETIC	L
73990412	TAMPER FABRICATE PHYSICAL EVID W/INTENT TO IMP	L
73990424	RACING W/O LICENSE	L
73990427	PRACTICE ACUPUNCTURE W/O LICENSE	L
73990435	SELL CHECKS W/O LICENSE	L
73990438	CONTEST AND GIFT GIVEAWAY ACT 3RD	L
73990442	FAIL COMPLY CHEM LAB APP REC KEEP REQ ENH	L
73990443	FAIL COMPLY CHEM LAB APP REC KEEP REQ	L
73990451	FAIL TO REGISTER AIRCRAFT/FAA	L
73990454	COMMODITY EXCHANGES	L
73990459	CRUELTY TO ANIMALS W/2 PREV CONVIC/SBI	L
73990462	REGULATION MUSIC/SKILL PLEASURE COIN-OP MACH E	L
73990471	RULE MAKING AUTHORITY BY COMPTROLLER	L
73990475	PRACTICING MEDICINE IN VIOLATION OF SUBTITLE	L
73990476	MEDICAL PRACTICE ACT W/PHYSICAL HARM	M
73990477	MEDICAL PRACTICE ACT W/FINANCIAL HARM	L
73990481	CHIROPRACTIC PRACTICE ACT W/O LICENSE ENH	L
73990484	PHYSICIANS ASST ACT W/O LICENSE	L
73990485	ACUPUNCTURE ACT W/O LICENSE	L
73990488	DENTAL HYGENISTS ACT VIOL W/PREV CONVIC	L

NCIC CODE	OFFENSE DESCRIPTION	RANK
73990489	DENTAL ASSISTANTS REGULATIONS	L
73990492	NURSING REGULATIONS W/PREV CONVIC	L
73990515	OCCUPATION RELATE TO LAW ENF/SECURITY W/CONVIC	L
73990525	BINGO REGULATIONS	L
73990532	COIN OPERATED MACHINE BY FRAUD LICENSE	L
73990534	COIN OPERATED MACHINE PROH TRANSACTIONS	L
73990539	SOLICIT PATIENTS W/PREV CONVIC	L
73990542	PRIVATE INVESTIGATOR/SECURITY AGENCY REG ENH	L
73990546	PRIVATE INVESTIG/SECUR AGENCY REG W/PREV CONV	L
73990548	DAMAGE FOR UNAUTHORIZED HARVESTING BY TRUSTEE	L
73990551	GRAIN WAREHOUSE W/O LICENSE	L
73990552	UNL DELIVERY OF GRAIN	M
73990553	DEPOSIT GRAIN W/O TITLE	M
73990554	INTERFER W/SEALED WAREHOUSE INSPECTION OR INV	L
73990561	CRUELTY TO ANIMAL W/2 PREV CONVIC	L
73990571	CONFIDENT OF PRECONFINEMENT DNA RECORDS	L
73990577	DENTISTRY ACT VIOL W/PREV CONV	L
73990578	PERFORMING SURGERY WHILE INTOXICATED	L
73990579	FINANCIAL SERVICES REGULATIONS OR LOSS OF <10K	L
73990580	FINANCIAL SERV REGULATIONS OR LOSS OF 10K>100K	L
73990581	FINANCIAL SERVICES REGULATIONS OF =>100K	M
73990591	INVESTIGATE FIRE SAFETY HAZARDS VIOL W/2 PREV	L
73990592	DENTAL LAB SERVICE VIOL OF 266.151/266.301	L
73990595	CRUELTY TO ANIMALS W/2 PREV CONV (2,3,4,9,10)	L
73990596	CRUELTY TO ANIMALS (PARAGRAPH 1,5,6,7,8)	L
73990597	CRUELTY TO ANIMALS W/2 PREV CONV (1,5,6,7,8)	L
73990600	SALVAGE VEHICLE LICENSE VIOLATION W/PREV CONV	L
73990601	UNAUTH CONTRACT W/BAIL BOND SURETY	L
73990602	CONTINUE ADEQUATE SERV DISC/REDU/IMPAR SERVICE	L
73990604	ASSEMBLE OPERATE AMUSEMENT RIDE W/INTOX 3RD/MO	L
73990606	NOTICE OF WHOLESALE WATER SUPPLY CONTRACT	L
73990608	EMERG RESPONSE PROVIDER LIC FALSE PRINTS/PHOTO	L
73990610	EMERG RESPONSE PROVIDER LIC VIOL W/PREV CONV	L
73990611	CHIROPRACTIC PRACTICE ACT WHILE INTOXICATED	L
73990616	MASSAGE THERAPY LICENSE/OWNER W/3+ PREV CONV	L
73990617	TAMPER W/DIRECT RECORD ELEC VOTE MACHINE	M
73990618	TAMPER W/DIRECT RECORD ELEC VOTE MACH ATTEMPT	L
73990619	TAMPER W/GOV SCHOOL RECORD LIC/SEAL/CERT/PERM	L
73990620	TAMPER W/GOVERN RECORD DEFRAUD/HARM	L
73990621	TAMPER W/GOVERN RECORD LIC/SEAL DEFRAUD/HARM	L
73990628	TAMPER W/GOV REC-INS DOC	L
73990629	TAMPER W/GOV REC-INS DOC	L

NCIC CODE	OFFENSE DESCRIPTION	RANK
73990630	TAMPER W/GOV REC-INS DOC-DEFRAUD/HARM	L
73990644	CRUELTY TO NON-LVSTOCK ANMLS:FAIL PROV W/2CONV	L
73990645	CRUELTY TO NON-LIVESTOCK ANIMALS: TORTURE	L
73990646	CRUELTY TO NON-LVSTOCK ANMLS:TORTURE W/2 CONV	L
73990650	INTOX MANSLTR CAUSE DEATH PEACE OFC/FIRE/EMS	H+
73990652	MOTOR VEHICLE/TRANSPORTATION REGULATION W/PREV	L
73990653	ACT AS INS AGENT W/REVOKED/SUSP LICENSE	L
73991000	ENGAGE IN ORGANIZED CRIMINAL ACTIVITY	L
73991000	ENGAGE IN ORGANIZED CRIMINAL ACTIVITY	L
73991003	ENGAGE IN ORGANIZED CRIMINAL ACTIVITY	M
73991004	ENGAGE IN ORGANIZED CRIMINAL ACTIVITY	M
73991005	ENGAGE IN ORGANIZED CRIMINAL ACTIVITY	H
73991011	EMPLOY WORKING AT RACE TRACK W/O LIC	L
73991022	INTEREST EMPLOYEES HUD PROPERTIES	L
73991029	MEDICAL PRACTICE ACT	L
73991029	MEDICAL PRACTICE ACT	L
73991031	FEE ON DELIVERY OF CERTAIN PETROLEUM PRODUCTS	L
73991032	INTENT KNOW UNAUTH DISCHARGE WASTE	L
73991036	SLANDER OR LIBEL OF BANKS	L
73991036	SLANDER OR LIBEL OF BANKS	L
73991042	TEXAS MENTAL HEALTH CODE VIOLATION	L
73991043	TEXAS MENTAL HEALTH CODE VIOL W/PREV CONV	L
73991044	ASSEMBLE/OPER AMUSE RIDE W/PREV INTOX MAN CONV	M
73991049	UNAUTHORIZED TRANS OR POSS OF DRIVER ED CERT	L
73991058	TAMP/FAB PHYS EVID W/INTENT TO IMPAIR HUM CORP	M
73991060	DOG FIGHTING:PARTICIP IN EARNINGS/PROVIDE BLDG	L
73991062	TEMP CARDBOARD TAG FOR DIST TO UNAUTH PERSON	L
73991063	ORGANIZED CRIM ACTIVITY-TEMP CARDBOARD TAG	L
73991064	CRUELTY TO LIVESTOCK ANIMALS	L
73991066	CRUELTY TO LIVESTOCK ANIM W/2 PREV CONV	L
73991067	CRUELTY TO LIVESTOCK ANIM W/2 PREV CONV	L
73991073	DIRECT ACTIVITIES OF STREET GANG	H
73991075	INTERF W/RADIO FREQ INTEND OFF/INTERF RESPONSE	L
73991076	TAMPER W/WRITTEN EVIDENTIARY REPORT	L
73991077	TAMPER W/CERT/INSP/MAINTENANCE REPORT	L
73991081	COERCE/SOLICIT/INDUCE GANG MEMBERSHIP THREAT	L
73991082	COERCE/SOLICIT/INDUCE GANG MEMBERSHIP CAUSE BI	M
73991083	COERCE/SOLICIT/INDUCE GANG MEMBERSHIP 2ND	M

Appendix 3

Board Members of the Board of Pardons and Parole

Board Members of the Board of Pardons and Parole

Board Members are vested with the sole responsibility of promulgating policy relative to parole and mandatory supervision considerations; vote cases requiring the full Board vote; determine conditions of parole; and vote on clemency matters.

Board members are appointed by the Governor with the advice and consent of the Senate for a six year term.

David G. Gutierrez– Chair Person

- ASSIGNMENT: Gatesville
- APPOINTED: 2009; appointed chair in 2015
- TERM EXPIRES: 2027
- EDUCATION: Bachelor of Science in Criminal Justice, Wayland Baptist University, Lubbock, Texas.
- BACKGROUND: In addition to his six years on the Board, Mr. Gutierrez served 33 years in Criminal Justice and Law Enforcement, including 11 years as Sheriff of Lubbock County. He is a former chair of the Texas Commission on Jail Standards and the Texas Correctional Office on Offenders with Medical or Mental Impairments (TCOOMMI) Advisory Board, and past president of both the Texas Corrections Association and the Texas Jail Association. He also has been a volunteer with Hospice of Lubbock, the American Heart Association, United Way, Lubbock Boy Scouts of America and Boys and Girls Clubs.

Elodia Brito

- ASSIGNMENT: Amarillo
- APPOINTED: 2022
- TERM EXPIRES: 2023
- EDUCATION: Bachelor of Science in Organizational Management, Lubbock Christian University, Lubbock, TX.
- BACKGROUND: Over 21 years of experience with the federal courts for the Northern District of Texas – specifically as a courtroom deputy for the U.S. Magistrate Judge in the Amarillo Division.

Carmella Jones

- ASSIGNMENT: Huntsville
- APPOINTED: 2018
- TERM EXPIRES: 2025
- EDUCATION: Attended Stephen F. Austin State University; Certification as Master Peace Officer, Master Jailer.
- BACKGROUND: Sheriff Jones was appointed to the Texas Commission on Jail Standards; a member of the Sheriffs' Association of Texas; and is a lifetime member of the Texas Jail Association.

Brian Long

- ASSIGNMENT: Palestine
- APPOINTED: 2017
- TERM EXPIRES: 2023
- EDUCATION: Brian Long has a Bachelor of Science degree with a major in Criminal Justice from the University of Texas at Tyler, in Tyler Texas.
- BACKGROUND: Brian has over 25 years of experience in the Criminal Justice/Parole fields, including work with the: Cherokee County Sheriff's Department; the Texas Department of Criminal Justice, Parole Division, as a Parole Officer and Unit Supervisor; and the Texas Board of Pardons and Paroles as a Hearing Officer.

Marsha Moberley

- ASSIGNMENT: Angleton
- APPOINTED: 2022
- TERM EXPIRES: 2025
- EDUCATION: Bachelor of Science with a major in Criminal Justice from East Carolina University in Greenville, North Carolina.
- BACKGROUND: Ms. Moberley has over 25 years of criminal justice experience, including 12 years as a Parole Commissioner with the Texas Board of Pardons and Paroles. Her experience in criminal justice includes North Carolina Juvenile Court Counselor, Texas Youth Commission Case Manager, Probation Officer for Young and Stephens counties, and Chief Juvenile Officer for Deaf Smith and Oldham counties. She additionally served as Chair of the Panhandle Chief Probation Officer's Association, and Chair of Panhandle Regional Planning Commission Criminal Justice Advisory Board.

Linda Molina

- ASSIGNMENT: San Antonio
- APPOINTED: 2021
- TERM EXPIRES: 2027
- EDUCATION: Juris Doctor (J.D.), Southern Methodist University, Dedman School of Law; Master of Arts in Spanish, University of Texas at San Antonio;
- Bachelor of Arts in English and Spanish, Southern Methodist University.
- BACKGROUND: Ms. Molina has practiced law for 20 years, serving as an Assistant District Attorney in Bexar County for 12 years and as an Assistant Attorney General in the Texas Attorney General's Office, Habeas Corpus Section. Ms. Molina also served as the Municipal Judge in Sandy Oaks, Texas. Most recently, she was a partner in her law firm, Duarte & Molina, and worked as a criminal defense attorney, handling adult and juvenile matters. Ms. Molina was appointed by Governor Abbott to the Texas Medical Board, where she sat as a Public Member of the Board, and was the Chair of the Licensure Committee and the Chair of the Boundaries Taskforce. She is also a past member of the Emerging Leader Board for Southern Methodist University, Dedman School of Law.

Ed Robertson

- ASSIGNMENT: Austin
- APPOINTED: 2015
- TERM EXPIRES: 20271
- EDUCATION: Master of Science-Urban Administration, Trinity University, San Antonio, Texas; Bachelor of Arts, University of Texas at Austin, Austin, Texas.
- BACKGROUND: Twenty-two year veteran of public service, including Office of the Governor, Legislative Budget Board and the City of Austin.

Parole Commissioners of the Board of Pardons and Parole

Parole Commissioners assist the board with parole and revocation decisions. The commissioners are appointed by the Chair.

Michael Adams

- ASSIGNMENT: Huntsville
- EMPLOYED: 2022
- EDUCATION: Bachelor of Liberal Arts, Wheeling University, Wheeling, West Virginia.
- BACKGROUND: Over 36 years in the Criminal Justice profession serving as a Parole Officer and Supervisor for the Texas Department of Criminal Justice, and Hearing Officer, Regional Operations Supervisor, and Director of Hearing Operations for the Texas Board of Pardons and Paroles.

Richard Aiello

- ASSIGNMENT: Austin
- EMPLOYED: 2022
- EDUCATION: Bachelor of Science in Criminal Justice, Southwest Texas State University, San Marcos, Texas.
- BACKGROUND: Over 30 years in the Criminal Justice profession serving as a Parole Officer for the Texas Department of Criminal Justice, and Hearing Officer and Analyst Supervisor for the Texas Board of Pardons and Paroles.

Jacqueline Bishop

- ASSIGNMENT: Huntsville
- EMPLOYED: 2022
- EDUCATION: Bachelor of Science in Criminal Justice, Southwest Texas State University, San Marcos, TX.
- BACKGROUND: Over 30 years of Criminal Justice experience.

Edward Davila

- ASSIGNMENT: Amarillo
- EMPLOYED: 2022
- EDUCATION: Bachelor of Arts in Sociology, St. Mary's University, San Antonio, TX.
- BACKGROUND: Over 33 years in the Criminal Justice profession, serving as a Parole Officer for the Texas Department of Criminal Justice, and a Board Analyst for the Texas Board of Pardons and Paroles.

Lee Anne Eck-Massingill

- ASSIGNMENT: Gatesville
- EMPLOYED: 2014
- EDUCATION: Bachelor of Science in Criminologoy and Corrections, Sam Houston State University, Huntsville, Texas; Minor in Psychology, Sam Houston State University, Huntsville, Texas.
- BACKGROUND: 25 years of Criminal Justice experience.

Ira Evans

- ASSIGNMENT: Angleton
- EMPLOYED: 2015
- EDUCATION: B.S.E.E. Prairie View A&M University, Prairie View, Texas; post graduate studies at Webster University, St. Louis, Missouri.
- BACKGROUND: Commissioned as a Field Artillery Officer in U.S. Army, Honorable Discharge from service. Eighteen years experience in Manufacturing and Technical Management in the private sector. Joined the Texas Board of Pardons and Paroles as an Institutional Parole Officer in 2002 and promoted to Board Analyst in 2010.

Mary J. Farley

- ASSIGNMENT: Huntsville
- EMPLOYED: 2019
- EDUCATION: Criminal Justice Studies, Central Texas College, Killeen, and University of Phoenix in Killeen, Texas.
- BACKGROUND: Over 28 years in the Corrections profession with 26 years as Jail Administrator at County Jail. Earned TCOLE Master Peace Officer and Master Jailer. She is past president of the Texas Jail Association. She is an alumnus of the inaugural class Jail Leadership Command Academy at Sam Houston State University. Prior to Corrections, Mary served in the U.S. Army as a medical specialist.

Sandra Fletcher

- ASSIGNMENT: Angleton
- EMPLOYED: 2022
- EDUCATION: Bachelor of Science in Criminal Justice, Southwest Texas State University, San Marcos, TX.
- BACKGROUND: Over 30 years of experience with the State of Texas serving as a District Parole Officer, Institutional Parole Officer, and Hearing Officer.

Troy Fox

- ASSIGNMENT: Austin
- EMPLOYED: 2012
- EDUCATION: Bachelor of Science in Criminology and Corrections from Sam Houston State University, Hunstville, Texas.
- BACKGROUND: Over 35 years experience in the corrections and criminal justice fields in positions ranging from probation officer to various management positions with the TDCJ-Parole Division and the Board of Pardons and Paroles, most recently serving as the BPP Board Administrator 2006-2012.

Raymond Gonzalez

- ASSIGNMENT: Amarillo
- EMPLOYED: 2016
- EDUCATION: Bachelor's degree in Criminal Justice, Sam Houston State University, Huntsville, Texas.
- BACKGROUND: Over 38 years of experience in Criminal Justice, which includes 20 years with the Texas Department of Criminal Justice-Parole Division in positions from a Parole Officer to Assistant Regional Supervisor; additionally he has worked in Correctional Institutional Division as an Assistant Warden. Mr. Gonzalez worked eight years as a Juvenile Halfway House Superintendent for the Texas Juvenile Justice Department.

James Paul Kiel, Jr.

- ASSIGNMENT: Palestine
- EMPLOYED: 2004
- EDUCATION: Bachelor of Science in Criminal Justice, Sam Houston State University, Huntsville, Texas.
- BACKGROUND: Over 40 years of experience in the Criminal Justice field, starting with the Texas Department of Corrections as a Correctional Officer and a Sociologist. Assigned to the TDCJ Parole Division as a Parole Officer, Unit Supervisor, Parole Supervisor and Assistant Regional Director. Various roles with the Board of Pardons and Paroles as a Board Member, Policy Board Member, and currently a Parole Commissioner.

Jeffrey Marton

- ASSIGNMENT: Amarillo
- EMPLOYED: 2021
- EDUCATION: Master's in Public Administration, Bachelor of Science in Criminal Justice & Correctional Management, Bellevue University, Bellevue, Nebraska.

- BACKGROUND: 39 years in the Criminal Justice profession serving in various positions for the Texas Department of Criminal Justice, Project Coordinator for Correctional Management Institute of Texas at Sam Houston State University, Assistant Supervisor for the Texas Juvenile Justice Department, and Unit Supervisor and Assistant Regional Supervisor for the Texas Board of Pardons and Paroles, Institutional Parole Operations.

Anthony Ramirez

- ASSIGNMENT: San Antonio
- EMPLOYED: 2012
- EDUCATION: Bachelor of Arts in Criminal Justice from the University of Texas at San Antonio.
- BACKGROUND: Over 22 years of experience in the criminal justice field, with 14 years in TDCJ-Parole Division positions including Parole Officer, Sex Offender Unit Supervisor, and Program Administrator overseeing the Internal Review and Field/Specialized Training programs. Served nearly eight years with Texas Lottery Commission Enforcement Division performing intake duties for complaints and investigations. Elected to two terms on Elgin City Council (2007-2011), serving as Mayor Pro-Tem in 2010.

Alfredo Salcido

- ASSIGNMENT: Huntsville
- EMPLOYED: 2023
- EDUCATION: Associate of Applied Science in Criminal Justice, Central Texas College, Killeen, TX.
- BACKGROUND: 35 years in the Law Enforcement profession.

Roel Tejada

- ASSIGNMENT: Gatesville
- EMPLOYED: 2014
- EDUCATION: Bachelors of Arts, St. Mary's University, San Antonio, Texas; Master's of Justice Administration, St. Mary's University, San Antonio, Texas
- BACKGROUND: Criminal Justice experience in both Juvenile and Adult systems with emphasis on Substance Abuse, Special Needs and Domestic Violence. Over 13 years of Administrative and Supervisory experience.

Appendix 4

Location of Voting Board Offices

Voting Board Locations

The Texas Board of Pardons and Paroles maintains headquarters in Austin and Huntsville under Presiding Officer David G. Gutierrez, along with Board offices each supervised by a board member. Generally, parole review cases are assigned to offices based on the TDCJ unit locations.

Mailing address for main office:
Texas Board of Pardons and Paroles
P. O. Box 13401
Austin, Texas 78711-3401
Phone: (512) 406-5452
Parole Status Line: (844) 512-0461

Austin Board Office

4616 W. Howard Lane, Suite 200
Austin, Texas 78728
Phone: (512) 671-2532
Fax: (512) 671-2497

Units Assigned to the Austin Board Office

- Bridgeport Unit*
- Coleman (Private) Prison
- Coleman Work Facility
- Crain Unit*
- Halbert SAFPF
- Hamilton Unit
- Hilltop Unit*
- Hobby Unit
- Hughes Unit*
- Luther Unit
- Marlin Unit
- Memorial Unit*
- Middleton Unit
- Mountain View Unit*
- Murray Unit*
- Pack Unit
- San Saba Unit
- Sanders Estes Unit

- Stevenson Unit
- Stiles Unit*
- Travis County State Jail

*Cases that involve Board Members only (SB 45 and HB 1914).*Cases that involve Board Members only (SB 45 and HB 1914)

Amarillo Board Office

5809 S. Western, Suite 200
Amarillo, TX 79110
Phone: (806) 359-7656
Fax: (806) 358-6455

Units Assigned to the Amarillo Board Office

- Allred Unit
- Clements Unit
- Dalhart Unit
- Daniel Unit
- Formby State Jail
- Fort Stockton Unit
- Jordan Unit
- Lynaugh Unit
- Mechler Unit
- Montford Unit
- Roach Unit
- Robertson Unit
- Rudd Unit
- Sanchez State Jail
- Smith Unit
- Wallace Unit
- Wheeler State Jail
- Wilderness 3 - San Angelo

Angleton Board Office

1212 N. Velasco, Suite 201
Angleton, TX 77515
Phone: (979) 849-3031
Fax: (979) 849-8741

Units Assigned to the Angleton Board Office

- Carole S. Young Medical Complex
- Clemens Unit
- Gib Lewis Unit
- Gist State Jail
- Goodman Unit
- Henley State Jail
- Hightower Unit
- Hospital - Galveston
- Jester III Unit
- LeBlanc Unit
- Lychner State Jail
- Mac Stringfellow Unit
- Plane State Jail
- Ramsey Unit
- Scott Unit
- Terrell Unit
- Vance Unit

Gatesville Board Office

545 State Hwy. 36 Bypass N., Suite A
Gatesville, TX 76528
Phone: (254) 865-8870
Fax: (254) 865-2629

Units Assigned to the Gatesville Board Office

- Bridgeport - Male & Female
- Choice Moore Unit
- Cole State Jail
- Crain Unit

- Havins Unit
- Hilltop Unit
- Hughes Unit
- Hutchins State Jail
- Kyle Unit
- Lindsey State Jail
- Memorial Unit*
- Mountain View Unit
- Murray Unit
- Sayle SAFPF
- Stiles Unit*
- Woodman State Jail

Huntsville Board Office

1022 Veterans Memorial Parkway, Suite A
Huntsville, Texas 77320
Phone: (936) 291-2161
Fax: (936) 291-8367

Units Assigned to the Huntsville Board Office

- Bell Unit
- Byrd Unit
- Diboll Unit
- Duncan Unit
- Ellis Unit
- Estelle Unit
- Ferguson Unit
- Goree Unit
- Holliday Unit
- Huntsville Unit
- Kegans State Jail
- Wainwright Unit
- Wynne Unit
- Federal (FCI)

Palestine Board Office

133 E. Reagan Street
Palestine, TX 75801
Phone: (903) 723-1068
Fax: (903) 723-1441

Units Assigned to the Palestine Board Office

- Beto Unit
- Billy Moore Unit
- Boyd Unit
- Bradshaw State Jail
- Coffield Unit
- East Texas Treatment Facility
- Gurney Unit
- Hodge Unit
- Johnston SAFPF
- Michael Unit
- Polunsky Unit
- Powledge Unit
- Skyview Unit
- Telford Unit

San Antonio Board Office

2902 N.E. Loop 410, Suite #206
San Antonio, TX 78218
Phone: (210) 564-3721
Fax: (210) 564-3726

Units Assigned to the San Antonio Board Office

- Briscoe Unit
- Connally Unit
- Cotulla Unit
- Dominguez State Jail
- Garza West Unit
- Glossbrenner SAFPF

- Lopez State Jail
- McConnell Unit
- Ney State Jail
- Segovia Unit
- Torres Unit
- Willacy County State Jail

Hearing Operations Locations

Hearing Operations Locations

Hearing officers for the Texas Board of Pardons and Paroles conduct hearings on alleged parole violations to determine whether an offense occurred and to make recommendations to the Board on revoking parole or issuing other sanctions. Parole hearings typically are held within county jails or TDCJ-CID units statewide. Hearing reports are presented to the parole panels for revocation decisions. Hearings Operations has offices in three regions: Dallas, Houston and San Antonio.

Batrice Murphy, Director of Hearing Operations
8610 Shoal Creek Boulevard
Austin, Texas 78757
Phone: 512-406-5452
Fax: 512-406-5482

Austin (Region I)

Heather Clark, Regional Operations Supervisor

Austin Regional Hearing Operations
3928 Promontory Point
Austin, Texas 78744
Phone: 512-462-3502
Fax: 512-445-0157

Abilene Hearing Operations
100 Chestnut, Ste. 205
Abilene, Texas 79602
Phone: 325-676-4204
Fax: 325-677-8960

Amarillo Hearing Operations
5809 South Western St., Ste. 200
Amarillo, Texas 79110
Phone: 806-457-8557
Fax: 806-457-8386

Arlington Hearing Operations
2500 NE Green Oaks Blvd., Suite 210
Arlington, Texas 76006
Phone: 817-633-3731
Fax: 817-640-8924

Corpus Christi Hearing Operations
422 Sunbelt Drive
Corpus Christi, Texas 78408
Phone: 361-888-5698
Fax: 361-906-3313

El Paso Hearing Operations
13 Founders Blvd.
El Paso, Texas
Phone: 915-778-4233
Fax: 915-772-4031

Harlingen Hearing Operations
232 Hanmore Dr.
Harlingen, Texas 78550
Phone: 956-428-0335
Fax: 956-428-2017

Odessa Hearing Operations
701 McDonald
Odessa, Texas 79761
Phone: 432-550-0131
Fax: 432 550-0012

San Angelo Hearing Operations
1070 Gateway Drive
San Angelo, Texas 76904
Phone: 325-947-8644
Fax: 325-947-8599

San Antonio Hearing Operations
2902 N.E. Loop 410, Suite #219
San Antonio, Texas 78218
Phone: 210-564-3737
Fax: 210-564-3728

Wichita Falls Hearing Operations
3100 Seymour Hwy, #118
Wichita Falls, Texas 76301
Phone: 940-322-2721
Fax: 940-766-4216

Houston (Region II)

Joel Butler, Regional Operations Supervisor

Houston Regional Hearing Operations
4949 W. 34th St., Ste. A-3
Houston, Texas 77092
Phone: 713-681-4828
Fax: 713-957–5780

Angleton Hearing Operations
1208 N. Velasco
Angleton, Texas 77515
Phone: 979-848-5710
Fax: 979-849-9289

Dallas Hearing Operations
1010 Cadiz, Ste.105
Dallas, Texas 75215
Phone: 214-428-8338
Fax: 214-426-6239

Huntsville Hearing Operations
1022 Veterans Memorial Parkway, Ste. A
Huntsville, Texas 77340
Phone: 936-291-2244
Fax: 936-291-6852

Paris Hearing Operations
3905 North Main Street
Paris, Texas 75460
Phone: 903-785-4492
Fax: 903-784-2056

Port Arthur Hearing Operations
4200 Jimmy Johnson Blvd., Suite B
Port Arthur, Texas 77642
Phone: 409-724-3029
Fax: 409-724-3037

Tyler Hearing Operations
517 N. Glenwood, Ste. A
Tyler, Texas 75702
Phone: 903-531-0057
Fax: 903-531-0134

Waco Hearing Operations
801 Austin, Suite 135
Waco, Texas 76701
Phone: 254-752-3753
Fax: 254-752-1104

Appendix 6

Institutional Parole Offices (IPO)

Institutional Parole Offices (IPO)

Institutional parole officers for the Texas Board of Pardons and Paroles gather information about offenders coming up for parole, interview offenders, and prepare detailed case summaries for the Parole Panel to review prior to voting. Their duties include:

- Identify victim information for referral to TDCJ-Victim Services
- Complete sex offender risk assessments
- Screen offenders for treatment program eligibility
- Respond to inquiries from offender families, general public, victims, and law enforcement agencies
- Deliver Status Letters to offenders
- Interview offenders who are eligible for parole
- Prepare detailed case summaries for Parole Panel review prior to voting.

With four regional offices and four satellite offices, the IPOs cover 104 prison units and 254 counties.

Clint Gunnels, IPO Director

Erica Montalvan, IPO Deputy Director

1022 Veterans Memorial Parkway, Suite A
Huntsville, TX 77320
Phone: 936- 437-2273
Fax: 936-291-6852

545 SH 36 Bypass N, Suite B
Gatesville, Texas 76528
Phone: 254-865-2720
Fax: 254-865-2575

Amarillo Institutional Parole Office (IPO)

Rueth Palad Farr, Regional Supervisor
Elizabeth Hartwell, Assistant Regional Supervisor

5809 S. Western, Ste. 130
Amarillo, TX 79110
Phone: 806-352-9500
Fax: 806-467-1348

Units Assigned to the Amarillo IPO

- Clements Unit
- Dalhart Unit
- Formby State Jail
- Fort Stockton Unit
- Jordan Unit
- Lynaugh Unit
- Mechler Unit
- Montford Unit
- Roach Unit
- Rudd Unit
- Sanchez State Jail
- Smith Unit
- Wheeler State Jail

Angleton Institutional Parole Office (IPO)

Margo Green, Regional Supervisor
Jimmy Guyton, Assistant Regional Supervisor

1208 N. Velasco
Angleton, TX 77515
Phone: 979-849-6491
Fax: 979-849-9289

Units Assigned to the Angleton IPO

- Clemens Unit
- Coleman Private
- Coleman Work Facility
- Dominguez State Jail
- Hospital Galveston
- Jester 3 Unit
- Joe Kegans State Jail
- Kyle Unit
- Lychner State Jail
- Mac Stringfellow Unit
- Memorial Unit
- Ramsey Unit
- Santa Maria State Jail
- Scott Unit
- Terrell Unit
- Travis County State Jail
- Vance Unit
- Young Medical Complex

Arlington Institutional Parole Office (IPO)

Kristi Mitchell, Regional Supervisor
Lee Foster, Assistant Regional Supervisor

2500 NE Green Oaks Blvd., Suite 210
Arlington, TX 76006
Phone: 817-640-8960
Fax: 817-640-8956

Units Assigned to the Arlington IPO

- Allred Unit
- Bridgeport Unit (Male)
- Choice Moore Unit
- Cole State Jail
- Estes Unit
- Hutchins State Jail
- Lindsey State Jail

Beeville Institutional Parole Office (IPO)

Margo Green, Regional Supervisor
Michael Ortiz, Assistant Regional Supervisor

2033 Independence Street, Building 2189
Beeville, TX 78102
Phone: 361-362-6511
Fax: 361-362-6364

Units Assigned to the Beeville IPO

- Briscoe Unit
- Connally Unit
- Cotulla Unit
- Garza West Unit
- Glossbrenner SAFPF
- Lopez State Jail
- McConnell Unit
- Ney State Jail
- Segovia Unit
- Stevenson Unit
- Torres Unit
- Willacy County State Jail

Gatesville Institutional Parole Office (IPO)

Rueth Palad Farr, Regional Supervisor
Joy Chandler, Assistant Regional Supervisor

545 State Hwy 36 Bypass N, Suite B
Gatesville, TX 76528
Phone: 254-865-2720
Fax: 254-865-8816

Units Assigned to the Gatesville IPO

- Crain Unit
    - Crain/Reception
    - Crain/Riverside
    - Crain/Sycamore
    - Crain/Terrace
    - Crain/Trusty Camp
    - Crain/Valley
- Daniel Unit
- Halbert SAFPF
- Havins Unit
- Hilltop Unit
- Hobby Unit
- Hughes Unit
- Marlin Unit
- Middleton Unit
- Mountain View Unit
- Murray Unit
- Robertson Unit
- San Saba Unit
- Sayle SAFPF
- Wallace Unit
- Wilderness 3 (San Angelo)
- Woodman State Jail

Huntsville Institutional Parole Office (IPO)

Jennifer Herrington, Regional Supervisor
Clint Adams, Assistant Regional Supervisor

1022 Veterans Memorial Parkway, Suite B
Huntsville, TX 77320
Phone: 936-437-5514
Fax: 936-437-5543

Units Assigned to the Huntsville IPO

- Bell Unit
- Byrd Unit
- Diboll Unit
- Duncan Unit
- Ellis Unit
- Estelle Unit
- Ferguson Unit
- Gib Lewis Unit
- Gist State Jail
- Goodman Unit
- Goree Unit
- Hamilton Unit
- Henley State Jail
- Hightower Unit
- Holliday Unit
- Huntsville Unit
- LeBlanc Unit
- Luther Unit
- Pack Unit
- Plane State Jail
- Polunsky Unit
- Stiles Unit
- Wainwright Unit
- Wynne Unit
- Federal (FCI)

Palestine Institutional Parole Office (IPO)

Kristi Mitchell, Regional Supervisor
Lee Foster, Assistant Regional Supervisor

P.O. Box 2045
Palestine, Texas 75802
Phone: 903-729-3698
Fax: 903-729-0431

Units Assigned to the Palestine IPO

- Allred
- Beto Unit
- Billy Moore Unit
- Boyd Unit
- Bridgeport
- Choice Moore Unit
- Coffield Unit
- Cole State Jail
- East Texas Treatment Facility
- Estes Unit
- Gurney Unit
- Hodge Unit
- Hutchins State Jail
- Johnston SAFPF
- Lindsey State Jail
- Michael Unit
- Powledge Unit
- Skyview Unit
- Telford Unit

Frequently Asked Questions

What is the difference between the Board of Pardons and Paroles and Parole Division?

The primary role of the board members and parole commissioners is the determination of which offenders are to be released on parole or discretionary mandatory supervision and the revocation of parole or mandatory supervision offenders for violations. Additionally, parole panels are responsible for determining the conditions of release and the imposition of any special conditions for parole or mandatory supervision offenders. The primary role of the

Parole Division is the supervision of offenders released from the Correctional Institutions Division on parole or mandatory supervision. The division also supervises offenders who are released from a county jail or another jurisdiction to Parole in Absentia.

How can I contact the Texas Board of Pardons and Paroles?

Anyone wishing to contact the Texas Board of Pardons and Paroles can submit their requests in writing to:

Texas Board of Pardons and Paroles
P. O. Box 13401, Capitol Station
Austin, Texas 78711
512-406-5452

Email: bpp-pio@tdcj.state.tx.us
Website: http://www.tdcj.state.tx.us/bpp/

How can I contact the Parole Division?

Anyone wishing to contact the Parole Division can submit their concerns in writing to:

Texas Department of Criminal Justice, Parole Division
Attention: Ombudsman
P.O. Box 13401, Capitol Station
Austin, Texas 78711
(512) 406-5795

Bilingual Staff Available – Se habla Espanol
Email address: parole.div@tdcj.state.tx.us

What is the phone number for the Parole Status Line?

The number for the Parole Status Line is: 844-512-0461

Where can I send my offender support letter and parole packet?

Offender support letters may be sent to the Texas Department of Criminal Justice to be placed in the offender's permanent file for review by the parole panel at the appropriate time.

Address letters to:
TDCJ-Parole Division
Attention: Correspondence
P.O. Box 13401, Capitol Station
Austin, Texas 78711

Include the offender's full name and their TDCJ number, SID number and/or date of birth.

Can any offender be paroled?

No. Offenders who are sentenced to death, or to life without parole are not eligible for parole. Also, State Jail convictions are not applicable for parole eligibility

How are Consecutive ("stacked") Sentences Used For Parole Eligibility?

If an offender is serving consecutive sentences and any of those offenses were committed before September 1, 1987, parole eligibility is based on the total number of years of the various sentences. For example, two 15-year sentences running consecutively would be considered one 30-year sentence for eligibility purposes. Once parole eligibility is met, these offenders need only be voted an approval for release one time in order to be released on supervision.

Offenders who are serving consecutive sentences in which all of the offenses were committed on or after September 1, 1987, must complete each sentence in the series before the next sentence begins. The sentence can be completed only by serving the sentence day for day until the maximum expiration date or by receiving a favorable vote from a parole panel for the sentence to "cease to operate" on a specified date. Time earning for parole review purposes on the next sentence in the series will begin on the date calculated by the CID-Classification and Records Office. The phrase "cease to operate" only means the next sentence in the sequence begins and does not mean the sentence is totally discharged. All sentences in the series are totaled to calculate the overall maximum discharge date of all the offenses. Mandatory supervision, if applicable, applies only to the last sentence in the series.

What are Full Board Parole Decisions-SB 45 and HB 1914?

In accordance with Texas Government Code Section 508.046, a two-thirds majority vote of the Board is necessary for parole decisions involving: offenders convicted of serving a sentence for a capital felony, an offense under Section 20A.03 [Continuous Trafficking of Persons], Section 21.02 [Continuous Sexual Abuse of Young Child or Children], Section 21.11(a)(1) [Indecency with a Child], or Section 22.021 [Aggravated Sexual Assault] of the Penal Code, or offenders required under Texas Government Code Section 508.145(c) to serve 35 calendar years before becoming eligible for release on parole.

These offenders, except capital felons serving a life sentence and those convicted of or serving a sentence for Aggravated Sexual Assault, are eligible for up to a 5 year set-off. Capital felons serving a life sentence and those offenders with Aggravated Sexual Assault offenses are eligible for up to a 10 year set-off.

What special conditions can the parole panel impose in addition to the rules stated previously?

A parole panel may add special release conditions for any offender. The most common special conditions include; sex offender requirements, intensive supervision, electronic monitoring, drug monitoring (urinalysis), or mandatory participation in drug/alcohol treatment, educational programs, or psychological counseling. A parole panel may also impose other conditions deemed appropriate to the individual and in the interest of society, including payment of court-ordered restitution to victims. A Super-Intensive Supervision Program (SISP) special condition requires violent/assaultive offenders to be placed on an SISP caseload upon release from prison.

When does release become effective?

A parole release becomes effective when the offender signs his or her release certificate. The certificate orders the release and tells the offender in clear and understandable language where to report and to whom. The certificate lists the conditions of release and gives the date on which the offender will discharge his or her sentence and be free from supervision. The certificate also includes a waiver of extradition. The parole certificate must be signed by the offender. Offenders released on mandatory supervision are given release certificates that provide parole office information and release conditions. Mandatory supervision offenders are not required to sign their release certificates, but they nevertheless must obey the rules and conditions of supervision and are subject to revocation if they violate the rules or conditions.

What is parole to a community-based facility (Residential Reentry Center/County Jail Work Release Program)?

Residential Reentry Center beds are designated for placement of parole and mandatory supervision offenders either immediately upon release from the Correctional Institutions Division (CID) or upon referral from field staff under specific circumstances. Specifically, some clients who need closer supervision and special services or who lack family and community resources are released to these facilities to ease the transition from prison life to community life. Residential Reentry Centers may provide intensive job search assistance and require offender participation in the savings program, which is described below in the 'rules' section. County jail work release beds are contractually arranged by Texas counties and TDCJ-PD. The program was developed to return the parole or mandatory supervision offender to the offender's county of residence.

What are the rules of a Residential Reentry Center/County Jail Work Release Program?

Each community-based facility has its own rules, but residents must abide by the following general rules:

- Upon release, go directly to the assigned facility and remain there until permission to move is granted by authorized parole officials;
- Obey all facility rules and attend required facility meetings;
- Cooperate with facility officials in monitoring one's whereabouts;
- Remain on the property at all times except for traveling to and from a job or as authorized by facility rules;
- Pay 25% of gross salary toward upkeep in the facility and any specified obligations incurred while a resident; and
- Save 33.3% of gross salary to be utilized in developing a residential plan to transition out of the facility.

Can probation violators be paroled?

Offenders imprisoned for probation violations are no longer probationers. They are therefore eligible for parole consideration or mandatory release in accordance with the same laws and policies that apply to all offenders.

What is "gate money"?

The Correctional Institutions Division provides $50 and a bus ticket to offenders released on parole or mandatory supervision to help with transportation to the community to which they will be paroled and with other expenses involved in resettling in the community. They receive an additional $50 upon reporting to their parole office. Clients who are not required to report to a Parole Officer immediately after release or who are released to a detainer or to an out-of-state plan receive the full $100 at time of release.

Can offenders be supervised in other states upon release?

Yes. Texas has an agreement with other states, the District of Columbia, Puerto Rico and the Virgin Islands to send and receive offenders for supervision. It is called the "Interstate Compact for Adult Offender Supervision". The website is www.interstatecompact.org. Offenders sent to other states must obey the rules of both Texas and the supervising state. Upon a decision from the parole panel, they must be returned to Texas to continue serving their sentences and are subject to revocation of their release if they violate the rules.

What is Parole in Absentia (PIA)?

Some offenders serve their Texas sentences while in the custody of federal facilities, prisons in other states, or city and county jails. The parole panel may conduct PIA reviews for such parole eligible offenders who are incarcerated in non-TDCJ facilities. The Institutional Parole Offices assist in tracking PIA reviews and in preparing the appropriate paperwork.

Appendix 8

Complete Parole Laws

CHAPTER 508. PAROLE AND MANDATORY SUPERVISION
SUBCHAPTER A. GENERAL PROVISIONS

Sec. 508.001. DEFINITIONS. In this chapter:

(1) "Board" means the Board of Pardons and Paroles.

(2) "Community supervision and corrections department" means a department established under Chapter 76.

(3) "Director" means the director of the pardons and paroles division.

(4) "Division" means the pardons and paroles division.

(5) "Mandatory supervision" means the release of an eligible inmate sentenced to the institutional division so that the inmate may serve the remainder of the inmate's sentence not on parole but under the supervision of the pardons and paroles division.

(6) "Parole" means the discretionary and conditional release of an eligible inmate sentenced to the institutional division so that the inmate may serve the remainder of the inmate's sentence under the supervision of the pardons and paroles division.

(7) "Parole officer" means a person appointed by the director and assigned the duties of assessment of risks and needs, investigation, case management, and supervision of releasees to ensure that releasees are complying with the conditions of parole or mandatory supervision.

(8) "Parole commissioner" means a person employed by the board to perform the duties described by Section 508.0441.

(9) "Releasee" means a person released on parole or to mandatory supervision.

(10) "Presiding officer" means the presiding officer of the Board of Pardons and Paroles.

Added by Acts 1997, 75th Leg., ch. 165, Sec. 12.01, eff. Sept. 1, 1997. Amended by Acts 1999, 76th Leg., ch. 62, Sec. 10.01, eff. Sept. 1, 1999; Acts 2003, 78th Leg., 3rd C.S., ch. 3, Sec. 11.02, eff. Jan. 11, 2004.

Sec. 508.002. CLEMENCY, COMMUTATION DISTINGUISHED. Neither parole nor mandatory supervision is a commutation of sentence or any other form of clemency.

Added by Acts 1997, 75th Leg., ch. 165, Sec. 12.01, eff. Sept. 1, 1997.

Sec. 508.003. INAPPLICABLE TO JUVENILES AND CERTAIN INMATES. (a) This chapter does not apply to an emergency absence under escort granted to an inmate by the institutional division under Section 501.006.

(b) Except as provided by Subsection (c), this chapter does not apply to release on parole from an institution for juveniles.

(c) The provisions of this chapter not in conflict with Section 508.156 apply to parole of a person from the Texas Youth Commission under that section.

Added by Acts 1997, 75th Leg., ch. 165, Sec. 12.01, eff. Sept. 1, 1997.

SUBCHAPTER B. BOARD OF PARDONS AND PAROLES

Sec. 508.031. COMPOSITION OF BOARD. (a) The board consists of seven members appointed by the governor with the advice and consent of the senate.

(b) Appointments to the board must be made without regard to the race, color, disability, sex, religion, age, or national origin of the appointed members.

Added by Acts 1997, 75th Leg., ch. 165, Sec. 12.01, eff. Sept. 1, 1997. Amended by Acts 1999, 76th Leg., ch. 554, Sec. 1, eff. Sept. 1, 1999; Acts 2003, 78th Leg., 3rd C.S., ch. 3, Sec. 11.03, eff. Jan. 11, 2004.

Sec. 508.032. REQUIREMENTS FOR MEMBERSHIP. (a) Board members must be representative of the general public.

(b) A member must have resided in this state for the two years before appointment.

(c)(1) A person who is a former employee of the department may not serve on the board before the second anniversary of the date the person terminated employment with the department.

(2) A person who is employed by the department on August 1, 2003, may not serve on the board before August 1, 2005.

(d) At any time not more than three members of the board may be former employees of the department.

(e) For purposes of Subsections (c) and (d), previous service as a board member is not considered to be employment with the department.

Added by Acts 1997, 75th Leg., ch. 165, Sec. 12.01, eff. Sept. 1, 1997. Amended by Acts 2003, 78th Leg., 3rd C.S., ch. 3, Sec. 11.04, eff. Jan. 11, 2004.

Sec. 508.033. DISQUALIFICATIONS. (a) A person is not eligible for appointment as a member of the board or for employment as a parole commissioner if the person or the person's spouse:

(1) is employed by or participates in the management of a business entity or other organization receiving funds from the department or the board;

(2) owns or controls, directly or indirectly, more than a 10-percent interest in a business entity or other organization:

(A) regulated by the department; or

(B) receiving funds from the department or the board; or

(3) uses or receives a substantial amount of tangible goods, services, or funds from the department or the board, other than compensation or reimbursement authorized by law for board membership, attendance, or expenses.

(b) In determining eligibility under Subsection (a)(3), the compensation or reimbursement that a board member's spouse or parole commissioner's spouse receives as an employee of the board or the department may not be considered. This subsection does not affect any restriction on employment or board membership imposed by any other law.

(c) A person may not serve as a parole commissioner, may not be a member of the board, and may not be an employee of the division or the board employed in a "bona fide executive, administrative, or professional capacity," as that phrase is used for purposes of establishing an exemption to the overtime provisions of the federal Fair Labor Standards Act of 1938 (29 U.S.C. Section 201 et seq.) and its subsequent amendments, if:

(1) the person is an officer, employee, or paid consultant of a Texas trade association in the field of criminal justice; or

(2) the person's spouse is an officer, manager, or paid consultant of a Texas trade association in the field of criminal justice.

(d) A person who is required to register as a lobbyist under Chapter 305 because of the person's activities for compensation in or on behalf of a profession related to the operation of the board may not:

(1) serve as a member of the board or as a parole commissioner; or

(2) act as the general counsel to the board or division.

(e) In this section, "Texas trade association" means a cooperative and voluntarily joined association of business or professional competitors in this state designed to assist its members and its industry or profession in:

(1) dealing with mutual business or professional problems; and

(2) promoting their common interests.

(f) A person who is a current or former employee of the department may not serve as a parole commissioner before the second anniversary of the date the person's employment with the department ceases, and a member of the board may not serve as a parole commissioner before the second anniversary of the date the person's membership on the board ceases.

Added by Acts 1997, 75th Leg., ch. 165, Sec. 12.01, eff. Sept. 1, 1997. Amended by Acts 1999, 76th Leg., ch. 62, Sec. 10.04, eff. Sept. 1, 1999; Acts 1999, 76th Leg., ch. 554, Sec. 2, eff. Sept. 1, 1999.

Amended by:

Acts 2007, 80th Leg., R.S., Ch. 1308, Sec. 33, eff. June 15, 2007.

Sec. 508.034. GROUNDS FOR REMOVAL. (a) It is a ground for removal from the board that a member:

(1) does not have at the time of taking office the qualification required by Section 508.032(b) for appointment to the board;

(2) is ineligible for membership under Section 508.033;

(3) is unable to discharge the member's duties for a substantial part of the term for which the member is appointed because of illness or disability; or

(4) is absent from more than half of the regularly scheduled board or panel meetings that the member is eligible to attend during each calendar year.

(b) The board administrator or the board administrator's designee shall provide to members of the board and to employees, as often as necessary, information regarding their qualification for office or employment under this chapter and their responsibilities under applicable laws relating to standards of conduct for state officers or employees.

(c) The validity of an action of the board or panel is not affected by the fact that the action is taken when a ground for removal of a board member exists.

(d) If the general counsel to the board has knowledge that a potential ground for removal exists, the general counsel shall notify the presiding officer of the board of the potential ground. The presiding officer shall notify the governor and the attorney general that a potential ground for removal exists. If the potential ground for removal involves the presiding officer, the general counsel to the board shall notify the governor and the attorney general that a potential ground for removal exists.

(e) It is a ground for removal from the board that a member fails to comply with policies or rules adopted by the board.

Added by Acts 1997, 75th Leg., ch. 165, Sec. 12.01, eff. Sept. 1, 1997. Amended by Acts 1999, 76th Leg., ch. 62, Sec. 10.05, eff. Sept. 1, 1999; Acts 1999, 76th Leg., ch. 554, Sec. 3, eff. Sept. 1, 1999; Acts 2001, 77th Leg., ch. 856, Sec. 1, eff. Sept. 1, 2001; Acts 2003, 78th Leg., 3rd C.S., ch. 3, Sec. 11.05, eff. Jan. 11, 2004.

Sec. 508.035. PRESIDING OFFICER. (a) The governor shall designate one member to serve as presiding officer of the board.

(b) The presiding officer serves in that capacity at the pleasure of the governor.

(c) The presiding officer reports directly to the governor and serves as the administrative head of the board.

(d) The presiding officer may:

(1) delegate responsibilities and authority to other members of the board, parole commissioners, or to employees of the board;

(2) appoint advisory committees from the membership of the board or from parole commissioners to further the efficient administration of board business; and

(3) establish policies and procedures to further the efficient administration of the business of the board.

Added by Acts 1997, 75th Leg., ch. 165, Sec. 12.01, eff. Sept. 1, 1997. Amended by Acts 2001, 77th Leg., ch. 856, Sec. 2, eff. Sept. 1, 2001; Acts 2003, 78th Leg., 3rd C.S., ch. 3, Sec. 11.06, eff. Jan. 11, 2004.

Sec. 508.036. GENERAL ADMINISTRATIVE DUTIES. (a) The presiding officer shall:

(1) develop and implement policies that clearly separate the policy-making responsibilities of the board and the management responsibilities of the board administrator, parole commissioners, and the staff of the board;

(2) establish caseloads and required work hours for members of the board and parole commissioners;

(3) update parole guidelines, assign precedential value to previous decisions of the board relating to the granting of parole and the revocation of parole or mandatory supervision, and develop policies to ensure that members of the board and parole commissioners use guidelines and previous decisions of the board and parole commissioners in making decisions under this chapter;

(4) require members of the board and parole commissioners to file activity reports that provide information on release decisions made by members of the board and parole commissioners, the workload and hours worked of the members of the board and parole commissioners, and the use of parole guidelines by members of the board and parole commissioners; and

(5) report at least annually to the governor and the legislature on the activities of the board and parole commissioners, parole release decisions, and the use of parole guidelines by the board and parole commissioners.

(b) The board shall:

(1) adopt rules relating to the decision-making processes used by the board and parole panels;

(2) prepare information of public interest describing the functions of the board and make the information available to the public and appropriate state agencies;

(3) comply with federal and state laws related to program and facility accessibility;

(4) prepare annually a complete and detailed written report that meets the reporting requirements applicable to financial reporting provided in the General Appropriations Act and accounts for all funds received and disbursed by the board during the preceding fiscal year; and

(5) develop and implement policies that provide the public with a reasonable opportunity to appear before the board and to speak on any issue under the jurisdiction of the board, with the exception of an individual parole determination or clemency recommendation.

(c) The board administrator shall prepare and maintain a written plan that describes how a person who does not speak English can be provided reasonable access to the board's programs and services.

(d) The board, in performing its duties, is subject to the open meetings law, Chapter 551, and the administrative procedure law, Chapter 2001. This subsection does not affect the provisions of Section 2001.223 exempting hearings and interviews conducted by the board or the division from Section 2001.038 and Subchapters C-H, Chapter 2001.

(e) The board, in accordance with the rules and procedures of the Legislative Budget Board, shall prepare, approve, and submit a legislative appropriations request that is separate from the legislative appropriations request for the department and is used to develop the board's budget structure. The board shall maintain the board's legislative appropriations request and budget structure separately from those of the department.

Added by Acts 1997, 75th Leg., ch. 165, Sec. 12.01, eff. Sept. 1, 1997. Amended by Acts 1999, 76th Leg., ch. 62, Sec. 10.06, eff. Sept. 1, 1999; Acts 2001, 77th Leg., ch. 856, Sec. 3, eff. Sept. 1, 2001; Acts 2003, 78th Leg., ch. 1170, Sec. 31.01, eff. Sept. 1, 2003; Acts 2003, 78th Leg., 3rd C.S., ch. 3, Sec. 11.07, eff. Jan. 11, 2004.

Amended by: Acts 2007, 80th Leg., R.S., Ch. 1308, Sec. 34, eff. June 15, 2007.

Acts 2007, 80th Leg., R.S., Ch. 1308, Sec. 35, eff. June 15, 2007.

Sec. 508.0362. TRAINING REQUIRED. (a)(1) A person who is appointed to and qualifies for office as a member of the board may not vote, deliberate, or be counted as a member in attendance at a meeting of the board until the person completes at least one course of a training program that complies with this section.

(2) A parole commissioner employed by the board may not vote or deliberate on a matter described by Section 508.0441 until the person completes at least one course of a training

program that complies with this section.

(b) A training program must provide information to the person regarding:

(1) the enabling legislation that created the board;

(2) the programs operated by the board;

(3) the role and functions of the board and parole commissioners;

(4) the rules of the board;

(5) the current budget for the board;

(6) the results of the most recent formal audit of the board;

(7) the requirements of the:

(A) open meetings law, Chapter 551;

(B) open records law, Chapter 552; and

(C) administrative procedure law, Chapter 2001;

(8) the requirements of the conflict of interest laws and other laws relating to public officials; and

(9) any applicable ethics policies adopted by the board or the Texas Ethics Commission.

(c) A person appointed to the board is entitled to reimbursement, as provided by the General Appropriations Act, for the travel expenses incurred in attending the training program regardless of whether the attendance at the program occurs before or after the person qualifies for office.

Added by Acts 1999, 76th Leg., ch. 62, Sec. 10.08, eff. Sept. 1, 1999.
Amended by Acts 1999, 76th Leg., ch. 554, Sec. 4, eff. Sept. 1, 1999; Acts 2003, 78th Leg., 3rd C.S., ch. 3, Sec. 11.08, eff. Jan. 11, 2004.

Sec. 508.037. TERMS; REMOVAL. (a) A board member holds office for a term of six years.

(b) The terms of one-third of the members expire February 1 of each odd-numbered year.

(c) The governor may remove a board member, other than a member appointed by another governor, at any time and for any reason.

Added by Acts 1997, 75th Leg., ch. 165, Sec. 12.01, eff. Sept. 1, 1997.

Sec. 508.038. VACANCIES. If a vacancy occurs, the governor shall appoint in the same manner as other appointments are made a person to serve the remainder of the unexpired term.

Added by Acts 1997, 75th Leg., ch. 165, Sec. 12.01, eff. Sept. 1, 1997.

Sec. 508.039. COMPENSATION. A board member is paid the salary the legislature determines in the General Appropriations Act.

Added by Acts 1997, 75th Leg., ch. 165, Sec. 12.01, eff. Sept. 1, 1997.

Sec. 508.040. PERSONNEL. (a) The presiding officer is responsible for the employment and supervision of:

(1) parole commissioners;

(2) a general counsel to the board;

(3) a board administrator to manage the day-to-day activities of the board;

(4) hearing officers;

(5) personnel to assist in clemency and hearing matters; and

(6) secretarial or clerical personnel.

(b) The board administrator or the board administrator's designee shall prepare and maintain a written policy statement that implements a program of equal employment opportunity under which all personnel decisions of the board are made without regard to race, color, disability, sex, religion, age, or national origin. The policy statement must include:

(1) personnel policies, including policies relating to recruitment, evaluation, selection, training, and promotion of personnel, that show the intent of the board to avoid the unlawful employment practices described by Chapter 21, Labor Code; and

(2) an analysis of the extent to which the composition of the board's personnel is in accordance with state and federal law and a description of reasonable methods to achieve compliance with state and federal law.

(c) The policy statement must be updated annually, be reviewed by the Commission on Human Rights for compliance with Subsection (b)(1), and be filed with the governor's office.

(d) The board administrator or the board administrator's designee shall develop an intra-agency career ladder program that addresses opportunities for mobility and advancement for employees within the board. The program shall require intra-agency posting of all positions concurrently with any public posting.

(e) The board administrator or the board administrator's designee shall develop a system of annual performance evaluations that are based on documented employee performance. All merit pay for board employees must be based on the system established under this subsection.

Added by Acts 1997, 75th Leg., ch. 165, Sec. 12.01, eff. Sept. 1, 1997. Amended by Acts 1999, 76th Leg., ch. 62, Sec. 10.09, eff. Sept. 1, 1999; Acts 1999, 76th Leg., ch. 554, Sec. 5, eff. Sept. 1, 1999; Acts 2003, 78th Leg., 3rd C.S., ch. 3, Sec. 11.09, eff. Jan. 11, 2004.

Sec. 508.041. DESIGNEE TRAINING; HANDBOOK. (a) The board shall develop and implement:

(1) a training program that each newly hired employee of the board designated to conduct hearings under Section 508.281 must complete before conducting a hearing without the assistance of a board member or experienced parole commissioner or designee; and

(2) a training program to provide an annual update to designees of the board on issues and procedures relating to the revocation process.

(b) The board shall prepare and biennially update a procedural manual to be used by designees of the board. The board shall include in the manual:

(1) descriptions of decisions in previous hearings determined by the board to have value as precedents for decisions in subsequent hearings;

(2) laws and court decisions relevant to decision making in hearings; and

(3) case studies useful in decision making in hearings.

(c) The board shall prepare and update as necessary a handbook to be made available to participants in hearings under Section 508.281, such as defense attorneys, persons released on parole or mandatory supervision, and witnesses. The handbook must describe in plain language the procedures used in a hearing under Section 508.281.

Added by Acts 1997, 75th Leg., ch. 165, Sec. 12.01, eff. Sept. 1, 1997. Amended by Acts 1999, 76th Leg., ch. 62, Sec. 10.10, eff. Sept. 1, 1999; Acts 2003, 78th Leg., 3rd C.S., ch. 3, Sec. 11.10, eff. Jan. 11, 2004.

Sec. 508.042. TRAINING PROGRAM FOR MEMBERS AND PAROLE COMMISSIONERS. (a) The board shall develop for board members and parole commissioners a comprehensive training and education program on the criminal justice system, with special emphasis on the parole process.

(b)(1) A new member may not participate in a vote of the board or a panel, deliberate, or be counted as a member in attendance at a meeting of the board until the member completes the program.

(2) A new parole commissioner may not participate in a vote of a panel until the commissioner completes the program. This subdivision does not apply to a new parole commissioner who as a board member completed the program.

Added by Acts 1997, 75th Leg., ch. 165, Sec. 12.01, eff. Sept. 1, 1997. Amended by Acts 1999, 76th Leg., ch. 62, Sec. 10.11, eff. Sept. 1, 1999; Acts 1999, 76th Leg., ch. 554, Sec. 6, eff. Sept. 1, 1999; Acts 2003, 78th Leg., 3rd C.S., ch. 3, Sec. 11.11, eff. Jan. 11, 2004.

Sec. 508.043. GIFTS AND GRANTS. The board may apply for and accept gifts or grants from any public or private source for use in any lawful purpose of the board.

Added by Acts 1997, 75th Leg., ch. 165, Sec. 12.01, eff. Sept. 1, 1997.

Sec. 508.044. POWERS AND DUTIES OF BOARD. A board member shall give full time to the duties of the member's office, including duties imposed on the board by the Texas Constitution and other law.

Added by Acts 1997, 75th Leg., ch. 165, Sec. 12.01, eff. Sept. 1, 1997. Amended by Acts 1999, 76th Leg., ch. 62, Sec. 10.12 to 10.14, eff. Sept. 1, 1999; Acts 2001, 77th Leg., ch. 856, Sec. 4, eff. Sept. 1, 2001; Acts 2003, 78th Leg., 3rd C.S., ch. 3, Sec. 11.12, eff. Jan. 11, 2004.

Sec. 508.0441. RELEASE AND REVOCATION DUTIES. (a) Board members and parole commissioners shall determine:

(1) which inmates are to be released on parole or mandatory supervision;

(2) conditions of parole or mandatory supervision, including special conditions;

(3) the modification and withdrawal of conditions of parole or mandatory supervision;

(4) which releasees may be released from supervision and reporting; and

(5) the continuation, modification, and revocation of parole or mandatory supervision.

(b) The board shall develop and implement a policy that clearly defines circumstances under which a board member or parole commissioner should disqualify himself or herself from voting on:

(1) a parole decision; or

(2) a decision to revoke parole or mandatory supervision.

(c) The board may adopt reasonable rules as proper or necessary relating to:

(1) the eligibility of an inmate for release on parole or release to mandatory supervision;

(2) the conduct of a parole or mandatory supervision hearing; or

(3) conditions to be imposed on a releasee.

(d) The presiding officer may provide a written plan for the administrative review of actions taken by a parole panel by a review panel.

(e) Board members and parole commissioners shall, at the direction of the presiding officer, file activity reports on duties performed under this chapter.

Added by Acts 1997, 75th Leg., ch. 165, Sec. 12.01, eff. Sept. 1, 1997. Amended by Acts 1999, 76th Leg., ch. 62, Sec. 10.12 to 10.14, eff. Sept. 1, 1999; Acts 2001, 77th Leg., ch. 856, Sec. 4, eff. Sept. 1, 2001. Redesignated from Government Code Sec. 508.044(b) to (f) and amended by Acts 2003, 78th Leg., 3rd C.S., ch. 3, Sec. 11.12, eff. Jan. 11, 2004.

Sec. 508.045. PAROLE PANELS. (a) Except as provided by Section 508.046, board members and parole commissioners shall act in panels composed of three in matters of:

(1) release on parole;

(2) release to mandatory supervision; and

(3) revocation of parole or mandatory supervision.

(b) The presiding officer shall designate the composition of each panel and shall designate panels composed of at least one board member and any combination of board members and parole commissioners.

(c) A parole panel may:

(1) grant, deny, or revoke parole;

(2) revoke mandatory supervision; and

(3) conduct parole revocation hearings and mandatory supervision revocation hearings.

Added by Acts 1997, 75th Leg., ch. 165, Sec. 12.01, eff. Sept. 1, 1997. Amended by Acts 2003, 78th Leg., 3rd C.S., ch. 3, Sec. 11.13, eff. Jan. 11, 2004.

Sec. 508.046. EXTRAORDINARY VOTE REQUIRED. To release on parole an inmate who was convicted of an offense under Section 21.02, 21.11(a)(1), or 22.021, Penal Code, or who is required under Section 508.145(c) to serve 35 calendar years before becoming eligible for release on parole, all members of the board must vote on the release on parole of the inmate, and at least two-thirds of the members must vote in favor of the release on parole. A member of the board may not vote on the release unless the member first receives a copy of a written report from the department on the probability that the inmate would commit an offense after being released on parole.

Added by Acts 1997, 75th Leg., ch. 165, Sec. 12.01, eff. Sept. 1, 1997.

Amended by:

Acts 2005, 79th Leg., Ch. 787, Sec. 3, eff. September 1, 2005.

Acts 2007, 80th Leg., R.S., Ch. 593, Sec. 3.38, eff. September 1, 2007.

Sec. 508.047. MEETINGS. (a) The members of the board shall meet at least once in each quarter of the calendar year at a site determined by the presiding officer.

(b) The members of the board are not required to meet as a body to perform the members' duties in clemency matters.

(c) A majority of each parole panel constitutes a quorum for the transaction of the panel's business. A panel's decision must be by majority vote.

(d) The members of a parole panel are not required to meet as a body to perform the members' duties, except to conduct a hearing under Section 508.281.

Added by Acts 1997, 75th Leg., ch. 165, Sec. 12.01, eff. Sept. 1, 1997. Amended by Acts 1999, 76th Leg., ch. 62, Sec. 10.15, eff. Sept. 1, 1999; Acts 2003, 78th Leg., 3rd C.S., ch. 3, Sec. 11.14, eff. Jan. 11, 2004.

Sec. 508.048. SUBPOENAS. (a) A parole panel may issue a subpoena requiring the attendance of a witness or the production of any record, book, paper, or document the panel considers necessary for investigation of the case of a person before the panel.

(b) A member of the board may sign a subpoena and administer an oath.

(c) A peace officer, parole officer, or community supervision and corrections department officer may serve the subpoena in the same manner as similar process in a court of record having original jurisdiction of criminal actions is served.

(d) A person who testifies falsely, fails to appear when subpoenaed, or fails or refuses to produce material under the subpoena is subject to the same orders and penalties to which a person taking those actions before a court is subject.

(e) On application of the board, a court of record having original jurisdiction of criminal actions may compel the attendance of a witness, the production of material, or the giving of testimony before the board, by an attachment for contempt or in the same manner as the court may otherwise compel the production of evidence.

Added by Acts 1997, 75th Leg., ch. 165, Sec. 12.01, eff. Sept. 1, 1997.

Sec. 508.0481. VICTIM'S RIGHT TO REPRESENTATION. (a) If a victim, close relative of a deceased victim, or guardian of a victim is required by a subpoena issued under Section 508.048 to appear at a hearing, the victim, relative, or guardian is entitled to representation by counsel at the hearing.

(b) This section does not require the state to provide representation by counsel to a victim, close relative of a deceased victim, or guardian of a victim.

(c) In this section, "victim," "close relative of a deceased victim," and "guardian of a victim" have the meanings assigned by Section 508.117.

Added by Acts 2001, 77th Leg., ch. 1034, Sec. 10, eff. Sept. 1, 2001.

Sec. 508.049. MISSION STATEMENT. (a) The board, after consultation with the governor and the Texas Board of Criminal Justice, shall adopt a mission statement that reflects the responsibilities for the operation of the parole process that are assigned to the board, the division, the department, or the Texas Board of Criminal Justice.

(b) The board shall include in the mission statement a description of specific locations at which the board intends to conduct business related to the operation of the parole process.

Added by Acts 1997, 75th Leg., ch. 165, Sec. 12.01, eff. Sept. 1, 1997. Amended by Acts 1999, 76th Leg., ch. 62, Sec. 10.16, eff. Sept. 1, 1999; Acts 2003, 78th Leg., 3rd C.S., ch. 3, Sec. 11.15, eff. Jan. 11, 2004.

Sec. 508.050. REPORT TO GOVERNOR. (a) On request of the governor, the board shall investigate a person being considered by the governor for:

(1) pardon;

(2) commutation of sentence;

(3) reprieve;

(4) remission of fine; or

(5) forfeiture.

(b) The board shall report to the governor on its investigation and make recommendations about the person to the governor.

Added by Acts 1997, 75th Leg., ch. 165, Sec. 12.01, eff. Sept. 1, 1997.

Sec. 508.051. SUNSET PROVISION. The Board of Pardons and Paroles is subject to review under Chapter 325 (Texas Sunset Act), but is not abolished under that chapter. The board shall be reviewed during the period in which the Texas Department of Criminal Justice is reviewed.

Added by Acts 1997, 75th Leg., ch. 165, Sec. 12.01, eff. Sept. 1, 1997. Amended by Acts 1999, 76th Leg., ch. 62, Sec. 10.17, eff. Sept. 1, 1999.

Sec. 508.052. COMPUTERS; OFFICE SPACE; OTHER EQUIPMENT. (a) The department by interagency contract may provide to the board necessary computer equipment and computer access to all computerized records and physical access to all printed records in the custody of the department that are related to the duties and functions of the board.

(b) The department by interagency contract may provide to the board necessary and appropriate:

(1) office space at locations designated by the presiding officer of the board; and

(2) utilities and communications equipment.

Added by Acts 1997, 75th Leg., ch. 165, Sec. 12.01, eff. Sept. 1, 1997.

Sec. 508.053. USE OF TECHNOLOGY. The board shall implement a policy requiring the board to use appropriate technological solutions to improve the board's ability to perform its functions. The policy must ensure that the public is able to interact with the board on the Internet.

Added by Acts 2007, 80th Leg., R.S., Ch. 1308, Sec. 36, eff. June 15, 2007.

Sec. 508.054. RECORDS OF COMPLAINTS. (a) The board shall maintain a system to promptly and efficiently act on complaints filed with the board. The board shall maintain information about parties to the complaint, the subject matter of the complaint, a summary of the results of the review or investigation of the complaint, and its disposition.

(b) The board shall make information available describing its procedures for complaint investigation and resolution.

(c) The board shall periodically notify the complaint parties of the status of the complaint until final disposition.

(d) This section does not apply to a complaint about an individual parole determination or clemency recommendation.

Added by Acts 2007, 80th Leg., R.S., Ch. 1308, Sec. 36, eff. June 15, 2007.

Sec. 508.055. NEGOTIATED RULEMAKING AND ALTERNATIVE DISPUTE RESOLUTION. (a) The board shall develop and implement a policy to encourage the use of:

(1) negotiated rulemaking procedures under Chapter 2008 for the adoption of board rules; and

(2) appropriate alternative dispute resolution procedures under Chapter 2009 to assist in the resolution of internal disputes under the board's jurisdiction.

(b) The board's procedures relating to alternative dispute resolution must conform, to the extent possible, to any model guidelines issued by the State Office of Administrative Hearings for the use of alternative dispute resolution by state agencies.

(c) The board shall designate a trained person to:

(1) coordinate the implementation of the policy adopted under Subsection (a);

(2) serve as a resource for any training needed to implement the procedures for negotiated rulemaking or alternative dispute resolution; and

(3) collect data concerning the effectiveness of those procedures, as implemented by the board.

Added by Acts 2007, 80th Leg., R.S., Ch. 1308, Sec. 36, eff. June 15, 2007.

SUBCHAPTER C. REPRESENTATION OF INMATES

Sec. 508.081. DEFINITIONS. In this subchapter:

(1) "Compensation" has the meaning assigned by Section 305.002.

(2) "Inmate" includes:

(A) an administrative releasee;

(B) an inmate imprisoned in the institutional division; and

(C) a person confined in a transfer facility or county jail awaiting:

(i) transfer to the institutional division; or

(ii) a revocation hearing.

(3) "Represent" means to directly or indirectly contact in person or by telephone, facsimile transmission, or correspondence a member or employee of the board or an employee of the department on behalf of an inmate.

Added by Acts 1997, 75th Leg., ch. 165, Sec. 12.01, eff. Sept. 1, 1997.

Sec. 508.082. RULES. The board shall adopt rules relating to:

(1) the submission and presentation of information and arguments to the board, a parole panel, and the department for and in behalf of an inmate; and

(2) the time, place, and manner of contact between a person representing an inmate and:

(A) a member of the board or a parole commissioner;

(B) an employee of the board; or

(C) an employee of the department.

Added by Acts 1997, 75th Leg., ch. 165, Sec. 12.01, eff. Sept. 1, 1997. Amended by Acts

1999, 76th Leg., ch. 62, Sec. 10.18, eff. Sept. 1, 1999; Acts 2003, 78th Leg., 3rd C.S., ch. 3, Sec. 11.16, eff. Jan. 11, 2004.

Sec. 508.083. ELIGIBILITY TO REPRESENT INMATES. (a) A person who represents an inmate for compensation must:

(1) be an attorney licensed in this state; and

(2) register with the division.

(b) A person serving as a member or employee of the board or the Texas Board of Criminal Justice may not, before the second anniversary of the date the person ceases to be a board member or employee:

(1) represent any person in a matter before the board or a parole panel; or

(2) receive compensation for services rendered on behalf of any person regarding a matter pending before the board or a parole panel.

(c) A person, other than a person subject to Subsection (b), who is employed by the department may not, before the second anniversary of the date the person terminates service with the department:

(1) represent an inmate in a matter before the board or a parole panel; or

(2) receive compensation for services rendered on behalf of any person regarding a matter pending before the board or a parole panel.

(d) Repealed by Acts 2003, 78th Leg., ch 1007, Sec. 2.

Added by Acts 1997, 75th Leg., ch. 165, Sec. 12.01, eff. Sept. 1, 1997. Amended by Acts 2003, 78th Leg., ch. 1007, Sec. 1, 2, eff. Sept. 1, 2003.

Sec. 508.084. FEE AFFIDAVIT. (a) A person required to register under Section 508.083, before the person first contacts a member of the board, an employee of the board, or an employee of the department on behalf of an inmate, shall file a fee affidavit with the department in a form prescribed by the department for each inmate the person represents for compensation.

(b) The fee affidavit must be written and verified and contain a statement of:

(1) the registrant's full name and address;

(2) the registrant's normal business, business phone number, and business address;

(3) the full name of any former member or employee of the board or the Texas Board of Criminal Justice or any former employee of the department with whom the registrant:

(A) is associated;

(B) has a relationship as an employer or employee; or

(C) maintains a contractual relationship to provide services;

(4) the full name and institutional identification number of the inmate the registrant represents;

(5) the amount of compensation the registrant has received or expects to receive in exchange for the representation; and

(6) the name of the person providing the compensation.

(c) If a registrant receives compensation in excess of the amount reported on the fee affidavit, the registrant shall file with the department, not later than the fifth day after the date the registrant receives compensation in excess of the reported amount, a supplemental fee affidavit in a form prescribed by the department indicating the total amount of compensation received for representing the inmate.

(d) For each fee affidavit and supplemental fee affidavit received, the department shall:

(1) keep a copy of the affidavit in a central location; and

(2) not later than the third day after the date the affidavit is filed, place a copy of the affidavit in the inmate's file that is reviewed by a parole panel or the board.

Added by Acts 1997, 75th Leg., ch. 165, Sec. 12.01, eff. Sept. 1, 1997.

Sec. 508.085. REPRESENTATION SUMMARY FORM. (a) A person required to register under Section 508.083 shall, for each calendar year in which the person represents an inmate, file a representation summary form with the division on a form prescribed by the division.

(b) The form must be filed not later than January 31 of the year succeeding the year for which the report is filed and must include a statement of:

(1) the registrant's full name and address;

(2) the registrant's normal business, business phone number, and business address;

(3) the full name of any former member or employee of the board or the Texas Board of Criminal Justice or any former employee of the department with whom the registrant:

(A) is associated;

(B) has a relationship as an employer or employee; or

(C) maintains a contractual relationship to provide services;

(4) the full name and institutional identification number of each inmate the registrant

represented in the previous calendar year; and

(5) the amount of compensation the registrant has received for representing each inmate in the previous calendar year.

(c) A person who files a form under this section and for whom the information required for the form has changed shall, not later than the 10th day after the date the information changes, file a supplemental statement with the division indicating the change.

Added by Acts 1997, 75th Leg., ch. 165, Sec. 12.01, eff. Sept. 1, 1997.

Sec. 508.086. CRIMINAL PENALTIES. (a) A former member or employee of the board or the Texas Board of Criminal Justice or a former employee of the department commits an offense if the former member or employee violates Section 508.083(b), (c), or (d).

(b) A person who represents an inmate for compensation commits an offense if the person is not an attorney licensed in this state.

(c) A person who is required to file an affidavit under Section 508.084(a) or (c) or a form or statement under Section 508.085 commits an offense if the person fails to file the affidavit, form, or statement.

(d) An offense under Subsection (a) is a Class A misdemeanor. An offense under Subsection (b) or (c) is a Class C misdemeanor.

Added by Acts 1997, 75th Leg., ch. 165, Sec. 12.01, eff. Sept. 1, 1997.

SUBCHAPTER D. PARDONS AND PAROLES DIVISION

Sec. 508.111. DIRECTOR. (a) The executive director shall hire the director of the division.

(b) The director is responsible for the administration of the division.

Added by Acts 1997, 75th Leg., ch. 165, Sec. 12.01, eff. Sept. 1, 1997.

Sec. 508.112. DUTY OF DIVISION. The division is responsible for the investigation and supervision of all releasees.

Added by Acts 1997, 75th Leg., ch. 165, Sec. 12.01, eff. Sept. 1, 1997.

Sec. 508.113. PAROLE OFFICERS, SUPERVISORS: QUALIFICATIONS. (a) This subsection and Subsection (b) apply only to a person employed as a parole officer or supervisor on or before September 1, 1990. A person may not be employed as a parole officer or supervisor, or be responsible for investigating or supervising a releasee, unless the person has:

(1) four years of successfully completed education in an accredited college or university;

(2) two years of full-time paid employment in responsible correctional work with adults or juveniles or in a related field; and

(3) any other qualifications that may be specified by the director.

(b) Additional experience in a category described by Subsection (a)(2) may be substituted year for year for the required college education, with a maximum substitution of two years.

(c) The director shall establish qualifications for parole officers and supervisors that are the same as qualifications for community supervision and corrections department officers imposed by Section 76.005. A person may not begin employment as a parole officer or supervisor after September 1, 1990, unless the person meets the qualifications established by the director.

(d) A person who is serving as a peace officer or as a prosecuting attorney may not act as a parole officer or be responsible for supervising a releasee.

Added by Acts 1997, 75th Leg., ch. 165, Sec. 12.01, eff. Sept. 1, 1997.

Sec. 508.1131. SALARY CAREER LADDER FOR PAROLE OFFICERS. (a) The executive director shall adopt a salary career ladder for parole officers. The salary career ladder must base a parole officer's salary on the officer's classification and years of service with the department.

(b) For purposes of the salary schedule, the department shall classify all parole officer positions as Parole Officer I, Parole Officer II, Parole Officer III, Parole Officer IV, or Parole Officer V.

(c) Under the salary career ladder adopted under Subsection (a), a parole officer to whom the schedule applies and who received an overall evaluation of at least satisfactory in the officer's most recent annual evaluation is entitled to an annual salary increase, during each of the officer's first 10 years of service in a designated parole officer classification as described by Subsection (b), equal to one-tenth of the difference between:

(1) the officer's current annual salary; and

(2) the minimum annual salary of a parole officer in the next highest classification.

Added by Acts 2007, 80th Leg., R.S., Ch. 1308, Sec. 37, eff. June 15, 2007.

Sec. 508.114. PAROLE OFFICERS, SUPERVISORS: ADDITIONAL DUTIES. (a) The judge of a court having original jurisdiction of criminal actions may, with the approval of the director, designate a parole officer or supervisor as a community supervision and corrections department officer. The director must give prior written approval for the payment of a proportional part of the salary paid to the parole officer or supervisor in compensation for service as a community supervision and corrections department officer. The director shall periodically report to the governor and the legislature the proportional salary payments.

(b) A parole officer or supervisor, on request of the governor or on order of the director, shall be responsible for supervising an inmate placed on conditional pardon or granted an emergency absence under escort.

Added by Acts 1997, 75th Leg., ch. 165, Sec. 12.01, eff. Sept. 1, 1997.

Sec. 508.1141. SPECIALIZED TRAINING; GANG MEMBERS. The department shall develop and provide specialized training for parole officers supervising releasees previously identified by the department as being members of prison gangs, criminal street gangs, or security threat groups.

Added by Acts 1999, 76th Leg., ch. 490, Sec. 1, eff. Sept. 1, 1999.

Sec. 508.1142. PAROLE OFFICER MAXIMUM CASELOADS. (a) The department shall adopt a policy that establishes guidelines for a maximum caseload for each parole officer of:

(1) 60 active releasees, if the releasees are not in a specialized program described by Subdivisions (2)-(6);

(2) 35 active releasees, if the releasees are in the special needs offender program;

(3) 35 active releasees, if the releasees are in the therapeutic community substance abuse aftercare treatment program;

(4) 24 active releasees, if the releasees are in the sex offender program;

(5) 20 active releasees, if the releasees are electronically monitored; and

(6) 11 active releasees, if the releasees are in the super-intensive supervision program.

(b) If the department is unable to meet the maximum caseload guidelines, the department shall submit a report to the Legislative Budget Board, at the end of each fiscal year in which the department fails to meet the guidelines, stating the amount of money needed by the department to meet the guidelines.

Added by Acts 2007, 80th Leg., R.S., Ch. 1421, Sec. 1, eff. June 15, 2007.

Sec. 508.115. NOTIFICATION OF RELEASE OF INMATE. (a) Not later than the 11th day before the date a parole panel orders the release on parole of an inmate or not later than the 11th day after the date the board recommends that the governor grant executive clemency, the division shall notify the sheriffs, each chief of police, the prosecuting attorneys, and the district judges in the county in which the inmate was convicted and the county to which the inmate is released that a parole panel is considering release on parole or the governor is considering clemency.

(b) In a case in which there was a change of venue, the division shall notify the sheriff, the prosecuting attorney, and the district judge in the county in which the prosecution was originated if, not later than the 30th day after the date the inmate was sentenced, those officials request in writing that the division give the officials notice under this section of a release of the inmate.

(c) Not later than the 10th day after the date a parole panel orders the transfer of an inmate to a halfway house under this chapter, the division shall give notice in accordance with Subsection (d) to:

(1) the sheriff of the county in which the inmate was convicted;

(2) the sheriff of the county in which the halfway house is located and each chief of police in the county; and

(3) the attorney who represents the state in the prosecution of felonies in the county in which the halfway house is located.

(d) The notice must state:

(1) the inmate's name;

(2) the county in which the inmate was convicted; and

(3) the offense for which the inmate was convicted.

Added by Acts 1997, 75th Leg., ch. 165, Sec. 12.01, eff. Sept. 1, 1997. Amended by Acts 1999, 76th Leg., ch. 62, Sec. 10.19, eff. Sept. 1, 1999; Acts 2001, 77th Leg., ch. 856, Sec. 5, eff. Sept. 1, 2001.

Sec. 508.116. PAROLE INFORMATION PROGRAM. (a) The division shall develop and implement a comprehensive program to inform inmates, the inmates' families, and other interested parties about the parole process.

(b) The division shall update the program annually.

Added by Acts 1997, 75th Leg., ch. 165, Sec. 12.01, eff. Sept. 1, 1997.

Sec. 508.117. VICTIM NOTIFICATION. (a) Before a parole panel considers for release on parole an inmate who is serving a sentence for an offense in which a person was a victim, the division, using the name and address provided on the victim impact statement, shall make a reasonable effort to notify:

(1) the victim;

(2) if the victim has a guardian, the guardian; or

(3) if the victim is deceased, a close relative of the deceased victim.

(b) A victim, guardian of a victim, or close relative of a deceased victim who would have been entitled to notification of parole consideration by the division but failed to provide a victim impact statement containing the person's name and address may file with the division a written request for notification. After receiving the written request, the division shall grant to the person all privileges, including notification under this section, to which the person would have been entitled had the person submitted a completed victim impact statement.

(c) If the notice is sent to a guardian or close relative of a deceased victim, the notice must contain a request by the division that the guardian or relative inform other persons having an interest in the matter that the inmate is being considered for release on parole.

(d) The failure of the division to comply with notice requirements of this section is not a ground for revocation of parole.

(e) Before an inmate is released from the institutional division on parole or to mandatory supervision, the pardons and paroles division shall give notice of the release to a person entitled to notification of parole consideration for the inmate under Subsection (a) or (b).

(f) Except as necessary to comply with this section, the board or the department may not disclose to any person the name or address of a person entitled to notice under this section unless:

(1) the person approves the disclosure; or

(2) a court determines that there is good cause for disclosure and orders the board or the department to disclose the information.

(g) In this section:

(1) "Close relative of a deceased victim" means a person who was:

(A) the spouse of the victim at the time of the victim's death;

(B) a parent of the deceased victim;

(C) an adult brother, sister, or child of the deceased victim; or

(D) the nearest relative of the deceased victim by consanguinity, if the persons described by Paragraphs (A) through (C) are deceased or are incapacitated due to physical or mental illness or infirmity.

(2) "Guardian of a victim" means a person who is the legal guardian of a victim, whether or not the legal relationship between the guardian and the victim exists because of the age of the victim or the physical or mental incompetency of the victim.

(2-a) "Sexual assault" includes an offense under Section 21.02, Penal Code.

(3) "Victim" means a person who:

(A) is a victim of sexual assault, kidnapping, aggravated robbery, or felony stalking; or

(B) has suffered bodily injury or death as the result of the criminal conduct of another.

Added by Acts 1997, 75th Leg., ch. 165, Sec. 12.01, eff. Sept. 1, 1997.

Amended by:

Acts 2007, 80th Leg., R.S., Ch. 593, Sec. 3.39, eff. September 1, 2007.

Acts 2007, 80th Leg., R.S., Ch. 826, Sec. 1, eff. June 15, 2007.

Acts 2007, 80th Leg., R.S., Ch. 1308, Sec. 38, eff. June 15, 2007.

Sec. 508.118. HALFWAY HOUSES. (a) The division, in conjunction with the institutional division, shall use halfway houses to divert from housing in regular units of the institutional division suitable low-risk inmates and other inmates who would benefit from a smoother transition from incarceration to supervised release.

(b) Before transferring an inmate to a halfway house, the division shall send to the director of the halfway house all information relating to the inmate that the division determines will aid the halfway house in helping the inmate make a transition from the institutional division to supervised release.

(c) The division is responsible for supervising an inmate:

(1) for whom a presumptive parole date has been established; and

(2) who is transferred into a preparole residence in a halfway house under Subchapter A, Chapter 499.

Added by Acts 1997, 75th Leg., ch. 165, Sec. 12.01, eff. Sept. 1, 1997.

Sec. 508.119. COMMUNITY RESIDENTIAL FACILITIES. (a) The purpose of a community residential facility is to provide housing, supervision, counseling, personal, social, and work adjustment training, and other programs to:

(1) releasees who are required by a parole panel as a condition of release on parole or to mandatory supervision to serve a period in a community residential facility; and

(2) releasees whose parole or mandatory supervision has been continued or modified under Section 508.283 and on whom sanctions have been imposed under that section.

(b) The division may establish and operate, or contract for the operation of, community residential facilities.

(c) The division may contract with a public or private vendor for the financing, construction, operation, or management of a community residential facility using a lease-purchase or installment sale contract to provide or supplement housing, board, or supervision for releasees placed in a community residential facility. A releasee housed or supervised in a facility operated by a vendor under a contract is subject to the same laws as if the housing or supervision were provided directly by the division.

(d) Unless the division or a vendor proposing to operate a community residential facility provides notice of a following proposed action and a hearing on the issues in the same manner as required under Section 509.010, the division may not:

(1) establish or contract for a community residential facility;

(2) change the use of a community residential facility;

(3) significantly increase the capacity of a community residential facility; or

(4) increase the capacity of a community residential facility to more than 500 residents, regardless of whether the increase is significant.

(e) Subsection (d) applies to any residential facility that the division establishes or contracts for under:

(1) this chapter;

(2) Subchapter C, Chapter 497; or

(3) Subchapter A, Chapter 499.

(f) The Texas Board of Criminal Justice shall adopt rules necessary for the management of a community residential facility.

(g) The division may charge to a releasee housed in a community residential facility a reasonable fee for the cost of housing, board, and the part of the administrative costs of the facility that is properly allocable to the releasee. The fee may not exceed the actual costs to the division for services to that releasee. The division may not deny placement in a community residential facility to a releasee because the releasee is unable to pay the fee.

(h) A parole panel or a designated agent of the division may grant a limited release to a releasee placed in a community residential facility to maintain or seek employment or participation in an education or training course or to seek housing after release from the facility.

(i) The notice required by Subsection (d) must clearly state that the proposed action concerns a facility in which persons who have been released from prison on parole or to mandatory supervision are to be housed.

Added by Acts 1997, 75th Leg., ch. 165, Sec. 12.01, eff. Sept. 1, 1997. Amended by Acts 1999, 76th Leg., ch. 62, Sec. 10.20, eff. Sept. 1, 1999.

SUBCHAPTER E. PAROLE AND MANDATORY SUPERVISION; RELEASE PROCEDURES

Sec. 508.141. AUTHORITY TO CONSIDER AND ORDER RELEASE ON PAROLE. (a) A parole panel may consider for release and release on parole an inmate who:

(1) has been sentenced to a term of imprisonment in the institutional division;

(2) is confined in a penal or correctional institution, including a jail in this state, a federal correctional institution, or a jail or a correctional institution in another state; and

(3) is eligible for release on parole.

(b) A parole is issued only on the order of a parole panel.

(c) Before releasing an inmate on parole, a parole panel may have the inmate appear before the panel and interview the inmate.

(d) A parole panel may release an inmate on parole during the parole month established for the inmate if the panel determines that the inmate's release will not increase the likelihood of harm to the public.

(e) A parole panel may release an inmate on parole only when:

(1) arrangements have been made for the inmate's employment or for the inmate's maintenance and care, which may include the issuance of payment for the cost of temporary post-release housing under Section 508.157; and

(2) the parole panel believes that the inmate is able and willing to fulfill the obligations of a law-abiding citizen.

(f) A parole panel may order a parole only for the best interest of society and not as an award of clemency.

(g) The board shall adopt a policy establishing the date on which the board may reconsider for release an inmate who has previously been denied release. The policy must require the board to reconsider for release an inmate serving a sentence for an offense listed in Section 508.149(a) during a month designated by the parole panel that denied release. The designated month must begin after the first anniversary of the date of the denial and end before the fifth anniversary of the date of the denial. The policy must require the board to reconsider for release an inmate other than an inmate serving a sentence for an offense listed in Section 508.149(a) as soon as practicable after the first anniversary of the date of the denial.

Added by Acts 1997, 75th Leg., ch. 165, Sec. 12.01, eff. Sept. 1, 1997. Amended by Acts 2003, 78th Leg., ch. 349, Sec. 1, eff. June 18, 2003; Acts 2003, 78th Leg., 3rd C.S., ch. 3, Sec. 11.17, eff. Jan. 11, 2004.

Amended by:

Acts 2009, 81st Leg., R.S., Ch. 944, Sec. 2, eff. June 19, 2009.

Sec. 508.142. PERIOD OF PAROLE. (a) The institutional division shall provide the board with sentence time credit information for each inmate who is eligible for release on parole.

(b) Good conduct time credit is computed for an inmate as if the inmate were confined in the institutional division during the entire time the inmate was actually confined.

(c) The period of parole is computed by subtracting from the term for which the inmate was sentenced the calendar time served on the sentence.

Added by Acts 1997, 75th Leg., ch. 165, Sec. 12.01, eff. Sept. 1, 1997.

Sec. 508.143. LEGAL CUSTODY OF RELEASEE. (a) A releasee while on parole is in the legal custody of the division.

(b) A releasee while on mandatory supervision is in the legal custody of the state.

Added by Acts 1997, 75th Leg., ch. 165, Sec. 12.01, eff. Sept. 1, 1997.

Sec. 508.144. PAROLE GUIDELINES. (a) The board shall:

(1) develop according to an acceptable research method the parole guidelines that are the basic criteria on which a parole decision is made;

(2) base the guidelines on the seriousness of the offense and the likelihood of a favorable parole outcome;

(3) ensure that the guidelines require consideration of an inmate's progress in any programs in which the inmate participated during the inmate's term of confinement; and

(4) implement the guidelines.

(b) If a board member or parole commissioner deviates from the parole guidelines in voting on a parole decision, the member or parole commissioner shall:

(1) produce a written statement describing in detail the specific circumstances regarding the departure from the guidelines;

(2) place a copy of the statement in the file of the inmate for whom the parole decision was made; and

(3) provide a copy of the statement to the inmate.

(c) The board shall keep a copy of a statement made under Subsection (b) in a central location.

(d) The board shall meet annually to review and discuss the parole guidelines developed under Subsection (a). The board may consult outside experts to assist with the review. The board must consider:

(1) how the parole guidelines serve the needs of parole decision-making;

(2) how well the parole guidelines reflect parole panel decisions; and

(3) how well parole guidelines predict successful parole outcomes.

(e) Based on the board's review of the parole guidelines under Subsection (d), the board may:

(1) update the guidelines by:

(A) including new risk factors; or

(B) changing the values of offense severity or risk factor scores; or

(2) modify the recommended parole approval rates under the guidelines, if parole approval rates differ significantly from the recommended rates.

(f) The board is not required to hold an open meeting to review the guidelines as required by Subsection (d), but any modifications or updates to the guidelines made by the board under Subsection (e) must occur in an open meeting.

Added by Acts 1997, 75th Leg., ch. 165, Sec. 12.01, eff. Sept. 1, 1997. Amended by Acts 2003, 78th Leg., 3rd C.S., ch. 3, Sec. 11.18, eff. Jan. 11, 2004.

Amended by:

Acts 2007, 80th Leg., R.S., Ch. 1308, Sec. 39, eff. June 15, 2007.

Sec. 508.1445. ANNUAL REPORT ON GUIDELINES REQUIRED. (a) The board annually shall submit a report to the Criminal Justice Legislative Oversight Committee, the lieutenant governor, the speaker of the house of representatives, and the presiding officers of the standing committees in the senate and house of representatives primarily responsible for criminal justice regarding the board's application of the parole guidelines adopted under Section 508.144.

(b) The report must include:

(1) a brief explanation of the parole guidelines, including how the board:

(A) defines the risk factors and offense severity levels; and

(B) determines the recommended parole approval rates for each guideline score;

(2) a comparison of the recommended approval rates under the parole guidelines to the actual approval rates for individual parole panel members, regional offices, and the state as a whole; and

(3) a description of instances in which the actual parole approval rates do not meet the recommended approval rates under the parole guidelines, an explanation of the variations, and a list of actions that the board has taken or will take to meet the guidelines.

Added by Acts 2007, 80th Leg., R.S., Ch. 1308, Sec. 40, eff. June 15, 2007.

Sec. 508.145. ELIGIBILITY FOR RELEASE ON PAROLE; COMPUTATION OF PAROLE ELIGIBILITY DATE. (a) An inmate under sentence of death, serving a sentence of life imprisonment without parole, serving a sentence for an offense under Section 21.02, Penal Code, or serving a sentence for an offense under Section 22.021, Penal Code, that is punishable under Subsection (f) of that section is not eligible for release on parole.

(b) An inmate serving a life sentence under Section 12.31(a)(1), Penal Code, for a capital felony is not eligible for release on parole until the actual calendar time the inmate has served, without consideration of good conduct time, equals 40 calendar years.

(c) An inmate serving a sentence under Section 12.42(c)(2), Penal Code, is not eligible for release on parole until the actual calendar time the inmate has served, without consideration of good conduct time, equals 35 calendar years.

(d) An inmate serving a sentence for an offense described by Section 3g(a)(1)(A), (C), (D), (E), (F), (G), (H), (I), (J), or (K), Article 42.12, Code of Criminal Procedure, or for an offense for which the judgment contains an affirmative finding under Section 3g(a)(2) of that article, is not eligible for release on parole until the inmate's actual calendar time served, without consideration of good conduct time, equals one-half of the sentence or 30 calendar years, whichever is less, but in no event is the inmate eligible for release on parole in less than two calendar years.

(d-1) Notwithstanding Subsection (d), for every 12 months that elapse between the date an arrest warrant is issued for the inmate following an indictment for the offense and the date the inmate is arrested for the offense, the earliest date on which an inmate is eligible for parole is delayed by three years from the date otherwise provided by Subsection (d), if the inmate is serving a sentence for an offense under Section 19.02, 22.011, or 22.021, Penal Code.

(e) An inmate serving a sentence for which the punishment is increased under Section 481.134, Health and Safety Code, is not eligible for release on parole until the inmate's actual calendar time served, without consideration of good conduct time, equals five years or the term to which the inmate was sentenced, whichever is less.

(f) Except as provided by Section 508.146, any other inmate is eligible for release on parole when the inmate's actual calendar time served plus good conduct time equals one-fourth of the sentence imposed or 15 years, whichever is less.

Added by Acts 1997, 75th Leg., ch. 165, Sec. 12.01, eff. Sept. 1, 1997. Amended by Acts 1999, 76th Leg., ch. 62, Sec. 10.21, eff. Sept. 1, 1999.

Amended by:

Acts 2005, 79th Leg., Ch. 787, Sec. 4, eff. September 1, 2005.

Acts 2005, 79th Leg., Ch. 787, Sec. 12, eff. September 1, 2005.

Acts 2007, 80th Leg., R.S., Ch. 405, Sec. 2, eff. September 1, 2007.

Acts 2007, 80th Leg., R.S., Ch. 593, Sec. 1.10, eff. September 1, 2007.

Acts 2009, 81st Leg., R.S., Ch. 146, Sec. 2, eff. September 1, 2009.

Acts 2009, 81st Leg., R.S., Ch. 765, Sec. 2, eff. September 1, 2009.

Acts 2009, 81st Leg., R.S., Ch. 1400, Sec. 3, eff. September 1, 2009.

Sec. 508.146. MEDICALLY RECOMMENDED INTENSIVE SUPERVISION. (a) An inmate other than an inmate who is serving a sentence of death or life without parole may be released on medically recommended intensive supervision on a date designated by a parole panel described by Subsection (e), except that an inmate with an instant offense that is an offense described in Section 3g, Article 42.12, Code of Criminal Procedure, or an inmate who has a reportable conviction or adjudication under Chapter 62, Code of Criminal Procedure, may only be considered if a medical condition of terminal illness or long-term care has been diagnosed by a physician, if:

(1) the Texas Correctional Office on Offenders with Medical or Mental Impairments, in cooperation with the Correctional Managed Health Care Committee, identifies the inmate as being:

(A) elderly, physically disabled, mentally ill, terminally ill, or mentally retarded or having a condition requiring long-term care, if the inmate is an inmate with an instant offense that is described in Section 3g, Article 42.12, Code of Criminal Procedure; or

(B) in a persistent vegetative state or being a person with an organic brain syndrome with significant to total mobility impairment, if the inmate is an inmate who has a reportable conviction or adjudication under Chapter 62, Code of Criminal Procedure;

(2) the parole panel determines that, based on the inmate's condition and a medical evaluation, the inmate does not constitute a threat to public safety; and

(3) the Texas Correctional Office on Offenders with Medical or Mental Impairments, in cooperation with the pardons and paroles division, has prepared for the inmate a medically recommended intensive supervision plan that requires the inmate to submit to electronic monitoring, places the inmate on super-intensive supervision, or otherwise ensures appropriate supervision of the inmate.

(b) An inmate may be released on medically recommended intensive supervision only if the inmate's medically recommended intensive supervision plan under Subsection (a)(3) is approved by the Texas Correctional Office on Offenders with Medical or Mental Impairments.

(c) The parole panel shall require as a condition of release under Subsection (a) that the releasee remain under the care of a physician and in a medically suitable placement. At least once each calendar quarter, the Texas Correctional Office on Offenders with Medical or Mental Impairments shall report to the parole panel on the releasee's medical and placement status. On the basis of the report, the parole panel may modify conditions of release and impose any condition on the releasee that a panel could impose on a releasee released under Section 508.145, including a condition that the releasee reside in a halfway house or community residential facility.

(d) The Texas Correctional Office on Offenders with Medical or Mental Impairments and the Texas Department of Human Services shall jointly request proposals from public or private vendors to provide under contract services for inmates released on medically recommended intensive supervision. A request for proposals under this subsection may require that the services be provided in a medical care facility located in an urban area. For the purposes of this subsection, "urban area" means the area in this state within a metropolitan statistical area, according to the standards of the United States Bureau of the Census.

(e) Only parole panels composed of the presiding officer of the board and two members appointed to the panel by the presiding officer may make determinations regarding the release of inmates on medically recommended intensive supervision under Subsection (a) or of inmates released pending deportation. If the Texas Council on Offenders with Mental Impairments identifies an inmate as a candidate for release under the guidelines established by Subsection (a)(1), the council shall present to a parole panel described by this subsection relevant information concerning the inmate and the inmate's potential for release under this section.

(f) An inmate who is not a citizen of the United States, as defined by federal law, who is not under a sentence of death or life without parole, and who does not have a reportable conviction or adjudication under Chapter 62, Code of Criminal Procedure, or an instant offense described in Section 3g, Article 42.12, Code of Criminal Procedure, may be released to immigration authorities pending deportation on a date designated by a parole panel described by Subsection (e) if the parole panel determines that on release the inmate would be deported to another country and that the inmate does not constitute a threat to public safety in the other country or this country and is unlikely to reenter this country illegally.

Added by Acts 1997, 75th Leg., ch. 165, Sec. 12.01, eff. Sept. 1, 1997. Amended by Acts 2001, 77th Leg., ch. 1435, Sec. 1, eff. Sept. 1, 2001; Acts 2003, 78th Leg., ch. 252, Sec. 1, eff. Sept. 1, 2003; Acts 2003, 78th Leg., ch. 856, Sec. 21, eff. Sept. 1, 2003.

Amended by:

Acts 2005, 79th Leg., Ch. 787, Sec. 5, eff. September 1, 2005.

Acts 2007, 80th Leg., R.S., Ch. 1247, Sec. 1, eff. September 1, 2007.

Sec. 508.147. RELEASE TO MANDATORY SUPERVISION. (a) Except as provided by Section 508.149, a parole panel shall order the release of an inmate who is not on parole to mandatory supervision when the actual calendar time the inmate has served plus any accrued good conduct time equals the term to which the inmate was sentenced.

(b) An inmate released to mandatory supervision is considered to be released on parole.

(c) To the extent practicable, arrangements for the inmate's proper employment, maintenance, and care must be made before the inmate's release to mandatory supervision.

Added by Acts 1997, 75th Leg., ch. 165, Sec. 12.01, eff. Sept. 1, 1997.

Sec. 508.148. PERIOD OF MANDATORY SUPERVISION. (a) The period of mandatory supervision is computed by subtracting from the term for which the inmate was sentenced the calendar time served on the sentence.

(b) The time served on mandatory supervision is computed as calendar time.

Added by Acts 1997, 75th Leg., ch. 165, Sec. 12.01, eff. Sept. 1, 1997.

Sec. 508.149. INMATES INELIGIBLE FOR MANDATORY SUPERVISION. (a) An inmate may not be released to mandatory supervision if the inmate is serving a sentence for or has been previously convicted of:

(1) an offense for which the judgment contains an affirmative finding under Section 3g(a)(2), Article 42.12, Code of Criminal Procedure;

(2) a first degree felony or a second degree felony under Section 19.02, Penal Code;

(3) a capital felony under Section 19.03, Penal Code;

(4) a first degree felony or a second degree felony under Section 20.04, Penal Code;

(5) an offense under Section 21.11, Penal Code;

(6) a felony under Section 22.011, Penal Code;

(7) a first degree felony or a second degree felony under Section 22.02, Penal Code;

(8) a first degree felony under Section 22.021, Penal Code;

(9) a first degree felony under Section 22.04, Penal Code;

(10) a first degree felony under Section 28.02, Penal Code;

(11) a second degree felony under Section 29.02, Penal Code;

(12) a first degree felony under Section 29.03, Penal Code;

(13) a first degree felony under Section 30.02, Penal Code;

(14) a felony for which the punishment is increased under Section 481.134 or Section 481.140, Health and Safety Code;

(15) an offense under Section 43.25, Penal Code;

(16) an offense under Section 21.02, Penal Code; or

(17) a first degree felony under Section 15.03, Penal Code.

(b) An inmate may not be released to mandatory supervision if a parole panel determines that:

(1) the inmate's accrued good conduct time is not an accurate reflection of the inmate's potential for rehabilitation; and

(2) the inmate's release would endanger the public.

(c) A parole panel that makes a determination under Subsection (b) shall specify in writing the reasons for the determination.

(d) A determination under Subsection (b) is not subject to administrative or judicial review, except that the parole panel making the determination shall reconsider the inmate for release to mandatory supervision at least twice during the two years after the date of the determination.

Added by Acts 1997, 75th Leg., ch. 165, Sec. 12.01, eff. Sept. 1, 1997. Amended by Acts 1999, 76th Leg., ch. 62, Sec. 10.22, eff. Sept. 1, 1999; Acts 2001, 77th Leg., ch. 786, Sec. 3, eff. June 14, 2001.

Amended by:

Acts 2007, 80th Leg., R.S., Ch. 593, Sec. 1.11, eff. September 1, 2007.

Acts 2009, 81st Leg., R.S., Ch. 146, Sec. 3, eff. September 1, 2009.

Sec. 508.150. CONSECUTIVE FELONY SENTENCES. (a) If an inmate is sentenced to consecutive felony sentences under Article 42.08, Code of Criminal Procedure, a parole panel shall designate during each sentence the date, if any, the inmate would have been eligible for release on parole if the inmate had been sentenced to serve a single sentence.

(b) For the purposes of Article 42.08, Code of Criminal Procedure, the judgment and sentence of an inmate sentenced for a felony, other than the last sentence in a series of consecutive sentences, cease to operate:

(1) when the actual calendar time served by the inmate equals the sentence imposed by the court; or

(2) on the date a parole panel designates as the date the inmate would have been eligible for release on parole if the inmate had been sentenced to serve a single sentence.

(c) A parole panel may not:

(1) consider consecutive sentences as a single sentence for purposes of parole; or

(2) release on parole an inmate sentenced to serve consecutive felony sentences before the date the inmate becomes eligible for release on parole from the last sentence imposed on the inmate.

(d) A parole panel may not use calendar time served and good conduct time accrued by an inmate that are used by the panel in determining when a judgment and sentence cease to operate:

(1) for the same purpose in determining that date in a subsequent sentence in the same series of consecutive sentences; or

(2) for determining the date an inmate becomes eligible for release on parole from the last sentence in a series of consecutive sentences.

Added by Acts 1997, 75th Leg., ch. 165, Sec. 12.01, eff. Sept. 1, 1997.

Sec. 508.151. PRESUMPTIVE PAROLE DATE. (a) For the purpose of diverting inmates to halfway houses under Section 508.118, a parole panel, after reviewing all available pertinent information, may designate a presumptive parole date for an inmate who:

(1) has never been convicted of an offense listed under Section 3g(a)(1), Article 42.12, Code of Criminal Procedure, or an offense under Section 21.02, Penal Code; and

(2) has never had a conviction with a judgment that contains an affirmative finding under Section 3g(a)(2), Article 42.12, Code of Criminal Procedure.

(b) The presumptive parole date may not be a date that is earlier than the inmate's initial parole eligibility date computed under Section 508.145.

(c) A parole panel may rescind or postpone a previously established presumptive parole date on the basis of a report from an agent of the division responsible for supervision or an agent of the institutional division acting in the case.

(d) If an inmate transferred to preparole status has satisfactorily served the inmate's sentence in the halfway house to which the inmate is assigned from the date of transfer to the presumptive parole date, without rescission or postponement of the date, the parole panel shall order the inmate's release on parole and issue an appropriate certificate of release. The releasee is subject to the provisions of this chapter governing release on parole.

Added by Acts 1997, 75th Leg., ch. 165, Sec. 12.01, eff. Sept. 1, 1997.

Amended by:

Acts 2007, 80th Leg., R.S., Ch. 593, Sec. 3.40, eff. September 1, 2007.

Sec. 508.152. PROPOSED PROGRAM OF INSTITUTIONAL PROGRESS. (a) Not later than the 120th day after the date an inmate is admitted to the institutional division, the department shall obtain all pertinent information relating to the inmate, including:

(1) the court judgment;

(2) any sentencing report;

(3) the circumstances of the inmate's offense;

(4) the inmate's previous social history and criminal record;

(5) the inmate's physical and mental health record;

(6) a record of the inmate's conduct, employment history, and attitude in the institutional division; and

(7) any written comments or information provided by local trial officials or victims of the offense.

(b) The department shall:

(1) establish for the inmate a proposed program of measurable institutional progress; and

(2) submit the proposed program to the board at the time of the board's consideration of the inmate's case for release.

(c) The board shall conduct an initial review of an eligible inmate not later than the 180th day after the date of the inmate's admission to the institutional division.

(d) Before the inmate is approved for release on parole, the inmate must agree to participate in the programs and activities described by the proposed program of measurable institutional progress.

(e) The institutional division shall:

(1) work closely with the board to monitor the progress of the inmate in the institutional division; and

(2) report the progress to the board before the inmate's release.

(f) An attorney representing the state in the prosecution of an inmate serving a sentence for an offense described by Section 508.187(a) shall provide written comments to the department on the circumstances related to the commission of the offense and other information determined by the attorney to be relevant to any subsequent parole decisions regarding the inmate.

Added by Acts 1997, 75th Leg., ch. 165, Sec. 12.01, eff. Sept. 1, 1997. Amended by Acts 2001, 77th Leg., ch. 978, Sec. 1, eff. Sept. 1, 2001.

Sec. 508.153. STATEMENTS OF VICTIM. (a) A parole panel considering for release on parole or mandatory supervision an inmate who is serving a sentence for an offense in which a person was a victim shall allow:

(1) the victim, a guardian of the victim, a close relative of the deceased victim, or a representative of the victim, the victim's guardian, or the victim's close relative to provide a written statement to the panel; and

(2) the victim, guardian of the victim, or close relative of the deceased victim to appear in person before the board members to present a statement of the person's views about:

(A) the offense;

(B) the inmate; and

(C) the effect of the offense on the victim.

(b) If more than one person is entitled to appear in person before the board members or parole commissioners, only the person chosen by all persons entitled to appear as the persons' sole representative may appear.

(c) The panel shall consider the statements and the information provided in a victim impact statement in determining whether to recommend an inmate for release on parole.

(d) This section does not limit the number of persons who may provide written statements for or against the release of the inmate on parole.

(e) In this section, "close relative of a deceased victim," "guardian of a victim," and "victim" have the meanings assigned by Section 508.117.

Added by Acts 1997, 75th Leg., ch. 165, Sec. 12.01, eff. Sept. 1, 1997. Amended by Acts 2001, 77th Leg., ch. 856, Sec. 6, eff. Sept. 1, 2001; Acts 2003, 78th Leg., 3rd C.S., ch. 3, Sec. 11.19, eff. Jan. 11, 2004.

Sec. 508.154. CONTRACT ON RELEASE. (a) An inmate to be released on parole shall be furnished a contract stating in clear and intelligible language the conditions and rules of parole.

(b) Acceptance, signing, and execution of the contract by the inmate to be paroled is a precondition to release on parole.

(c) An inmate released to mandatory supervision shall be furnished a written statement stating in clear and intelligible language the conditions and rules of mandatory supervision.

(d) A releasee while on parole or mandatory supervision must be amenable to the conditions of supervision ordered by a parole panel.

Added by Acts 1997, 75th Leg., ch. 165, Sec. 12.01, eff. Sept. 1, 1997.

Sec. 508.155. COMPLETION OF PAROLE PERIOD. (a) To complete a parole period, a releasee must serve the entire period of parole.

(b) The time on parole is computed as calendar time.

(c) The division may allow a releasee to serve the remainder of the releasee's sentence without supervision and without being required to report if a parole supervisor at the regional level has approved the releasee's early release from supervision under Section 508.1555.

(d) The division may require a person released from supervision and reporting under Subsection (c) to resubmit to supervision and resume reporting at any time and for any reason.

Added by Acts 1997, 75th Leg., ch. 165, Sec. 12.01, eff. Sept. 1, 1997.

Amended by:

Acts 2007, 80th Leg., R.S., Ch. 1308, Sec. 41, eff. June 15, 2007.

Sec. 508.1555. PROCEDURE FOR THE EARLY RELEASE FROM SUPERVISION OF CERTAIN RELEASEES. (a) A parole officer annually shall identify the releasees under the parole officer's supervision who are eligible for early release from supervision under Section 508.155(c). A releasee is eligible for early release if:

(1) the releasee has been under supervision for at least one-half of the time that remained on the releasee's sentence when the releasee was released from imprisonment;

(2) during the preceding two-year period, the releasee has not committed any violation of the rules or conditions of release;

(3) during the period of supervision the releasee's parole or release to mandatory supervision has not been revoked; and

(4) the division determines:

(A) that the releasee has made a good faith effort to comply with any restitution order imposed on the releasee by a court; and

(B) that allowing the releasee to serve the remainder of the releasee's sentence without supervision and reporting is in the best interest of society.

(b) After identifying any releasees who are eligible for early release under Subsection (a), the parole officer shall review the eligible releasees, including any releasees the parole officer has previously declined to recommend for early release, to determine if a recommendation for early release from supervision is appropriate. In conducting the review and determining recommendations, the parole officer shall consider whether the releasee:

(1) has a low risk of recidivism as determined by an assessment developed by the department; and

(2) has made a good faith effort to comply with the conditions of release.

(c) A parole officer shall forward to the parole supervisor at the regional level any recommendations for early release the parole officer makes under Subsection (b). If the parole supervisor approves the recommendation, the division shall allow a releasee to serve the remainder of the releasee's sentence without supervision and without being required to report as authorized by Section 508.155.

Added by Acts 2007, 80th Leg., R.S., Ch. 1308, Sec. 42, eff. June 15, 2007.

Sec. 508.156. DETERMINATE SENTENCE PAROLE. (a) Before the release of a person who is transferred under Section 61.081(f) or 61.084(g), Human Resources Code, to the division for release on parole, a parole panel shall review the person's records and may interview the person or any other person the panel considers necessary to determine the conditions of parole. The panel may impose any reasonable condition of parole on the person that the panel may impose on an adult inmate under this chapter.

(b) The panel shall furnish the person with a written statement clearly describing the conditions and rules of parole. The person must accept and sign the statement as a precondition to release on parole.

(c) While on parole, the person remains in the legal custody of the state and shall comply with the conditions of parole ordered by a panel under this section.

(d) The period of parole for a person released on parole under this section is the term for which the person was sentenced less calendar time served at the Texas Youth Commission and in a juvenile detention facility in connection with the conduct for which the person was adjudicated.

(e) If a parole panel revokes the person's parole, the panel may require the person to serve the remaining portion of the person's sentence in the institutional division. The remaining portion of the person's sentence is computed without credit for the time from the date of the person's release to the date of revocation. The panel may not recommit the person to the Texas Youth Commission.

(f) For purposes of this chapter, a person released from the Texas Youth Commission on parole under this section is considered to have been convicted of the offense for which the person has been adjudicated.

Added by Acts 1997, 75th Leg., ch. 165, Sec. 12.01, eff. Sept. 1, 1997.

Amended by: Acts 2007, 80th Leg., R.S., Ch. 263, Sec. 19, eff. June 8, 2007.

For expiration of Subsections (f) and (g), see Subsection (g).

Sec. 508.157. TEMPORARY HOUSING ON RELEASE. (a) This section applies only to inmates who are eligible for release on parole or to mandatory supervision and to releasees.

(b) The department may issue payment for the cost of temporary post-release housing for an inmate described by Subsection (a) or for a releasee that meets any conditions or requirements imposed by a parole panel and is located in the county of legal residence of the inmate or releasee.

(c) The amount of payment issued under Subsection (b) may not exceed an amount that is equal to the cost the department would incur to incarcerate the inmate for the period for which the payment is issued.

(d) The department shall issue payment under Subsection (b) out of funds appropriated by the legislature to the department for use in administering the parole system with respect to the housing of inmates on their release.

(e) The executive director of the Texas Department of Criminal Justice shall adopt rules as necessary to implement this section, including rules that ensure that the food, hygiene, and clothing needs of an inmate or releasee on whose behalf payment is issued under this section are adequately met during the period for which the payment is issued

(f) Not later than September 30, 2010, for the first report and September 30, 2011, for the second report, the department shall submit to the Criminal Justice Legislative Oversight Committee a report that covers the period of August 1 of the year preceding the year in which the report is submitted through September 1 of the year in which the report is submitted and that includes:

(1) the total number of inmates and releasees on whose behalf payment is issued under this section;

(2) the total dollar amount of payments issued under this section; and

(3) the county of release and the county of legal residence of each inmate or releasee on whose behalf payment is issued under this section.

(g) This subsection and Subsection (f) expire January 1, 2012.

Added by Acts 2009, 81st Leg., R.S., Ch. 944, Sec. 1, eff. June 19, 2009.

SUBCHAPTER F. MANDATORY CONDITIONS OF PAROLE OR MANDATORY SUPERVISION

Sec. 508.181. RESIDENCE DURING RELEASE. (a) Except as provided by Subsections (b) and (c), a parole panel shall require as a condition of parole or mandatory supervision that the releasee reside in the county in which:

(1) the releasee resided at the time of committing the offense for which the releasee was sentenced to the institutional division; or

(2) the releasee committed the offense for which the releasee was sentenced to the institutional division, if the releasee was not a resident of this state at the time of committing the offense.

(b) A parole panel may require a releasee to reside in a county other than the county required under Subsection (a) to:

(1) protect the life or safety of:

(A) a victim of the releasee's offense;

(B) the releasee;

(C) a witness in the case; or

(D) any other person; or

(2) increase the likelihood of the releasee's successful completion of parole or mandatory supervision, because of:

(A) written expressions of significant public concern in the county in which the releasee would otherwise be required to reside;

(B) the presence of family members or friends in the other county who have expressed a willingness to assist the releasee in successfully completing the conditions of the releasee's parole or mandatory supervision;

(C) the verified existence of a job offer in the other county; or

(D) the availability of a treatment program, educational program, or other social service program in the other county that is not available in the county in which the releasee is otherwise required to reside under Subsection (a).

(c) At any time after a releasee is released on parole or to mandatory supervision, a parole panel may modify the conditions of parole or mandatory supervision to require the releasee to reside in a county other than the county required by the original conditions. In making a decision under this subsection, a parole panel must consider the factors listed under Subsection (b).

(d) If a parole panel initially requires the releasee to reside in a county other than the county required under Subsection (a), the parole panel shall subsequently require the releasee to reside in the county described under Subsection (a) if the requirement that the releasee reside in the other county was based on:

(1) the verified existence of a job offer under Subsection (b)(2)(C) and the releasee is no longer employed or actively seeking employment; or

(2) the availability of a treatment program, educational program, or other social service program under Subsection (b)(2)(D) and the releasee:

(A) no longer regularly participates in the program as required by a condition of parole or mandatory supervision; or

(B) has successfully completed the program but has violated another condition of the releasee's parole or mandatory supervision.

(e) If a parole panel requires the releasee to reside in a county other than the county required under Subsection (a), the panel shall:

(1) state in writing the reason for the panel's decision; and

(2) place the statement in the releasee's permanent record.

(f) This section does not apply to a decision by a parole panel to require a releasee to serve the period of parole or mandatory supervision in another state.

(g) The division shall, on the first working day of each month, notify the sheriff of any county in which the total number of sex offenders under the supervision and control of the division residing in the county exceeds 10 percent of the total number of sex offenders in the state under the supervision and control of the division. If the total number of sex offenders under the supervision and control of the division residing in a county exceeds 22 percent of the total number of sex offenders in the state under the supervision and control of the division, a parole panel may require a sex offender to reside in that county only as required by Subsection (a) or for the reason stated in Subsection (b)(2)(B). In this subsection, "sex offender" means a person who is released on parole or to mandatory supervision after serving a sentence for an offense described by Section 508.187(a).

(h) If a parole panel requires a releasee to reside in a county other than the county required under Subsection (a), the division shall include the reason for residency exemption in the required notification to the sheriff of the county in which the defendant is to reside, the chief of police of the municipality in which the halfway house is located, and the attorney who represents the state in the prosecution of felonies in that county.

Added by Acts 1997, 75th Leg., ch. 165, Sec. 12.01, eff. Sept. 1, 1997. Amended by Acts 1999, 76th Leg., ch. 62, Sec. 10.23, 10.24, eff. Sept. 1, 1999.

Sec. 508.182. PAROLE SUPERVISION FEE; ADMINISTRATIVE FEE. (a) A parole panel shall require as a condition of parole or mandatory supervision that a releasee pay to the division for each month during which the releasee is under parole supervision:

(1) a parole supervision fee of $10; and

(2) an administrative fee of $8.

(b) A fee under this section applies to an inmate released in another state who is required as a condition of the inmate's release to report to a parole officer or supervisor in this state for parole supervision.

(c) On the request of the releasee, a parole panel may allow the releasee to defer one or more payments under this section. The releasee remains responsible for payment of the fee and shall pay the amount of the deferred payment not later than the second anniversary of the date the payment becomes due.

(d) The Texas Board of Criminal Justice shall adopt rules relating to the method of payment required of the releasee.

(e) The division shall remit fees collected under this section to the comptroller. The comptroller shall deposit the fees collected under:

(1) Subsection (a)(1) in the general revenue fund; and

(2) Subsection (a)(2) in the compensation to victims of crime fund.

(f) In a parole or mandatory supervision revocation hearing under Section 508.281 at which it is alleged only that the releasee failed to make a payment under this section, it is an affirmative defense to revocation that the releasee is unable to pay the amount as ordered by a parole panel. The releasee must prove the affirmative defense by a preponderance of the evidence.

Added by Acts 1997, 75th Leg., ch. 165, Sec. 12.01, eff. Sept. 1, 1997.

Sec. 508.183. EDUCATIONAL SKILL LEVEL. (a) A parole panel shall require as a condition of release on parole or release to mandatory supervision that an inmate demonstrate to the parole panel whether the inmate has an educational skill level that is equal to or greater than the average skill level of students who have completed the sixth grade in a public school in this state.

(b) If the parole panel determines that the inmate has not attained that skill level, the parole panel shall require as a condition of parole or mandatory supervision that the inmate as a releasee attain that level of educational skill, unless the parole panel determines that the inmate lacks the intellectual capacity or the learning ability to ever achieve that level of skill.

Added by Acts 1997, 75th Leg., ch. 165, Sec. 12.01, eff. Sept. 1, 1997.

Sec. 508.184. CONTROLLED SUBSTANCE TESTING. (a) A parole panel shall require as a condition of parole or mandatory supervision that a releasee submit to testing for controlled substances on evidence that:

(1) a controlled substance is present in the releasee's body;

(2) the releasee has used a controlled substance; or

(3) the use of a controlled substance is related to the offense for which the releasee was convicted.

(b) The Texas Board of Criminal Justice by rule shall adopt procedures for the administration of a test required under this section.

Added by Acts 1997, 75th Leg., ch. 165, Sec. 12.01, eff. Sept. 1, 1997.

Sec. 508.185. SUBSTANCE ABUSE TREATMENT. (a) A parole panel shall require as a condition of release on parole or release to mandatory supervision that an inmate who immediately before release is a participant in the program established under Section 501.0931 participate as a releasee in a drug or alcohol abuse continuum of care treatment program.

(b) The Texas Commission on Alcohol and Drug Abuse shall develop the continuum of care treatment program.

Added by Acts 1997, 75th Leg., ch. 165, Sec. 12.01, eff. Sept. 1, 1997.

Sec. 508.186. SEX OFFENDER REGISTRATION. A parole panel shall require as a condition of parole or mandatory supervision that a releasee required to register as a sex offender under Chapter 62, Code of Criminal Procedure:

(1) register under that chapter; and

(2) submit a blood sample or other specimen to the Department of Public Safety under Subchapter G, Chapter 411, for the purpose of creating a DNA record of the releasee, unless the releasee has already submitted the required specimen under other state law.

Added by Acts 1997, 75th Leg., ch. 165, Sec. 12.01, eff. Sept. 1, 1997. Amended by Acts 1999, 76th Leg., ch. 62, Sec. 10.25, eff. Sept. 1, 1999; Acts 2001, 77th Leg., ch. 211, Sec. 16, eff. Sept. 1, 2001; Acts 2003, 78th Leg., ch. 1300, Sec. 9, eff. Sept. 1, 2003.

Amended by:

Acts 2005, 79th Leg., Ch. 1008, Sec. 1.06, eff. September 1, 2005.

Sec. 508.1861. PROHIBITIONS ON INTERNET ACCESS FOR CERTAIN SEX OFFENDERS. (a) This section applies only to a person who, on release, will be required to register as a sex offender under Chapter 62, Code of Criminal Procedure, by court order or otherwise, and:

(1) is serving a sentence for an offense under Section 21.11, 22.011(a)(2), 22.021(a)(1)(B), 33.021, or 43.25, Penal Code;

(2) used the Internet or any other type of electronic device used for Internet access to commit the offense or engage in the conduct for which the person is required to register under Chapter 62, Code of Criminal Procedure; or

(3) is assigned a numeric risk level of three based on an assessment conducted under Article 62.007, Code of Criminal Procedure.

(b) If the parole panel releases on parole or to mandatory supervision a person described by Subsection (a), the parole panel as a condition of parole or mandatory supervision shall prohibit the releasee from using the Internet to:

(1) access material that is obscene as defined by Section 43.21, Penal Code;

(2) access a commercial social networking site, as defined by Article 62.0061(f), Code of Criminal Procedure;

(3) communicate with any individual concerning sexual relations with an individual who is younger than 17 years of age; or

(4) communicate with another individual the releasee knows is younger than 17 years of age.

(c) The parole panel may modify at any time the condition described by Subsection (b)(4) if:

(1) the condition interferes with the releasee's ability to attend school or become or remain employed and consequently constitutes an undue hardship for the releasee; or

(2) the releasee is the parent or guardian of an individual who is younger than 17 years of age and the releasee is not otherwise prohibited from communicating with that individual.

Added by Acts 2009, 81st Leg., R.S., Ch. 755, Sec. 10, eff. September 1, 2009.

Sec. 508.187. CHILD SAFETY ZONE. (a) This section applies only to a releasee serving a sentence for an offense under:

(1) Section 43.25 or 43.26, Penal Code;

(2) Section 21.02, 21.11, 22.011, 22.021, or 25.02, Penal Code;

(3) Section 20.04(a)(4), Penal Code, if the releasee committed the offense with the intent to violate or abuse the victim sexually; or

(4) Section 30.02, Penal Code, punishable under Subsection (d) of that section, if the releasee committed the offense with the intent to commit a felony listed in Subdivision (2) or (3).

(b) A parole panel shall establish a child safety zone applicable to a releasee if the panel determines that a child as defined by Section 22.011(c), Penal Code, was the victim of the offense, by requiring as a condition of parole or mandatory supervision that the releasee:

(1) not:

(A) supervise or participate in any program that includes as participants or recipients persons who are 17 years of age or younger and that regularly provides athletic, civic, or cultural activities; or

(B) go in, on, or within a distance specified by the panel of premises where children commonly gather, including a school, day-care facility, playground, public or private youth center, public swimming pool, or video arcade facility; and

(2) attend for a period of time determined necessary by the panel psychological counseling sessions for sex offenders with an individual or organization that provides sex offender treatment or counseling as specified by the parole officer supervising the releasee after release.

(c) A parole officer who under Subsection (b)(2) specifies a sex offender treatment provider to provide counseling to a releasee shall:

(1) contact the provider before the releasee is released;

(2) establish the date, time, and place of the first session between the releasee and the provider; and

(3) request the provider to immediately notify the officer if the releasee fails to attend the first session or any subsequent scheduled session.

(d) At any time after the imposition of a condition under Subsection (b)(1), the releasee may request the parole panel to modify the child safety zone applicable to the releasee because the zone as created by the panel:

(1) interferes with the releasee's ability to attend school or hold a job and consequently constitutes an undue hardship for the releasee; or

(2) is broader than necessary to protect the public, given the nature and circumstances of the offense.

(e) A parole officer supervising a releasee may permit the releasee to enter on an event-by-event basis into the child safety zone that the releasee is otherwise prohibited from entering if:

(1) the releasee has served at least two years of the period of supervision imposed on release;

(2) the releasee enters the zone as part of a program to reunite with the releasee's family;

(3) the releasee presents to the parole officer a written proposal specifying:

(A) where the releasee intends to go within the zone;

(B) why and with whom the releasee is going; and

(C) how the releasee intends to cope with any stressful situations that occur;

(4) the sex offender treatment provider treating the releasee agrees with the officer that the releasee should be allowed to attend the event; and

(5) the officer and the treatment provider agree on a chaperon to accompany the releasee, and the chaperon agrees to perform that duty.

(f) In this section, "playground," "premises," "school," "video arcade facility," and "youth center" have the meanings assigned by Section 481.134, Health and Safety Code.

Added by Acts 1997, 75th Leg., ch. 165, Sec. 12.01, eff. Sept. 1, 1997. Amended by Acts 2001, 77th Leg., ch. 978, Sec. 2, eff. Sept. 1, 2001.

Amended by:

Acts 2007, 80th Leg., R.S., Ch. 593, Sec. 3.41, eff. September 1, 2007.

Sec. 508.188. COMMUNITY SERVICE FOR CERTAIN RELEASEES. A parole panel shall require as a condition of parole or mandatory supervision that a releasee for whom the court has made an affirmative finding under Article 42.014, Code of Criminal Procedure, perform not less than 300 hours of community service at a project designated by the parole panel that primarily serves the person or group that was the target of the releasee.

Added by Acts 1997, 75th Leg., ch. 165, Sec. 12.01, eff. Sept. 1, 1997.

Sec. 508.189. PAROLE FEE FOR CERTAIN RELEASEES. (a) A parole panel shall require as a condition of parole or mandatory supervision that a releasee convicted of an offense under Section 21.02, 21.08, 21.11, 22.011, 22.021, 25.02, 43.25, or 43.26, Penal Code, pay to the division a parole supervision fee of $5 each month during the period of parole supervision.

(b) The division shall send fees collected under this section to the comptroller. The comptroller shall deposit the fees in the general revenue fund to the credit of the sexual assault program fund established under Section 44.0061, Health and Safety Code.

Added by Acts 1997, 75th Leg., ch. 165, Sec. 12.01, eff. Sept. 1, 1997.

Amended by:

Acts 2007, 80th Leg., R.S., Ch. 593, Sec. 3.42, eff. September 1, 2007.

Sec. 508.190. AVOIDING VICTIM OF STALKING OFFENSE. (a) A parole panel shall require as a condition of parole or mandatory supervision that a releasee serving a sentence for an offense under Section 42.072, Penal Code, not:

(1) communicate directly or indirectly with the victim;

(2) go to or near the residence, place of employment, or business of the victim; or

(3) go to or near a school, day-care facility, or similar facility where a dependent child of the victim is in attendance.

(b) If a parole panel requires the prohibition contained in Subsection (a)(2) or (3) as a condition of parole or mandatory supervision, the parole panel shall specifically describe the prohibited locations and the minimum distances, if any, that the releasee must maintain from the locations.

Added by Acts 1999, 76th Leg., ch. 62, Sec. 10.26, eff. Sept. 1, 1999.

Sec. 508.191. NO CONTACT WITH VICTIM. (a) If a parole panel releases a defendant on parole or to mandatory supervision, the panel shall require as a condition of parole or mandatory supervision that the defendant not intentionally or knowingly communicate directly or indirectly with a victim of the offense or intentionally or knowingly go near a residence, school, place of employment, or business of a victim. At any time after the defendant is released on parole or to mandatory supervision, a victim of the offense may petition the panel for a modification of the conditions of the defendant's parole or mandatory supervision allowing the defendant contact with the victim subject to reasonable restrictions.

(b) Notwithstanding Subsection (a), a defendant may participate in victim-offender mediation authorized by Section 508.324 on the request of the victim or a guardian of the victim or a close relative of a deceased victim.

(c) In this section, "victim" has the meaning assigned by Article 56.01(3), Code of Criminal Procedure.

Added by Acts 1999, 76th Leg., ch. 62, Sec. 10.27, eff. Sept. 1, 1999.

SUBCHAPTER G. DISCRETIONARY CONDITIONS OF PAROLE OR MANDATORY SUPERVISION

Sec. 508.221. CONDITIONS PERMITTED GENERALLY. A parole panel may impose as a condition of parole or mandatory supervision any condition that a court may impose on a defendant placed on community supervision under Article 42.12, Code of Criminal Procedure, including the condition that a releasee submit to testing for controlled substances or submit to electronic monitoring if the parole panel determines that without testing for controlled substances or participation in an electronic monitoring program the inmate would not be released on parole.

Added by Acts 1997, 75th Leg., ch. 165, Sec. 12.01, eff. Sept. 1, 1997.

Sec. 508.222. PAYMENT OF CERTAIN DAMAGES. A parole panel may require as a condition of parole or mandatory supervision that a releasee make payments in satisfaction of damages for which the releasee is liable under Section 500.002.

Added by Acts 1997, 75th Leg., ch. 165, Sec. 12.01, eff. Sept. 1, 1997.

Sec. 508.223. PSYCHOLOGICAL COUNSELING. A parole panel may require as a condition of parole or mandatory supervision that a releasee serving a sentence for an offense under Section 42.072, Penal Code, attend psychological counseling sessions of a type and for a duration as specified by the parole panel, if the parole panel determines in consultation with a local mental health services provider that appropriate mental health services are available through the Texas Department of Mental Health and Mental Retardation in accordance with Section 534.053, Health and Safety Code, or through another mental health services provider.

Added by Acts 1997, 75th Leg., ch. 165, Sec. 12.01, eff. Sept. 1, 1997. Amended by Acts 1999, 76th Leg., ch. 62, Sec. 10.28, eff. Sept. 1, 1999.

Sec. 508.224. SUBSTANCE ABUSE COUNSELING. A parole panel may require as a condition of parole or mandatory supervision that the releasee attend counseling sessions for substance abusers or participate in substance abuse treatment services in a program or facility approved or licensed by the Texas Commission on Alcohol and Drug Abuse if:

(1) the releasee was sentenced for an offense involving a controlled substance; or

(2) the panel determines that the releasee's substance abuse was related to the commission of the offense.

Added by Acts 1997, 75th Leg., ch. 165, Sec. 12.01, eff. Sept. 1, 1997.

Sec. 508.225. CHILD SAFETY ZONE. (a) If the nature of the offense for which an inmate is serving a sentence warrants the establishment of a child safety zone, a parole panel may establish a child safety zone applicable to an inmate serving a sentence for an offense listed in Section 3g(a)(1), Article 42.12, Code of Criminal Procedure, or for which the judgment contains an affirmative finding under Section 3g(a)(2), Article 42.12, Code of Criminal Procedure, by requiring as a condition of parole or release to mandatory supervision that the inmate not:

(1) supervise or participate in any program that includes as participants or recipients persons

who are 17 years of age or younger and that regularly provides athletic, civic, or cultural activities; or

(2) go in or on, or within a distance specified by the panel of, a premises where children commonly gather, including a school, day-care facility, playground, public or private youth center, public swimming pool, or video arcade facility.

(b) At any time after the imposition of a condition under Subsection (a), the inmate may request the parole panel to modify the child safety zone applicable to the inmate because the zone as created by the panel:

(1) interferes with the ability of the inmate to attend school or hold a job and consequently constitutes an undue hardship for the inmate; or

(2) is broader than is necessary to protect the public, given the nature and circumstances of the offense.

(c) This section does not apply to an inmate described by Section 508.187.

(d) In this section, "playground," "premises," "school," "video arcade facility," and "youth center" have the meanings assigned by Section 481.134, Health and Safety Code.

Added by Acts 1999, 76th Leg., ch. 56, Sec. 2, eff. Sept. 1, 1999.

Sec. 508.226. ORCHIECTOMY AS CONDITION PROHIBITED. A parole panel may not require an inmate to undergo an orchiectomy as a condition of release on parole or to mandatory supervision.

Added by Acts 1999, 76th Leg., ch. 62, Sec. 10.29, eff. Sept. 1, 1999. Renumbered from Sec. 508.225 by Acts 2001, 77th Leg., ch. 1420, Sec. 21.001(45), eff. Sept. 1, 2001.

Sec. 508.227. ELECTRONIC MONITORING OF CERTAIN MEMBERS OF CRIMINAL STREET GANG. (a) This section applies only to a releasee who:

(1) is identified as a member of a criminal street gang in an intelligence database established under Chapter 61, Code of Criminal Procedure; and

(2) has three or more times been convicted of, or received a grant of deferred adjudication community supervision or another functionally equivalent form of community supervision or probation for, a felony offense under the laws of this state, another state, or the United States.

(b) A parole panel may require as a condition of release on parole or to mandatory supervision that a releasee described by Subsection (a) submit to tracking under an electronic monitoring service or other appropriate technological service designed to track a person's location.

Added by Acts 2009, 81st Leg., R.S., Ch. 1130, Sec. 20, eff. September 1, 2009.

SUBCHAPTER H. WARRANTS

Sec. 508.251. ISSUANCE OF WARRANT OR SUMMONS. (a) In a case of parole or mandatory supervision, the director or a designated agent of the director or, in another case, the board on order by the governor, may issue a warrant as provided by Section 508.252 for the return of:

(1) a releasee;

(2) an inmate released although not eligible for release;

(3) a resident released to a preparole or work program;

(4) an inmate released on emergency reprieve or on emergency absence under escort; or

(5) a person released on a conditional pardon.

(b) A warrant issued under Subsection (a) must require the return of the person to the institution from which the person was paroled or released.

(c) Instead of the issuance of a warrant under this section, the division may issue to the person a summons requiring the person to appear for a hearing under Section 508.281 unless the person is a releasee who is on intensive supervision or superintensive supervision, who is an absconder, or who is determined by the division to be a threat to public safety. The summons must state the time, date, place, and purpose of the hearing.

(d) A designated agent of the director acts independently from a parole officer and must receive specialized training as determined by the director.

Added by Acts 1997, 75th Leg., ch. 165, Sec. 12.01, eff. Sept. 1, 1997. Amended by Acts 2003, 78th Leg., ch. 264, Sec. 1, eff. Sept. 1, 2003.

Sec. 508.252. GROUNDS FOR ISSUANCE OF WARRANT OR SUMMONS. A warrant or summons may be issued under Section 508.251 if:

(1) there is reason to believe that the person has been released although not eligible for release;

(2) the person has been arrested for an offense;

(3) there is a document that is self-authenticating as provided by Rule 902, Texas Rules of Evidence, stating that the person violated a rule or condition of release; or

(4) there is reliable evidence that the person has exhibited behavior during the person's release that indicates to a reasonable person that the person poses a danger to society that warrants the person's immediate return to custody.

Added by Acts 1997, 75th Leg., ch. 165, Sec. 12.01, eff. Sept. 1, 1997. Amended by Acts 1999, 76th Leg., ch. 62, Sec. 10.30, eff. Sept. 1, 1999; Acts 2003, 78th Leg., ch. 264, Sec. 2, eff. Sept. 1, 2003.

Sec. 508.253. EFFECT ON SENTENCE AFTER ISSUANCE OF WARRANT. If it appears a releasee has violated a condition or provision of the releasee's parole or mandatory supervision, the date of the issuance of the warrant to the date of the releasee's arrest is not counted as a part of the time served under the releasee's sentence.

Added by Acts 1997, 75th Leg., ch. 165, Sec. 12.01, eff. Sept. 1, 1997.

Sec. 508.254. DETENTION UNDER WARRANT. (a) A person who is the subject of a warrant may be held in custody pending a determination of all facts surrounding the alleged offense, violation of a rule or condition of release, or dangerous behavior.

(b) A warrant authorizes any officer named by the warrant to take custody of the person and detain the person until a parole panel orders the return of the person to the institution from which the person was released.

(c) Pending a hearing on a charge of parole violation, ineligible release, or violation of a condition of mandatory supervision, a person returned to custody shall remain confined.

Added by Acts 1997, 75th Leg., ch. 165, Sec. 12.01, eff. Sept. 1, 1997.

Sec. 508.255. STATUS AS FUGITIVE FROM JUSTICE. (a) After the issuance of a warrant, a person for whose return a warrant was issued is a fugitive from justice.

(b) The law relating to the right of the state to extradite a person and return a fugitive from justice and Article 42.11, Code of Criminal Procedure, relating to the waiver of all legal requirements to obtain extradition of a fugitive from justice from another state to this state, are not impaired by this chapter and remain in full force and effect.

Added by Acts 1997, 75th Leg., ch. 165, Sec. 12.01, eff. Sept. 1, 1997.

Sec. 508.256. WITHDRAWAL OF WARRANT. At any time before setting a revocation hearing date under Section 508.282, the division may withdraw a warrant and continue supervision of a releasee.

Added by Acts 1997, 75th Leg., ch. 165, Sec. 12.01, eff. Sept. 1, 1997.

SUBCHAPTER I. HEARINGS AND SANCTIONS

Sec. 508.281. HEARING. (a) A releasee, a person released although ineligible for release, or a person granted a conditional pardon is entitled to a hearing before a parole panel or a designated agent of the board under the rules adopted by the board and within a period that permits a parole panel, a designee of the board, or the department to dispose of the charges within the periods established by Sections 508.282(a) and (b) if the releasee or person:

(1) is accused of a violation of the releasee's parole or mandatory supervision or the person's conditional pardon, on information and complaint by a peace officer or parole officer; or

(2) is arrested after an ineligible release.

(b) If a parole panel or designated agent of the board determines that a releasee or person granted a conditional pardon has been convicted of a felony offense committed while an administrative releasee and has been sentenced to a term of confinement in a penal institution, the determination is considered to be a sufficient hearing to revoke the parole or mandatory supervision or recommend to the governor revocation of a conditional pardon without further hearing, except that the parole panel or designated agent shall conduct a hearing to consider mitigating circumstances if requested by the releasee or person granted a conditional pardon.

(c) If a hearing before a designated agent of the board is held under this section for a releasee who appears in compliance with a summons, the sheriff of the county in which the releasee is required to appear shall provide the designated agent with a place at the county jail to hold the hearing. Immediately on conclusion of a hearing in which the designated agent determines that a releasee has violated a condition of release, a warrant may be issued requiring the releasee to be held in the county jail pending:

(1) the action of a parole panel on any recommendations made by the designated

agent; and

(2) if subsequently ordered by the parole panel, the return of the releasee to the institution from which the releasee was released.

Added by Acts 1997, 75th Leg., ch. 165, Sec. 12.01, eff. Sept. 1, 1997. Amended by Acts 1999, 76th Leg., ch. 62, Sec. 10.31, eff. Sept. 1, 1999; Acts 2003, 78th Leg., ch. 264, Sec. 3, eff. Sept. 1, 2003; Acts 2003, 78th Leg., 3rd C.S., ch. 3, Sec. 11.20, eff. Jan. 11, 2004.

Sec. 508.2811. PRELIMINARY HEARING. A parole panel or a designee of the board shall provide within a reasonable time to an inmate or person described by Section 508.281(a) a preliminary hearing to determine whether probable cause or reasonable grounds exist to believe that the inmate or person has committed an act that would constitute a violation of a condition of release, unless the inmate or person:

(1) waives the preliminary hearing; or

(2) after release:

(A) has been charged only with an administrative violation of a condition of release; or

(B) has been adjudicated guilty of or has pleaded guilty or nolo contendere to an offense committed after release, other than an offense punishable by fine only involving the operation of a motor vehicle, regardless of whether the court has deferred disposition of the case, imposed a sentence in the case, or placed the inmate or person on community supervision.

Added by Acts 1999, 76th Leg., ch. 62, Sec. 10.32, eff. Sept. 1, 1999.

Sec. 508.282. DEADLINES. (a) Except as provided by Subsection (b), a parole panel, a designee of the board, or the department shall dispose of the charges against an inmate or person described by Section 508.281(a):

(1) before the 41st day after the date on which:

(A) a warrant issued as provided by Section 508.251 is executed, if the inmate or person is arrested only on a charge that the inmate or person has committed an administrative violation of a condition of release, and the inmate or person is not charged before the 41st day with the commission of an offense described by Section 508.2811(2)(B); or

(B) the sheriff having custody of an inmate or person alleged to have committed an offense after release notifies the department that:

(i) the inmate or person has discharged the sentence for the offense; or

(ii) the prosecution of the alleged offense has been dismissed by the attorney representing the state in the manner provided by Article 32.02, Code of Criminal Procedure; or

(2) within a reasonable time after the date on which the inmate or person is returned to the custody of the department, if:

(A) immediately before the return the inmate or person was in custody in another state or in a federal correctional system; or

(B) the inmate or person is transferred to the custody of the department under Section 508.284.

(b) A parole panel, a designee of the board, or the department is not required to dispose of the charges against an inmate or person within the period required by Subsection (a) if:

(1) the inmate or person is in custody in another state or a federal correctional institution;

(2) the parole panel or a designee of the board is not provided a place by the sheriff to hold the hearing, in which event the department, parole panel, or designee is not required to dispose of the charges against the inmate or person until the 30th day after the date on which the sheriff provides a place to hold the hearing; or

(3) the inmate or person is granted a continuance by a parole panel or a designee of the board in the inmate's or person's hearing under Section 508.281(a), but in no event may a parole panel, a designee of the board, or the department dispose of the charges against the person later than the 15th day after the date on which the parole panel, designee, or department would otherwise be required to dispose of the charges under this section, unless the inmate or person is released from custody and a summons is issued under Section 508.251 requiring the inmate or person to appear for a hearing under Section 508.281.

(c) In Subsections (a), (b), and (f), charges against an inmate or person are disposed of when:

(1) the inmate's or person's conditional pardon, parole, or release to mandatory supervision is:

(A) revoked; or

(B) continued or modified and the inmate or person is released from the county jail;

(2) the warrant for the inmate or person issued under Section 508.251 is withdrawn; or

(3) the inmate or person is transferred to a facility described by Section 508.284 for further proceedings.

(d) A sheriff, not later than the 10th day before the date on which the sheriff intends to release from custody an inmate or person described by Section 508.281(a) or transfer the inmate or person to the custody of an entity other than the department, shall notify the department of the intended release or transfer.

(e) If a warrant for an inmate or person issued under Section 508.251 is withdrawn, a summons may be issued requiring the inmate or person to appear for a hearing under Section 508.281.

(f) A parole panel, a designee of the board, or the department shall dispose of the charges against a releasee for whom a warrant is issued under Section 508.281(c) not later than the 31st day after the date on which the warrant is issued.

Added by Acts 1997, 75th Leg., ch. 165, Sec. 12.01, eff. Sept. 1, 1997. Amended by Acts 1999, 76th Leg., ch. 62, Sec. 10.33, eff. Sept. 1, 1999; Acts 2003, 78th Leg., ch. 264, Sec. 4, eff. Sept. 1, 2003; Acts 2003, 78th Leg., ch. 1194, Sec. 1, eff. Sept. 1, 2003.

Sec. 508.283. SANCTIONS. (a) After a parole panel or designated agent of the board has held a hearing under Section 508.281, in any manner warranted by the evidence:

(1) the board may recommend to the governor to continue, revoke, or modify the conditional pardon; and

(2) a parole panel may continue, revoke, or modify the parole or mandatory supervision.

(b) If the parole, mandatory supervision, or conditional pardon of a person described by Section 508.149(a) is revoked, the person may be required to serve the remaining portion of the sentence on which the person was released. The remaining portion is computed without credit for the time from the date of the person's release to the date of revocation.

(c) If the parole, mandatory supervision, or conditional pardon of a person other than a person described by Section 508.149(a) is revoked, the person may be required to serve the remaining portion of the sentence on which the person was released. For a person who on the date of issuance of a warrant or summons initiating the revocation process is subject to a sentence the remaining portion of which is greater than the amount of time from the date of the person's release to the date of issuance of the warrant or summons, the remaining portion is to be served without credit for the time from the date of the person's release to the date of revocation. For a person who on the date of issuance of the warrant or summons is subject to a sentence the remaining portion of which is less than the amount of time from the date of the person's release to the date of issuance of the warrant or summons, the remaining portion is to be served without credit for an amount of time equal to the remaining portion of the sentence on the date of issuance of the warrant or citation.

(d) If a warrant is issued charging a violation of a release condition or a summons is issued for a hearing under Section 508.281, the sentence time credit may be suspended until a determination is made in the case. The suspended time credit may be reinstated if the parole, mandatory supervision, or conditional pardon is continued.

(e) If a person's parole or mandatory supervision is modified after it is established that the person violated conditions of release, the board may require the releasee to remain under custodial supervision in a county jail for a period of not less than 60 days or more than 180 days. A sheriff is required to accept an inmate sanctioned under this subsection only if the commissioners court of the county in which the sheriff serves and the Texas Department of Criminal Justice have entered into a contract providing for the housing of persons sanctioned under this subsection.

Added by Acts 1997, 75th Leg., ch. 165, Sec. 12.01, eff. Sept. 1, 1997. Amended by Acts 1999, 76th Leg., ch. 62, Sec. 10.34, eff. Sept. 1, 1999; Acts 2001, 77th Leg., ch. 856, Sec. 7, eff. Sept. 1, 2001; Acts 2001, 77th Leg., ch. 1197, Sec. 1, eff. Sept. 1, 2001; Acts 2003, 78th Leg., ch. 1275, Sec. 2(62), eff. Sept. 1, 2003.

Sec. 508.284. TRANSFER PENDING REVOCATION HEARING. The department, as provided by Section 508.282(c), may authorize a facility that is otherwise required to detain and house an inmate or person to transfer the inmate or person to a correctional facility operated by the department or under contract with the department if:

(1) the department determines that adequate space is available in the facility to which the inmate or person is to be transferred; and

(2) the facility to which the inmate or person is to be transferred is located not more than 150 miles from the facility from which the inmate or person is to be transferred.

Added by Acts 1999, 76th Leg., ch. 62, Sec. 10.35, eff. Sept. 1, 1999.

SUBCHAPTER J. MISCELLANEOUS

Sec. 508.311. DUTY TO PROVIDE INFORMATION. On request of a member of the board or employee of the board or department, a public official of the state, including a judge, district attorney, county attorney, or police officer, who has information relating to an inmate eligible for parole shall send to the department in writing the information in the official's possession or under the official's control.

Added by Acts 1997, 75th Leg., ch. 165, Sec. 12.01, eff. Sept. 1, 1997.

Sec. 508.312. INFORMATION ON RECIDIVISM OF RELEASEES. The Texas Board of Criminal Justice shall collect information on recidivism of releasees under the supervision of the division and shall use the information to evaluate operations.

Added by Acts 1997, 75th Leg., ch. 165, Sec. 12.01, eff. Sept. 1, 1997.

Sec. 508.313. CONFIDENTIAL INFORMATION. (a) All information obtained and maintained, including a victim protest letter or other correspondence, a victim impact statement, a list of inmates eligible for release on parole, and an arrest record of an inmate, is confidential and privileged if the information relates to:

(1) an inmate of the institutional division subject to release on parole, release to mandatory

supervision, or executive clemency;

(2) a releasee; or

(3) a person directly identified in any proposed plan of release for an inmate.

(b) Statistical and general information relating to the parole and mandatory supervision system, including the names of releasees and data recorded relating to parole and mandatory supervision services, is not confidential or privileged and must be made available for public inspection at any reasonable time.

(c) The department, on request or in the normal course of official business, shall provide information that is confidential and privileged under Subsection (a) to:

(1) the governor;

(2) a member of the board or a parole commissioner;

(3) the Criminal Justice Policy Council in performing duties of the council under Section 413.017; or

(4) an eligible entity requesting information for a law enforcement, prosecutorial, correctional, clemency, or treatment purpose.

(d) In this section, "eligible entity" means:

(1) a government agency, including the office of a prosecuting attorney;

(2) an organization with which the department contracts or an organization to which the department provides a grant; or

(3) an organization to which inmates are referred for services by the department.

(e) This section does not apply to information relating to a sex offender that is authorized for release under Chapter 62, Code of Criminal Procedure.

(f) This section does not apply to information that is subject to required public disclosure under Section 552.029.

Added by Acts 1997, 75th Leg., ch. 165, Sec. 12.01, eff. Sept. 1, 1997. Amended by Acts 1999, 76th Leg., ch. 62, Sec. 10.36, eff. Sept. 1, 1999; Acts 1999, 76th Leg., ch. 783, Sec. 3, eff. Aug. 30, 1999; Acts 2001, 77th Leg., ch. 856, Sec. 8, eff. Sept. 1, 2001;

Acts 2003, 78th Leg., ch. 6, Sec. 3, eff. April 10, 2003; Acts 2003, 78th Leg., 3rd C.S., ch. 3, Sec. 11.21, eff. Jan. 11, 2004.

Sec. 508.314. ACCESS TO INMATES. The department shall:

(1) grant to a member or employee of the board access at all reasonable times to any inmate;

(2) provide for the member or employee or a representative of the member or employee facilities for communicating with or observing an inmate; and

(3) furnish to the member or employee:

(A) any report the member or employee requires relating to the conduct or character of an inmate; or

(B) other facts a parole panel considers pertinent in determining whether an inmate will be released on parole.

Added by Acts 1997, 75th Leg., ch. 165, Sec. 12.01, eff. Sept. 1, 1997.

Sec. 508.315. ELECTRONIC MONITORING PROGRAMS. (a) To establish and maintain an electronic monitoring program under this chapter, the department may:

(1) fund an electronic monitoring program in a parole office;

(2) develop standards for the operation of an electronic monitoring program in a parole office; and

(3) fund the purchase, lease, or maintenance of electronic monitoring equipment.

(b) In determining whether electronic monitoring equipment should be leased or purchased, the department shall consider the rate at which technological change makes electronic monitoring equipment obsolete.

Added by Acts 1997, 75th Leg., ch. 165, Sec. 12.01, eff. Sept. 1, 1997.

Sec. 508.316. SPECIAL PROGRAMS. (a) The department may contract for services for releasees if funds are appropriated to the department for the services, including services for releasees who have a history of:

(1) mental impairment or mental retardation;

(2) substance abuse; or

(3) sexual offenses.

(b) The department shall seek funding for a contract under this section as a priority item.

Added by Acts 1997, 75th Leg., ch. 165, Sec. 12.01, eff. Sept. 1, 1997.

Sec. 508.317. INTENSIVE SUPERVISION PROGRAM; SUPER-INTENSIVE SUPERVISION PROGRAM. (a) The department shall establish a program to provide intensive supervision to inmates released under Subchapter B, Chapter 499, and other inmates determined by a parole panel or the department to require intensive supervision.

(b) The Texas Board of Criminal Justice shall adopt rules that establish standards for determining which inmates require intensive supervision.

(c) The program must provide the level of supervision the department provides that is higher than any level of supervision other than the level of supervision described by Subsection (d).

(d) The department shall establish a program to provide super-intensive supervision to inmates released on parole or mandatory supervision and determined by parole panels to require super-intensive supervision. The program must provide the highest level of supervision provided by the department.

Added by Acts 1997, 75th Leg., ch. 165, Sec. 12.01, eff. Sept. 1, 1997. Amended by Acts 1999, 76th Leg., ch. 62, Sec. 10.37, eff. Sept. 1, 1999.

Sec. 508.318. CONTINUING EDUCATION PROGRAM. (a) The Texas Board of Criminal Justice and the Texas Education Agency shall adopt a memorandum of understanding that establishes the respective responsibilities of the board and the agency in implementing a continuing education program to increase the literacy of releasees.

(b) The Texas Board of Criminal Justice and the agency shall coordinate the development of the memorandum of understanding and each by rule shall adopt the memorandum.

Added by Acts 1997, 75th Leg., ch. 165, Sec. 12.01, eff. Sept. 1, 1997.

Sec. 508.319. PROGRAM TO ASSESS AND ENHANCE EDUCATIONAL AND VOCATIONAL SKILLS. (a) The department, with the assistance of public school districts, community and public junior colleges, public and private institutions of higher education, and other appropriate public and private entities, may establish a developmental program based on information obtained under Section 508.183 for an inmate to be released to the supervision of the division.

(b) The developmental program may provide the inmate with the educational and vocational training necessary to:

(1) meet the average skill level required under Section 508.183; and

(2) acquire employment while in the custody of the division to lessen the likelihood that the inmate will return to the institutional division.

(c) To decrease state expense for a program established under this section, the Texas Workforce Commission shall provide to the department and the other entities described by Subsection (a) information relating to obtaining financial assistance under applicable programs of public or private entities.

(d) The department may establish a developmental program similar to the program described by Subsection (a) for inmates released from the institutional division who will not be supervised by the department.

Added by Acts 1997, 75th Leg., ch. 165, Sec. 12.01, eff. Sept. 1, 1997.

Sec. 508.320. CONTRACTS FOR LEASE OF FEDERAL FACILITIES. (a) The department may contract with the federal government for the lease of a military base or other federal facility that is not being used by the federal government.

(b) The department may use a facility leased under this section to house releasees in the custody of the division.

(c) The department may not enter into a contract under this section unless funds have been appropriated specifically to make payments on a contract under this section.

(d) The department shall attempt to enter into contracts that will provide the department with facilities located in various parts of the state.

Added by Acts 1997, 75th Leg., ch. 165, Sec. 12.01, eff. Sept. 1, 1997.

Sec. 508.321. REPORTING, MANAGEMENT, AND COLLECTION SERVICES. The department, with the approval of the Texas Board of Criminal Justice, may contract with a public or private vendor to provide telephone reporting, automated caseload management, or collection services for:

(1) fines, fees, restitution, or other costs ordered to be paid by a court; or

(2) fees collected by the division.

Added by Acts 1997, 75th Leg., ch. 165, Sec. 12.01, eff. Sept. 1, 1997.

Sec. 508.322. RELEASEE RESTITUTION FUND. (a) The releasee restitution fund is a fund outside the treasury and consists of restitution payments made by releasees. Money in the fund may be used only to pay restitution as required by a condition of parole or mandatory supervision to victims of criminal offenses.

(b) The comptroller is the trustee of the releasee restitution fund as provided by Section 404.073.

(c) When a parole panel orders the payment of restitution from a releasee as provided by Article 42.037(h), Code of Criminal Procedure, the department shall:

(1) collect the payment for disbursement to the victim;

(2) deposit the payment in the releasee restitution fund; and

(3) transmit the payment to the victim as soon as practicable.

(d) If a victim who is entitled to restitution cannot be located, immediately after receiving a final payment in satisfaction of an order of restitution for the victim, the department shall attempt to notify the victim of that fact by certified mail, mailed to the last known address of the victim. If a victim then makes a claim for payment, the department promptly shall remit the payment to the victim.

(e) Money that remains unclaimed shall be transferred to the compensation to victims of crime auxiliary fund on the fifth anniversary of the date the money was deposited to the credit of the releasee restitution fund.

Added by Acts 1997, 75th Leg., ch. 165, Sec. 12.01, eff. Sept. 1, 1997. Amended by Acts 2001, 77th Leg., ch. 856, Sec. 9, eff. Sept. 1, 2001.

Sec. 508.323. AUDIT. The financial transactions of the division and the board are subject to audit by the state auditor in accordance with Chapter 321.

Added by Acts 1997, 75th Leg., ch. 165, Sec. 12.01, eff. Sept. 1, 1997.

Sec. 508.324. VICTIM-OFFENDER MEDIATION. If the pardons and paroles division receives notice from the victim services office of the department that a victim of the defendant, or the victim's guardian or close relative, wishes to participate in victim-offender mediation with a person released on parole or to mandatory supervision, the division shall cooperate and assist the person if the person chooses to participate in the mediation program provided by the office. The pardons and paroles division may not require the defendant to participate and may not reward the person for participation by modifying conditions of release or the person's level of supervision or by granting any other benefit to the person.

Added by Acts 1999, 76th Leg., ch. 62, Sec. 10.38, eff. Sept. 1, 1999.

Appendix 9

Glossary of Terms

Board
Refers to the Texas Board of Pardons and Paroles.

Correctional Institutions Division (CID)
The Correctional Institutions Division (CID) of the Texas Department of Criminal Justice is responsible for the confinement of adult felony offenders who are sentenced to prison.

CUFI
Designates the date on which an offender serving consecutive or cumulative sentences will satisfy the current sentence and begin to serve the next sentence in the series. The cause number on the approved sentence will be indicated in the vote.

Deny Mandatory Supervision
A parole panel decision to deny mandatory supervision release when the panel concludes that the accrued good time is not an accurate reflection of the offender's potential for rehabilitation and that release would endanger the public. It applies to those offenders with mandatory release eligible offenses committed on or after September 1, 1996.

Discretionary Mandatory Supervision (DMS)
A form of release that applies to certain offenders who are incarcerated for an offense committed on or after September 1, 1996 and are eligible for release on mandatory supervision. Those offenders must be approved by a parole panel for mandatory supervision release. See also HB 1433.

Fiscal Year (FY)
The Board's fiscal year runs from September 1 of one year through August 31 of the following year.

House Bill 1433 (HB 1433)
The law passed during the 74th Legislature that requires parole panels to review scheduled mandatory supervision releases if offenses were committed on or after September 1, 1996. Specifically, HB 1433 authorizes a parole panel to review and deny mandatory supervision releases on a case-by-case basis when it determines that an offender's good conduct time does not accurately reflect the potential for rehabilitation and that the offender's release would endanger the public. See also Discretionary Mandatory Supervision.

In-Prison Therapeutic Community (IPTC)
An intensive substance abuse treatment program housed in various TDCJ-CID units. As a condition of release from an IPTC, an offender is required to

participate in an Aftercare Program at a Transitional Treatment Center (TTC).

Intermediate Sanction Facility (ISF)
A secure facility under contract with or operated by TDCJ that serves as a confinement alternative for offenders under active supervision who have violated one or more release conditions but have no pending charges. An ISF provides an effective addition to the range of sanctions available for parole supervision.

Mandatory Supervision (MS)
The release by law of an eligible offender when calendar time served plus good conduct time credit equals the length of the sentence. The amount of good conduct time credits determines the length of time the offender serves under the supervision of the TDCJ-Parole Division.

Medically Recommended Intensive Supervision(MRIS) Program
Under this program, offenders who are mentally ill, mentally retarded, elderly, terminally ill, physically handicapped, or require long-term care are considered for release by a parole panel. The panel, based on the offender's condition and medical evaluation, may release an offender who does not constitute a threat to public safety or a threat to commit an offense.

Next Review (NR) Date
A parole panel decision to deny parole and to set a new date for review in one to five years, depending on the offense.

Offender
A person incarcerated in the prison system, other penal institution or jail, or a person released to parole or mandatory supervision.

Parole
The discretionary and conditional release of an eligible offender to serve the remainder of the sentence under the supervision of the TDCJ-Parole Division.

Parole in Absentia (PIA)
The release of an offender, eligible for parole or mandatory supervision, serving a Texas sentence in an institution other than a Texas state prison, i.e., an out-of-state prison, federal facility, or municipal or county jail.

Parole Panel
A three-member panel consisting of at least one board member and any combination of board members and parole commissioners.

Release to Mandatory Supervision (RMS)
A decision by a parole panel to release an offender to mandatory supervision under the provisions of HB 1433 (discretionary mandatory supervision law).

Senate Bill 45 (SB 45)
Passed during the 74th Legislature, this law requires a two-thirds affirmative vote of the board members to parole offenders with certain capital felony and sex offense convictions.

Senate Bill 880 (SB 880)
Passed during the 78th Legislature, this law reduced the hearing process for certain parole violators from 60 to 41 days.

Serve-All (SA)
A Serve-All vote means an offender is denied parole and that no further parole reviews will be scheduled on the current sentence. In no event, shall a serve-all be voted if the offender's projected release date is greater than five years for offenders serving sentences listed in Texas Government Code, §508.149(a), or greater than one year for offenders not serving sentences under that section.

Sex Offender
A classification applied to offenders who have been sentenced for a sexual offense, been convicted of an offense involving sexually deviant behavior, displayed sexually deviant behavior in committing any offense, or admitted sexually deviant behavior. Also refers to any offender who has a previous period of supervision revoked due to a technical violation that involved sexually deviant or offensive behavior without a legal conviction or offender admission.

State Jail Division
The division of TDCJ that provides community oriented, cost-effective incarceration and rehabilitation for offenders who commit certain low-level, non-violent offenses. Parole panels do not make release decisions on state jail offenders.

Substance Abuse Felony Punishment Facility (SAFPF)
A secure chemical-dependence treatment facility under contract with the TDCJ for non-violent offenders. An offender may be placed in a SAFPF by a parole panel as a condition of parole or mandatory supervision following a hearing.

Super Intensive Supervision Program (SISP)
The highest level of supervision and offender accountability under the TDCJ Parole Division, created by the 75th Legislature for potentially dangerous offenders released on parole or mandatory supervision.

Texas Department of Criminal Justice (TDCJ)
An umbrella agency that includes the Community Justice Assistance Division, the Correctional Institutions Division, and the Parole Division.

Made in the USA
Monee, IL
03 May 2026

49450255R00168